Praise for *Giving Up Whiteness*

"With a deep, genuine rumbling in his belly for racial equality and justice, Jeff James offers a hard look at history, the racial invention of whiteness, the structures built around the protection of white supremacy, and a hopeful posture toward a more beautiful world where racism is confronted, condemned, and overcome."

—Jen Hatmaker, *New York Times* bestselling author of
For the Love, Of Mess and Moxie, and
Fierce, Free and Full of Fire

"Contrary to the opinion of many, you can give up whiteness. Jeff James, while taking us on a very personal journey of his own, provides us with both solid research and compelling reasons to do so."

—Skot Welch, principal at Global Bridgebuilders
and author of *Plantation Jesus*

"A devastating contradiction throughout history is that the Christian faith holds the keys to defeating racism, yet the Christian church has often been one of the biggest obstructers in this battle. *Giving Up Whiteness* is a very personal and honest journey through how the idolatry of 'whiteness' has influenced one man, but also holds powerful clues for fighting this ongoing evil."

—Jefferson Bethke, *New York Times* bestselling author of
Jesus > Religion and *To Hell with the Hustle*

"Jeff James is doing something in writing *Giving Up Whiteness* that I've longed to see since I began studying race and culture from a psychological perspective and helping organizations become more culturally competent. I've long been troubled by so many initiatives labeled as 'increasing diversity' that only focus on 'otherness' of minorities but does not invite those labeled as White to explore what this identity means to them and what meaning it holds in our country and all of our institutions. I'm going to add this book to my toolbox, making it required reading for individuals and organizations who are genuinely invested in understanding and dismantling racism and the insidious notion of White Supremacy. This book is going to help change the conversation about race!"

—Nicole Cutts, PhD, success coach, diversity
trainer, and CEO of Cutts Consulting

"Often the best solutions are discovered by embracing an entirely different perspective on a problem. *Giving Up Whiteness* offers a compelling and unique perspective on why our culture continues to stumble on our journey to equality. This book will make you think about race and racism in a different way."

—Jacquelline Fuller, president, Google.org

"With the spirit of an explorer, James invites us into his quest to discover what divesting from whiteness looks like and whether or not it's even possible. Personal storytelling at its best!"

—Debby Irving, author of *Waking Up White*

"In *Giving Up Whiteness*, Jeff James reminds us that as beneficiaries of exploitation and systemic discrimination, all white Americans need to do more. In other words, if you are not part of the solution, you are part of the problem."

—Mary Mazzio, director/producer of *A Most Beautiful Thing*

GIVING UP WHITENESS

GIVING UP
WHITENESS

one man's journey

JEFF JAMES

 Broadleaf Books

Minneapolis

GIVING UP WHITENESS
One Man's Journey

Published in association with Illuminate Literary Agency (www.illuminate literary.com).

Some names in this book have been changed to protect individuals' privacy.

Cover design and art: James Kegley

Print ISBN: 978-1-5064-6402-2
eBook ISBN: 978-1-5064-6403-9

To Crystal
This was one of your wildest ideas—
and that's saying a lot

To Soni, Sonora, Shelby, Bella, and Gabby
With hope for a better world in which you may shine your lights

CONTENTS

PART I

Just Another Toe on the Foot

1

Crystal's Text Message

> The monster has always been
> well-dressed and well-loved.
> —Austin Channing Brown, *I'm Still Here*

I f you were to look at a picture of me or to see me across the room, you would think to yourself, "There's a white guy."

But that would only be because you were socialized to think so. I'm not objectively "white" in skin color; in fact, like most people deemed white, I have skin that is various shades of beige, depending on which body part gets more of the sunshine that activates my limited measure of melanin. In fact, if you had spotted me prior to the 17th century—maybe at a religious procession or a beheading in the town square of one of my European ancestors (you know, just a typical day of entertainment in medieval history)—the racial concept of "white" wouldn't have crossed your mind at all. You may have attempted to classify me as belonging to one of many European "races" based on my hair color, facial features, and skin tone. Perhaps I might be Anglo-Saxon, descended from Germanic people who migrated to the British Isles; or I might be a Frank, another Germanic tribe that took over Roman Gaul after the Roman Empire. Or my dark hair and brown eyes may have led you to classify me as an Indo-European tribe member from Italy, or possibly an ancient Greek. Those were just a few of the dozens of "races" that were commonly recognized in earlier eras. A few centuries later, most of them were lumped into a new racial category deemed first "Caucasian," then "white."

Crystal, a creative, intelligent, hilarious, tall, beautiful, spiritual, justice-seeking woman—who society would categorize as "biracial" under its current racial labeling system—is one of my most thought-provoking friends. One day after I moved to Nashville in 2015, I heard the news of a white supremacist's killing of nine members of Emanuel AME Church in Charleston, South Carolina. This news, combined with a string of highly publicized shootings of unarmed African Americans by law enforcement officers, led me, along with many others, to feel deep anguish and frustration.

Several pickup truck owners in my new Southern community, however, were apparently feeling their own frustration. The Confederate flag that lay draped around the killer's shoulders in his Facebook photos was being scrutinized more intensely. Was it truly an appropriate symbol to fly over the South Carolina state Capitol? After the state's Republican then-governor Nikki Haley and its legislature agreed that the flag should be taken down, I noticed a copious number of large Confederate flags flying from truck beds around my new neighborhood.

I texted Crystal.

These shootings are insane. I want to find a way for white people to be anti-racist. What can I do?

It's very simple.

White people are not white. Get rid of whiteness.

If you are considered white, you may feel disorientation and even defensiveness about Crystal's challenge. I did. Like most people, I assumed that racial categories were immutable. I had heard of some people attempting to "pass" as another race, and I certainly have been on board for arguing that all races are equal. But to question the very *reality* of race? To be challenged to shed my whiteness as a solution to what our society was facing? Did that mean everyone should be challenged to "give up" their race, or just white people? It was jarring to consider.

Of course, that was Crystal's point.

If my circle of friends is any indication, not many 50-year-old white guys ponder the issue of how we came to be classified as white. I can tell by the odd looks and awkward silences I get when I bring it up. It's just assumed to be a fact of life, like breathing or resenting Tom Brady and the New England Patriots. The origins of race, and whether racial categories are even a valid way to classify people, are not topics that most white people have had to ponder. When race comes up, many of us want to change the subject, because we assume something controversial is about to be said—something that will make us feel guilty.

Most of us also want to see ourselves as champions of equality. Everyone, regardless of race, should be considered equal and treated the same, right? Although this assumption is actually a relatively new development among white people, one that arose during my lifetime, we seem to keep stumbling over ourselves in terms of living this out economically, spiritually, and politically. We assumed that we could cling to our racial identities and just start treating each other better.

But a funny thing has held us back—something we haven't really wanted to admit. We white people like our whiteness and the way we've architected this American culture around it. It works for us. It's odd but true: in these modern times, most of "us" have been just fine with opening entry into this world of whiteness to "others" with different skin colors—as long as it was on "our" terms.

Crystal's challenge to me—her white friend who had become so concerned about why this approach hasn't been working so well—was to go deeper. What is "whiteness" anyway? Why was it invented? (And yes, as we'll see, it *was* invented.) Is the existence of whiteness—and perhaps in response, the invention of blackness and other human-created racial categories—the very obstacle to the kind of equality we fooled ourselves into thinking was achieved with the election of President Barack Obama?

The wild pendulum swing of who got elected next is probably a clue.

This book is the story of how I took up Crystal's challenge. After four years of exploring whether her dare was viable and discovering just how deeply a racial lens had shaped my, "I'm one of the good guys" assumptions, I can report one thing for sure: It's not very simple. Along this journey, I learned more about myself, my country, my faith, and the origins and applications of race than I ever imagined possible. I learned answers to questions I never even thought to ask. I learned why *who* classifies you and *how* you are classified carries an immense set of made-up assumptions that lead to a collection of privileges or oppressions, often ebbing and flowing to various extremes, depending on the era you live in and on what piece of soil you reside.

That racial categories carry varying levels of privilege is not a secret to most who are paying attention these days, of course. What *was* surprising to me, and what I eventually found immensely hopeful, is that we have a say in whether we continue to accept this false and destructive human classification called "race." To be clear, this challenge was far different from "not seeing color," a hollow attempt at papering over obvious differences in skin hues, as well as the cultural realities that have risen up around them. No, this was a dare to confront white supremacy by deconstructing its very foundation: *whiteness.*

So many friends of color have expressed the exhaustion of having to explain, educate, and speak on behalf of their entire race-categorized community to well-meaning white folks like me. That saddens me greatly. Another underlying motivation for this book is to identify my blindness, so others can identify it in themselves. By sharing what I've learned, I hope to reduce even a tiny bit of the workload on people of color.

Really, though, I felt compelled to explore Crystal's challenge and determine for myself: Could I shed this whiteness, this racial construct set before me? I owed my friend an answer.

✸ ✸ ✸

Before Crystal's text challenge, I had always considered myself part of the solution—not the problem. Experiences from my youth, along with some quality parenting from my mother and father, had planted within me a deep awareness and even sensitivity about injustice and inequality. These seeds from my youth blossomed into an attraction to the words of Martin Luther King Jr. and Malcolm X when I was in college. Yet like many white people who grew up in the cocoon of a white-centric community, I wasn't fully aware of the systemic powers of whiteness. Racism meant you were mean, not that you benefited from a centuries-old structure of domination against people of color.

A few years prior to meeting Crystal, I attended an anti-racism training event called Damascus Road. My congregation, Circle of Hope in Philadelphia, where I lived at the time, offered to send a team for the weekend event. When our church leaders asked for volunteers, I felt compelled to raise my hand. As it turns out, Circle of Hope, despite its funky, hipster Center City Philadelphia vibe, was a church plant of the Brethren in Christ, a denomination with roots in Ana-baptist and Mennonite traditions. The church's relationship to Ana-baptist principles began to explain why a commitment to equality, nonviolence, and justice was prevalent, but it didn't exempt our com-munity from the common misunderstandings, biases, and sometimes egotistical stubbornness that race so artfully inflames. There weren't a lot of people of color who attended the congregation at the time, but some who did had been expressing frustration with their experiences at the church, despite its stated values. I felt like this Damascus Road experience could be a game-changer for me and the congregation.

Small teams of five to 10 members, mostly from churches and schools around the city, gathered in a library meeting room at Phila-delphia Mennonite High School in the Germantown neighborhood. To begin, Conrad Moore, one of our leaders, walked us through a visualization exercise. On a large sheet of paper posted on the wall, he drew a rudimentary sketch of a community with shops, office build-ings, stick people, cars, and stoplights. He asked us to imagine that this was an under-resourced community—a "ghetto," a barrio, or a trailer park. Next, he asked us to describe what we would most often see in the way of buildings, stores, schools, or parks. A few people mumbled some initial ideas, which led others to chime in as we lost our new group inhibitions: "Graffiti." "Run-down houses." "Empty storefronts." "Liquor stores." "Homeless people." "Trash." Then he asked, "Why are people in this community poor?"

"A lack of jobs." "Inadequate schools." "Drugs." "Poor personal decisions."

We watched as he drew a giant foot at the top of the paper. It hovered menacingly in the white space above the community.

"What institutions have influence or power over these areas?" Conrad asked.

We shared our collective list: banks, developers, government officials, public works boards, boards of education, law enforcement, healthcare conglomerates, media, religious leaders, real estate brokers, transportation officials. The list continued, and it was surprisingly long. I realized how little I had considered the influence of those who make decisions that affect our communities—whether our community is a well-resourced or poorly resourced one.

"Who primarily runs these institutions?" Conrad inquired.

We could see where this was headed. Most, if not all, were run by white people who didn't live in the community.

A few white attendees began to loosen up. In hopeful tones, they pointed out that things were changing. They shared examples of African Americans who now held leadership roles with local banks, school boards, and even City Hall. After all, Philadelphia had elected its first black mayor, Wilson Goode, in 1984, and the current mayor at that time, John Street, was African American. Even the police commissioner, Richard Neal, was African American.

Aha! Progress against the giant Foot! Still, the group quickly realized that the powers that shaped the circumstances of poor neighborhoods had been in place for generations. While a few of the institutional forces were now managed by people of color, that was a relatively recent development.

Conrad wasn't quite done with his point. He described the role of gatekeepers: those who have a semblance of power but are bound to fulfill the policies and preferences of their bosses up the chain. "Who does the Latino regional manager of Philadelphia Electric work for?" he asked. A white vice president, most likely, and ultimately a white CEO, was the obvious answer.

"Who does the African American CEO of a regional bank work for?"

"Shareholders," someone responded. Not surprisingly, the vast majority of investors, especially the ones with a high enough concentration of ownership to influence corporate policy, were white and very wealthy. Only 9% of African Americans and 7% of Hispanics at the time owned any stocks at all.[1] What shareholders—wealthy and divorced from any familial or emotional connection to a poor community—would want their bank to invest equitably in struggling neighborhoods to ensure equal access to resources? Shareholders want a return; wealthy suburban branches making loans to already-resourced folks would certainly deliver a higher return.

The Foot that Conrad had drawn over the community was becoming clearer. Beyond the institutions that were supposed to be "helping," who owned the liquor stores that were so prevalent in this and other poor neighborhoods? The porn outlets and strip clubs? The waste treatment plants? The overpriced corner convenience stores, which in some cases, were the only place to find food for miles?

Who had passed the laws that were now sending an immense number of African Americans to jail for small-scale drug crimes at rates far higher than white drug offenders? Who were the people investing in and benefiting from that sharp rise in for-profit private prisons, funded by massive government contracts to house those inmates?

"Most of the institutions with power over poor communities have accountability outside of the community," Conrad explained. "Some of them may even have completely good intentions. But without accountability and personal experience within the community, how effectively do those intentions get executed?"

I immediately thought of my home state of West Virginia, and the many run-down, hollowed-out coal towns now rife with poverty, abandoned homes and buildings, trash-strewn streams, and growing levels of drug addiction. For generations, my home in Appalachia had faced its own Foot, in the form of out-of-state landowners and coal-mining interests. Local gatekeepers were accountable to them instead of to the community. The Foot that kept communities poor represented the combined effects of these institutional systems of racism and classism on communities of under-resourced people, many of whom were people of color.

We learned much more over this emotional weekend. During one particularly intense session, white folks met together in one room while people of color met in another to address the unique ways race and racism had affected us—sometimes without us being aware of it. It was heartbreaking to hear the stories from people of color in the follow-up joint session. Tearfully, they confessed how much internal oppression they carried with them, tattooed on their psyches by the Foot—to the point where they also distrusted brown and black people who looked like them. The European-American participants' eyes were opened to the concept of privileges we didn't even realize we had, such as: shopping without someone following us; driving through any neighborhood unfettered by a police stop, even if our registration tags were a month overdue; knowing that if we didn't get a job, most likely it was because another candidate was better suited, and we would have many more opportunities; and if we *did* get the job, not having to worry that it was because we were a "diversity" hire, with our qualifications and merit forever questioned by co-workers.

The term *white privilege* wasn't as prevalent at this time, and the term *white supremacy* was reserved for those overt racists with the white hoods. That weekend, however, we received a thorough education on the realities of privilege and control—as well as the powerlessness that comes with the lack of both—especially for people of color in a white-dominated culture that holds the keys.

The Damascus Road experience was mind- and heart-opening. Even though most of the white participants had entered the process with good intentions, we quickly realized that our definition of racism had been very personal. If we had a black friend, or if we felt no animosity toward any racial group, we didn't think we were racist. However, people of color in the group were much more concerned with the Foot. They asked themselves if they had the same access to resources, such as loans or education; if they were protected and treated the same way by police; or if the media was consistently projecting a narrative about people who looked like them that was at worst, inaccurate, and at best, incomplete. The white folks had entered the weekend thinking that as long as we were kind and fair, we were innocent. We hadn't fathomed how the Foot was positioned on the necks of so many people in the room. Most of us hadn't even understood there was such a thing as the Foot.

I had a profound change in perspective that weekend—one that would lead to a deep commitment to standing with my friends of color and defeating that Foot. I didn't realize yet that I was still a toe on it.

✦ ✦ ✦

Crystal and I met in the wake of a disturbing incident after I'd moved back home to Charleston, West Virginia, in the mid-2000s. A 20-year-old African American resident, Megan Williams, reported to police that she had been held captive, tortured, sexually assaulted, and denigrated with racial slurs for weeks in Logan, West Virginia, a small coal-mining community an hour south of Charleston. The odd twist was that she'd had a prior relationship with the perpetrators, which led the local prosecuting attorney to decline adding hate crime violations to the kidnapping and assault charges.

A bizarre and explosive situation for the normally quiet region, it attracted national media attention. It also attracted the concern of national civil rights groups, ranging from traditional organizations such as the Southern Christian Leadership Conference and the National Conference of Black Mayors to more confrontational groups such as Black Lawyers for Justice and the New Black Panther Party. The Reverend Al Sharpton made an appearance. Tensions between these national players and local groups such as the Black Ministerial Alliance began to rise, further complicating the situation.[2]

I had just moved back to West Virginia, where I'd grown up, after having lived in Philadelphia for 13 years. One of my goals in returning, after having built a career at Microsoft during the 1990s, was to find ways to help the local economy innovate, diversify, and encourage entrepreneurship. Toward that goal, I, and other native West Virginians who had also recently moved back home, launched Create West Virginia, an initiative that sought to spark job opportunities and growth beyond the traditional extraction industries. As a co-founder and leader of the group, I was invited by the Charleston Chamber of Commerce to brainstorm ways for the region to address the fallout from the Megan Williams incident. It was at this meeting that I met Crystal.

The child of an African American father and a European-American mother, unwed teenagers hell-bent on challenging 1970s social norms in Appalachia, Crystal grew up in the region at the same time as a famous athlete, NFL superstar Randy Moss. Both had experienced deep racism in their respective local high schools. Whereas Moss funneled his rage from those experiences into athletic excellence and the occasional outlandish behavior off the field, Crystal sought to escape the area by becoming a model. She ended up walking the runway for the likes of Calvin Klein in New York, and later worked as a catalog and magazine model in Atlanta and Dallas. Along the way, she had her own children, and like many West Virginia natives, found her way home to Charleston to raise them and to make sense of her complicated relationship with Appalachia.

As I soon learned, Crystal is a fighter and a survivor. After returning to West Virginia, she faced down the demons of childhood sexual abuse from her stepfather, and, like the persistent widow in Jesus's parable, she would not rest until the local district attorney took up her cause. After 18 long years of seeking justice, she finally saw her stepfather held to account for his actions.

Pain is often the catalyst for stunning creativity, and in Crystal's case, she turned to poetry and activism. Her poetry began to earn accolades. She was accepted into the Affrilachian Poets society—a group whose moniker served as a defiant claim that there were more than just poor white folks in Appalachia. African American Appalachians had a story to tell from the mountains as well. Crystal was a tireless activist for other victims of abuse. She was an advocate for saving West Virginia's mountains from mountaintop removal coal mining. She was even the lead plaintiff in a lawsuit when the local water company let a chemical leak contaminate the entire Kanawha Valley's water supply, an incident that made worldwide news.

I don't remember much of what was said in that first meeting with Crystal, but it did lead to a growing recognition of our mutual hopes and dreams for our home state, and over time, a professional relationship and friendship. We worked on a consulting project for the National Council of the Boy Scouts of America that involved a significant effort to infuse more awareness and commitment to diversity in the organization and in the kids they served. We partnered on a "Soul of Coal" event to bring recognition to African American coal miners, as well as a research project through the Charleston Area

Alliance to recommend ways the region could attract and retain more diverse professionals.

Throughout our work on these and other projects, I remember feeling a mix of hope and unease. I wanted Crystal, as well as other friends of color, to recognize my deeply held commitment to the cause of diversity and equality. But often we would find ourselves at odds emotionally or philosophically on issues relating to race. Crystal would share deep frustration and sometimes anger at how the Boy Scouts were dragging their feet to attract and serve children of color; I tended to zero in on the progress they had made, feeling encouraged by their good intentions and progress in certain areas, such as outreach to Latino communities. She would point out issues she saw in how the Create West Virginia board of directors was set up and operated (a board in which she was a founding member and the only person of color). She also noticed missed opportunities at our conferences to showcase speakers who represented more diverse views. As the leader of the group, I would often take these observations as personal critiques, and feel hurt.

Despite the pitfalls and emotional ups and downs, I appreciated Crystal's willingness to hang in there with our friendship and collaboration. She never failed to throw me into "growth opportunities" (that's code for downright uncomfortable situations), such as recruiting me to speak on a panel at West Virginia State University on the use of the n-word in today's hip-hop music and culture. ("You want me to do *what*?")

I began to realize that having a friend like Crystal may be the only hope people like me have to outgrow the cloak of white assumptions and privileges draped over us at birth. The problem was, I saw the frustration and exhaustion of this overcoming her. Crystal was often *the* one person well-meaning white people sought out to explain a difference, or provide a recommendation, or seek validation. Crystal was often the only friend of color, board member of color, or "who can we ask?" contact that white leaders in the community knew well enough to engage. Yet without her sacrifice, without the sacrifice of other people of color who are willing to play those roles time after time, far fewer white people—including me—would have any semblance of a clue.

More often than not, Crystal's insights would irritate progressive individuals or groups as much as conservative ones. Crystal questioned local organizations, like Create West Virginia or women's rights groups, who saw themselves as champions of equality. Why, she would ask, did the community achievement awards always feature two accomplished, professional white women (the "helpers"), and one underprivileged woman of color (the "helped")? Why would there not be at least one professional person of color honored for "helping" a poorer white woman who "overcame"? Why were leaders frustrated with the difficulty of finding a token person of color for the board of directors when they didn't include any people of color in their circles of relationships, the very source of all their other board members?

When Crystal's challenge arrived on my iPhone, I knew it was time to harness my lifetime of emotional and intellectual turmoil on this topic into something far deeper that could change my life and, God willing, help me make a more educated attempt at making a difference. One of those quotes attributed to Confucius claims, "True wisdom is knowing what you don't know." I was still clueless, but at least now I recognized that I was clueless.

By now I knew enough to realize that attempting to "help" from a position of power or superiority (however subconscious) would not fly. Now I had to find out what this mysterious force called whiteness really was, and how it was sabotaging my own life and our society.

2

Red Hill's Privileges

You inherit your environment just as much as your genes.
—Johnny Rich, *The Human Script*

A certain pang of anxiety would enter my heart every now and then, as I began my journey to take up Crystal's dare to give up whiteness. It usually happened after I explained this journey to white friends. "Is she challenging black people to give up their blackness?" some of them would ask. It's one of the most human reactions when confronted with a challenge, even indirectly: "Why don't I exercise more? Why don't *you* exercise more?"

I knew early in life why racism and treating others unequally was wrong. I knew that it had led to an entirely different experience for people in the United States who weren't considered white. I was beginning to admit, however, that I didn't really know the extent of the difference. I didn't understand how the very existence of whiteness—not just those mean old Southern segregationists, Klan members, or mysterious racist institutions and systems of the Foot—set the stage for where we as humans stood with each other.

Crystal's text triggered a deeper question that I had never fully asked: How did I *become* white? To take up her challenge, I knew I had to go back to the beginning.

✹ ✹ ✹

As a young boy, I loved the crunching sound of gravel underneath the wheels of my dad's car as it climbed up Red Hill, a little patch of rural heaven just outside of Parkersburg, West Virginia, where my grandparents on my father's side lived. Dad and his three siblings grew up on this hill, in what amounted to a shack with an outhouse. Later, my Grandpa Archie built a new house (with indoor plumbing!) by hand on the same spot, with the help of family and friends. When I was a child, the anticipation of seeing my cousins, in the warm glow of James family love and humor, for one summer reunion and one Christmas gathering each year, made the nausea-inducing, 90-minute drive through the West Virginia hills worth it.

My grandparents were not educated or wealthy people. They were simple Appalachians living simple, rural lives. Grandpa held a sixth-grade education and had worked in a variety of factories. Grandma Hazel, with her high school education, worked in a nursing home. Times were not easy, especially during World War II. My dad told stories of having to walk to school all spring in bare feet, after some-one stole his only pair of rationed shoes. The James family's life was rooted in their simple Christian faith and a sense of humor that I'm proud to see making an appearance in my own children. Humor is a true generational blessing in the James family. Grandpa's ornery laugh and unique cadence of praying during family reunions, along with Grandma's doting and the five-dollar bills she'd tuck into birthday cards, will always be treasured memories.

Somehow the humble couple raised four children in that tiny house on Red Hill; and in the course of one generation, all four of them leaped into the next strata of the American Dream, with bachelor's, master's, and professional degrees. Archie's and Hazel's parenting and constant prayers produced a college professor (my dad), an ordained pastor with a master's degree in divinity (Uncle Ronnie), a nurse (Aunt Clara), and an administrative professional (Aunt Mary Kay). After that, a brood of educated grandchildren took their place in the world as oceanographers, physical therapists, teachers, attorneys, nurses, financial managers, farm owners, and marketing professionals. The great-grandchildren of Archie and Hazel—my children and those of my cousins—seem to be carrying on the upward trajectory quite nicely.

The journey toward the American Dream wasn't easy—certainly not for Archie and Hazel. But it was available, with a few obstacles moved out of the way by an encouraging spiritual community, a can-do culture, a helpful US government that provided the GI Bill to help pay for college degrees, easy access to housing loans, and institutions ready to hire you if you showed a modest ability to jump through the right hoops. The American dream was within grasp—if you were considered white.

✱ ✱ ✱

The images in my dad's home movies are grainy and nostalgic, like all the 8-mm films that fathers of people my age shot in the 1960s and 1970s. In one clip, with the herky-jerky, quick start–quick stop style of those old reel movies, I am running gleefully down a sidewalk with my friend, a four-year-old African American girl. I have no idea today what her name is or where she could be now. But in that moment, we were in that completely unselfconscious zone that makes early childhood so conducive to joy.

Looking back through a childhood largely contained by whiteness, I had a few key experiences that likely prompted me to be open to Crystal's challenge. My father, a college professor at Glenville State College in Glenville, West Virginia, took classes toward his PhD at West Virginia University in Morgantown during the summers. During one wonderful period, moments of which are caught on one of Dad's reels, we lived in Morgantown for a full year. I attended first grade in this college town of 25,000, which to my young eyes seemed like New York City compared to my hometown of 2,000.

The graduate student apartment building where we lived in Morgantown was a different world than my normal homogenous existence in Glenville. Morgantown, like many larger college towns in the 1970s, had begun to show signs of global diversity. In those days, many international students matriculated to American colleges. At dinnertime, the hallways of our apartment building overflowed with the aroma of dishes from China, Kenya, Afghanistan, and Iran. The three-story building included a little community area consisting of a multipurpose room, a couple of picnic tables, a volleyball pit, and a metal swing and slide set that would be considered a death trap by today's standards. Each summer evening, the boys from the complex would meet at the dirt pile underneath the second-floor porch that jutted out from the building, dig for a batch of the colorful orange clay that lay beneath the dirt, and shape our collection of animals, monsters, and forts. I didn't realize it at the time, but these diverse play times were like small glitches in the code of an otherwise effective virtual reality program shaping whiteness in my young mind.

Before long, my parents' best friends in Morgantown became the Omars, a warm and wonderful Muslim family from Afghanistan. Sharifa, the mother, taught me to write my name in Arabic, a skill I shared proudly with my Nana and Papa Allen (my mom's parents), teachers, and anyone else who would indulge me. The father, Mohammed, who retired after many years as a physician in West Virginia, simply went by "Omar." Their two daughters, Hossai and Hoggai, became my frequent playmates.

A pang of sadness always hit me when those summers ended, and we packed up to return to Glenville. As much as I liked my big yard, larger house, and neighborhood friends in my hometown, each fall it was hard not to yearn for those Morgantown smells, interesting playmates, and summer evenings in the clay pit.

Glenville, unlike Morgantown, was a typical homogeneous West Virginia community. The one exception was the small state college on the hill overlooking the town. Although lily-white and rural Appalachian through-and-through—Glenville was 99% white at the time—the college made Glenville somewhat unique, compared to neighboring counties and communities with no such infusion of young people. In the 1960s, students of color (a handful at first) began showing up on GSC's tiny campus on the hill. Coaches started recruiting more African American athletes. A small group of international students from Iran, Japan, and China launched their higher education pursuits in the unlikely little Appalachian town. Looking back, I wonder what was going through the minds of these brave young people as the final leg of their long journey took them down a winding country road into the tiny, nearly all-white hamlet of Glenville. Of course, in those days there were no college rating websites that could be used to check out the campus situation. Many students of color likely had no idea what they were getting themselves into.

Because I'd rubbed shoulders with a more diverse group of children in Morgantown, it seems strange to me that I can't recall when I became aware of race. The civil rights era was in full swing in 1966, the year I was born, although I remained unaware of the movement for years. My parents, as was the polite, semi-conservative norm of that time and place, never mentioned race or seemed to be guided by its mysterious powers of separation as it related to offering Christian kindness to the handful of local college students of color. I'm quite sure my realization of the very concept of race must have come from interactions with friends in Glenville at some point.

Gilmer County High School remained almost entirely all-white during my years there in the 1980s. Our student body included two Filipino siblings, children of the local doctor and his wife, who set up shop in town. A biracial young woman attended our school for a year or two, then disappeared, then reappeared. A mixed-race younger boy also attended for a time. Through my white eyes, they seemed to have friends and to be accepted in the intimate halls of our 400-person high school. But what was their actual experience? I didn't know them well enough to be a confidante and learn otherwise.

It wasn't until the summer after my high school graduation that I became aware of the ugly, willful, hateful kind of white supremacy that makes any compassionate or thoughtful person recoil. My friend arranged for a small group of us to get jobs at a local natural gas drilling and pipeline company the summer before my first year of college. It paid slightly more than minimum wage, which seemed like a fortune to us. Our job would be to check into the local station at 7:30 am, receive our assignments, and then ride with the older work-ers either to an oil tank to paint, or to a swath of hilly forest to cut brush off the right-of-way where gas lines snaked through mountains underground. It was hot, sometimes difficult work done on muggy, 90-degree summer days, but not without plenty of time to goof off, tell exaggerated stories, or pine for girls who had caught our attention at the swimming pool.

Not long into this summer job, I noticed how frequently the older workers tossed around the n-word. Most of these men lived in rural parts of the county rather than in town. Most had worked at the gas company for a decade or more. None had extended their educations beyond high school, but they were proud of what they did for a living and how the work provided for their families. Everyone knew how difficult it was to land a steady job with livable wages in our part of the country.

Three of us were college-aged summer workers: blue-collar interns, if you will. As unlikely as it seems now, our ages and exposure to local college students at Glenville State had extended our cultural experiences far beyond these men. Having been exposed to people of color as a young child, I didn't understand the white supremacy–laced vitriol against people of different colors and cultures that we heard from these men daily. I saw no evidence that the white folks around me had any more intelligence, work ethic, or morality than the people they derided. Almost any comment from these men regarding local college students, sports teams, or the world outside of Gilmer County had a tinge of exasperation and disdain. The world "out there" just didn't make sense, and somehow black people and "foreigners" had something to do with it—never mind that few, if any of them, had ever actually met an African American person or a person from another country.

Heaven help any local white girl who was seen associating with one of the African American students from the college. One morning some of the men deliberated on what would possess the daughter of a local prominent business owner to become a "n***er-loving whore." She had been spotted riding in the car with a black male college student. The men combined their disgust with less-than-veiled glee about how it must have enraged her father. Sometimes it was difficult to determine where the racism toward people of color versus the disdain toward other members in the upper-socioeconomic levels of their own race ranked in their minds.

Our band of young laborers would sometimes muster up the courage or outrage to speak up against these kinds of racist conversations. These older men did not hesitate to mock us, and they held sway over what kind of unpleasant work we might be assigned that day. Still, we often found it unbearable to hear the hateful comments coming out of their mouths. In our boldest moments, we would point out that we knew some of the people they derided, and that they were not anything like what these men spewed. In our less audacious moments, we would shake our heads and walk away from the conversation.

One of the men was clearly the most irritable and open with his race-based hatred. He also happened to be the most intimidating. He didn't take kindly to us youngsters and our pushback on his worldview. The man had biceps like cantaloupes, and he was missing a finger from a mysterious work-related accident that we were afraid to ask about. He would often chide us for our naiveté and mock our friendships with black students from the college. In one lengthy conversation held at a worksite deep in the woods—somehow such a location made these conversations even more distressing; we had the sense that if we irritated this guy too much, no one would ever find us again—he berated us continually, challenging us to admit that there must be a group in the world that we held animosity toward. He seemed to be searching manically for a fissure in our self-righteous armor.

I was the one who finally cracked. Wanting to satisfy him enough to leave us alone, I said, "I don't know; maybe Iranians." This was only a few years after the Ayatollah had released the hostages in Iran, so they seemed like a fair group to throw under the bus to get this guy off our backs.

"There you go," he said, satisfied. "You're no better than me."

Another foul incident that summer informed my understanding of the role race played in the world. Softball teams and tournaments had become a huge fad in our region in the 1980s. Seemingly, every man in the county was on a softball team; and every weekend there was another tournament to attend. Many wives and girlfriends followed their men from town to town to cheer them; others said goodbye to their guys for the weekend and left them to their own devices. My friends and I were all on a team made up of younger guys. We often played against teams made up of gritty, older men like those we worked with. In small towns all over West Virginia, we would stay in cheap hotels, play our scheduled opponent, and generally kill time between games.

It may be difficult for those not from a small state like West Virginia to understand how distinct the dynamics can be in different pockets of a region. To me, Idaho is Idaho; I'm sure many see West Virginia as a homogenous place within its borders as well. The racist attitudes of our co-workers notwithstanding, our part of the state was mostly homogenous and therefore free from much of the public angst and demonstrations over civil rights and integration. Southern West Virginia was a different story. This region of the state was somewhat diverse, having attracted African Americans—along with Italians, Poles, and even Lebanese—to work in the coal mines in the late 1800s and early 1900s. The counties and small towns here seemed rougher and tougher to me than the area in which I'd grown up. Here, school segregation had been very real. While during 1960s-era efforts to desegregate, the region never made the national news like Birmingham and Little Rock had, it still tilted its affections more toward the South than the rest of the state did. Here, the occasional Confederate flag draped from a roadside house or blazed across a pickup truck window. Never mind that West Virginia was formed by and fought for the Union during the Civil War. (Well, at least half the state did. The other half, sometimes split within the same household, fought Confederate.)

This time our tournament was held in one of the larger communities in the southern coalfields. Our team had one African American player. The Friday night before our first game Saturday morning, our band of gangly young men headed out from the Holiday Inn to a local dance club we had heard about. We found the club, and one by one our team members paid the cover charge and entered.

Until our African American friend attempted to enter. Then the bouncer declared, "We're full."

I remember feeling a deep sting of embarrassment. Then I felt fury. Did that just happen? We argued with the bouncer. Yep, that just happened. The bouncer seemed to feel no shame about what was going on.

As a white, sheltered 18-year-old kid, I felt shocked by such real, tangible acts of racism. Those experiences belonged in the history films I had seen in school. Despite my experience with the racist gas company workers, I still assumed the "separate but equal" and "whites here, colored over there" kind of apartheid was over in America. This was 1985, not 1965; the memo must have been slow in getting to this club.

Half of us returned to the hotel with our black teammate in indignant protest. The other half of the team stayed, apparently having no problem with the club's arrangement.

3

The Measure of Whiteness

> Yeah, I love being famous. It's almost
> like being white, y'know?
>
> —Chris Rock

It's so easy to put unpleasant details out of our minds, isn't it? All that distasteful business about slavery and segregation in the South; it's over, so let's move on. Frankly, it's soothing to just believe that things are better now, and we can all get on with life. During the 2016 election year, about 80% of white people reported believing that African Americans are treated equally with whites in areas such as applying for a mortgage loan, being considered for a job, or shopping in stores or restaurants. About half of white people believe African Americans are treated equally by law enforcement officers and the courts.[1]

It didn't take much study during my personal journey to find clear, measurable evidence that most white people are just plain wrong in these beliefs. For those brave enough to review it, the evidence will leap out and slap you out of a majority-induced stupor. The Foot leaves a measurable print.

As I've mentioned, by the time I met Crystal, it wasn't as if I hadn't been aware of these disparities for quite some time. Yet if I was going to attempt to understand why I should consider giving up my race ID card and all its benefits, I decided I should probably be aware of the value that card represented. How valuable is being white toward achieving America's shared promise of life, liberty, and the pursuit of happiness? As humbly as the James family's history began, how much did the "white" element of our identity make it easier to rise so rapidly from lower socioeconomic levels to higher levels of education and stable middle-class (in some cases, upper middle-class) life? Was it just Grandpa and Grandma's faith and commitment to education for their children that did the trick? Could any family—black or white—with the same values expect the same trajectory?

Hailing from one of the poorest regions of the United States, I have always been sensitive to bias. To a certain extent, being Appalachian created more empathy in me, but it also complicated my journey to understand whiteness and its privileges. I was aware that generations of white West Virginians have been stuck in the cycles of poverty, especially in the most southern and rural counties. But does the persistent presence of white poverty in places like Appalachia prove that success or failure—at least as defined in economic and social-class terms—is color-blind?

What is the true value of whiteness in today's world?

***

The subjective concepts of joy and happiness are tough to measure. Basically, all you can do is ask someone if they feel those emotions. But social scientists are getting crafty about measuring them. Emiliana Simon-Thomas, the science director of the Greater Good Science Center at the University of California, Berkeley, teaches a class called "The Science of Happiness." She and other researchers have identified their definition of happiness, which includes the level of satisfaction and meaning in your life. According to Simon-Thomas, it's the propensity to feel positive emotions, the capacity to recover quickly from negative emotions, and holding a sense of purpose. Happiness is not having a lot of privilege or money. It's not constant pleasure. It's a broader thing, involving our ability to connect with others, to have meaningful relationships, to have a community. Time and again— across decades of research and across all studies—people who say they're happy have strong connections with community and with other people. That's sort of the recipe for happiness."[2]

So how much do race and racism screw up a person's ability to have meaningful connections with others, to have a community, to maintain positive emotions, and to live with a sense of purpose?

Economic threats wreak havoc on all the personal and social elements that make up long-term happiness. Economic hardship forces a single mom to work two jobs instead of being there to read to her kids. It inhibits people from planting roots through friendships in a community or school, because they're constantly being evicted or forced to move to another job. It can lead to crime, which sends away too many fathers and mothers, who then live behind bars with little hope of influencing their children in a positive way. Poverty—in other words—throws a lot of impediments between a person and life, liberty, and the pursuit of happiness.

Racism, experienced through both individual and systematic expressions, has condemned generations of people of color to lives of poverty, both real and relative, at a measurably higher rate than those considered white. And this lack of basic economic well-being has fostered deep anxiety and struggle among generations of people in our country and in other regions of the world. The chain reaction has been well-documented through the impact of: stress on health, socioeconomic factors on stress, and racism on socioeconomic status.[3] Again, that may seem obvious; but I don't think many people in middle- to upper-class environments and hailing from European roots are willing to connect the dots as closely as we must on this topic.

Over the past two decades, more lower- to middle-class white folks, especially those with limited education levels, have experienced economic threat levels that most African Americans and Latinx folks have faced for a long time. According to the Pew Research Center, the Great Recession of 2008 cut the overall net wealth—a measure of all assets, including real estate and investments—of lower-class white families from $42,700 per family to $19,600 by 2013.[4] For many pundits, that was the initial narrative explaining the populist, nationalist Trump phenomenon. The theory was that, with their class and income expectations threatened, a large number of white people— many self-proclaimed Christian white people—lined up to support a man who had little to nothing in common with their economic plight or religious values. No matter that the candidate willingly plucked those strings of insecurity by blaming the bogeymen of immigrants (*brown* immigrants!) and elitists around the world who were taking advantage of the good ole US of A.

Meanwhile, black and brown citizens experienced, relatively speaking, less wealth reduction during the same period—although it was wealth they never really had to lose in the first place. African American net wealth went from an average of $4,300 to $3,500 and the wealth of Latinx families from $8,400 to $6,800. Comparatively speaking, the white demographic, especially at the lower-class levels, perceived a lot more loss, even though they were still two to five times better off than people of color. Still, loss stings, even if it's relative to what you're used to, right?

But wait a minute. Deeper studies have shown that Trump voters were slightly *more* affluent and educated than the average American.[5] Plenty of highly educated, well-earning, middle- to upper-class white Americans lined up behind Trump. Outside of those who were primarily one-issue voters seeking to tip the Supreme Court against abortion (voters who, by the way, had many pro-life GOP presidential candidates to choose from in the primaries), did most of these voters react based on the *fear* of losing social status, not necessarily the *reality* of losing economic status? "My vote was my only way to say: I am here, and I count," said one Trump voter in New York.[6] This white woman felt like she was invisible; that she didn't count. Based on conversations I've had with several white folks with a self-perception of persecution and loss of status, it's safe to assume that she felt like people of color counted more now in this country, that they were somehow getting the benefits that she no longer was.

Who's right? And how much does getting to the truth matter to me as a white-labeled person determining whether to give up this identity? How does the truth matter to the future of whiteness as a racial category in general, and to the future of our country?

With such a clear tie between economic security, happiness, and health, exactly how much has racism robbed Americans with ancestry beyond European roots of their happiness? And how much has it benefited me and others considered white? Recent losses among white folks in real or perceived status (and therefore happiness) notwithstanding, the more I learned the statistics, the more the enormity of this truth came into focus: Racism has cheated and is still cheating millions of Americans out of the core promise in our country's

Declaration of Independence (notwithstanding that ugly reference griping about the King's support for "the merciless Indian Savages").

To get a sense of the magnitude of the economic disparity enabled by race, let's start with the beginning of our country and work our way to the present day. Two economists have determined the economic worth of the labor of enslaved people in modern dollars, from the beginning of the practice of slavery in the United States in 1619 until the official (if not actual) end of slavery after the Civil War in 1865.

The value of all that free labor, at 2018 currency value? *Thirteen trillion dollars.*[7]

Setting aside how offensive and impossible it is to place a dollar value on even one human life and that individual's suffering and loss of happiness, it is mind-boggling to consider the economic role that enslaved people played in the making of America's overall white economy, and the destruction that slavery wrought on the economy of those who weren't white. For some perspective, $13 trillion is roughly 75% of 2016's entire Gross Domestic Product in the United States. For those concerned over unfair "wealth redistribution" policies in today's political debate, the value of free labor via slavery is, by far, the greatest wealth redistribution in American history.

Much of that slave-derived wealth was concentrated in the South. But not all of it. Enslaved people's labor accounted for roughly 50% of the wealth of the South in 1860 at the outbreak of the Civil War, and about 19% of the wealth of the entire United States. Many cotton plantations and other industries located in the South were financed by bankers and had their biggest apparel-manufacturing customers in the North. In fact, one of the biggest concentrations of opposition against Abraham Lincoln and abolition wasn't in the South; it was in New York City.[8]

Northern business tycoons had deep ties to the Southern slave economy and lobbied against outlawing the practice of owning black and brown people. This included textile manufacturers in New England, who relied on slave-picked cotton to build their industry; insurance companies such as New York Life and Aetna, which sold policies that protected the value of slaves for slaveholders; and banks such as JP Morgan Chase and FleetBoston, which actually financed slave traders and accepted enslaved people as collateral on loans (and these lenders ended up owning slaves themselves when certain loans were in default and humans became their property).[9]

In other words, slavery and its ramifications weren't just Southern problems. They were and are United States problems.

✳ ✳ ✳

Once again, some may be thinking, "So what? That's all over now. I haven't owned any slaves or discriminated like those rascally Southern rebels. My family didn't own slaves. We're cool now. Black people basically get the same protections and benefits as everyone else these days, right? Stop whining; there's no excuse for not bucking up and making a decent life in this great country of ours. Let's move on."

I heard this so often during informal interviews with white acquaintances during my journey that I decided I needed to study the logic of the "hey, it wasn't me" argument. Why should modern white people feel guilty and be asked to sacrifice their own pursuit of happiness, so others get an advantage (which is the core of most anti-affirmative action arguments)?

"History is who we are and why we are the way we are," historian David McCullough has noted. In other words, the issue isn't one of guilt and blame over the past; it's one of equity and justice today. White people are still benefiting from the fruits of racism past and present. If you need some facts on the matter to make up your mind, consider these recent data points:

* Black and Hispanic families, on average, hold less than 10% of the net worth that white families have, even when compared across the same levels of education. (You'll learn why in the coming chapters.)[10]

* An extensive study of available research in hiring discrimination (over 55,000 applicants and over 26,000 positions) found that white applicants received 36% more callbacks (invitations to interview after an initial resumé is sent) even when qualifications were equivalent. This advantage has not changed since the issue has been researched beginning in 1989.[11]

* Despite improvements from the Affordable Care Act, people of color represent more than half of the nonelderly, uninsured population in the United States.[12]

* The Stanford Open Policing Project has thoroughly analyzed police traffic-stop data from 20 states, covering more than 60 million state patrol stops. While addressing the extremely complex challenges in measuring bias, the study found significant racial disparities in policing across white, black, and Hispanic drivers. Black drivers are 20% more likely to get a ticket instead of a warning after being pulled over for speeding than white drivers, while Hispanics are 30% more likely to receive a ticket than white drivers. Both black and Hispanic motorists can expect to be searched about twice as often as white drivers.[13]

* According to the United States Sentencing Commission, African American men are sentenced to 20% longer prison sentences for the exact same crimes compared to white men. (More on this and other justice data points later.)[14]

Diving back into American history, I was curious about how these disparities tracked against the lived experience of different races and ethnicities across generations in the United States. After all, these vast differences in life experience didn't appear overnight, and they are clearly continuing to impact our lives today. Current and future disparities sit on the foundations of historic policies and practices.

How have racial attitudes and practices, as applied to tangible elements of a healthy, happy life, affected different Americans? I couldn't find a holistic view of these factors in my research, so I decided to knit together data points that have been tracked throughout American history. These numbers, easily pulled from US Census and National Center for Education Statistics reports, tell a story of a powerful generational head start for Americans considered to be white—a story that explains the persistent disparities we still observe today. Despite what many might assume, none of the implications of this long-running story were erased by Abraham Lincoln's moves toward freedom or Lyndon Johnson's presidential signatures on key civil rights legislation (see chart 1).

Chart 1: Overview of racial disparity data, 1800–2020

	ca. 1800	ca. 1870	ca. 1910 (my grandparents' generation)	ca. 1940 (my parents' generation)
Literacy and Education	Limited to white males. 55% of white children enrolled in school; 2% of African American children enrolled. Illegal to teach slaves to read.	About the same rate of white children enrolled as in 1800. White adults had 88.5% literacy rate. Africans Americans had 10% school attendance and 20.1% literacy.	Whites reached 95% literacy, 13.5% high school and 2.7% college attainment. No data on African American degree attainment available; 69.5% literacy.	White Americans attained a 98% literacy rate and 75% attend school, with 26% achieving a high school degree. African Americans had a 78% literacy rate and 7.7% held a high school degree. "Separate but equal" was still the law of the land, especially in Southern states.
Political Representation	White, property-owning males allowed to vote. Slaves counted as three-fifths of a person with zero voice.	Property requirement eliminated in most states by 1828. The 14th and 15th Amendments secured voting rights for African Americans. More than ½ million voted in the South before 1877 but then voting participation plummeted again to 10%—thanks to Jim Crow restrictions.	Voting virtually nonexistent for black citizens in the South. Some 50,000 Klansmen march through Washington, D.C., in a 1925 show of force. Hispanics and Asians don't yet appear in government data.	Only 3% of African Americans of voting age in Southern states were registered to vote.
Access to Opportunity	Limited opportunities for free blacks in the North; African Americans limited to slavery in the South.	Initial burst of opportunity during Reconstruction for African Americans; quickly taken back after 1877. Thousands of black citizens re-enslaved through enforcement of nuisance laws and prisoner-leasing.	Most skilled or desirable jobs in public and private sector limited to whites. Hiring, housing, and other forms of discrimination based on race were legal. Black prisoner-leasing continued in the South.	Median family income is $1,368, but not yet analyzed by race. Federal government jobs slowly opened to African Americans. The US military desegregated in 1948. Black prisoner-leasing continued in South.

	ca. 1960 (my generation)	ca. 2000 (my children's generation)	ca. 2020
Literacy and Education	Now 43.2% of white Americans held a high school degree and 8.1% a college degree. Still only 21.7% of African Americans held a high school diploma and 3.5% a four-year college degree.	At this point 88.4% of white Americans held a high school degree; 28.1% a college degree. 78.9% of African Americans earned a high school degree and 16.6% a college degree. Hispanics reached 57% high school completion and 10.6% college, and Asians 85.7% and 44.5%, respectively, for each degree.	Every racial category has experienced significant increases in high school and college degree attainment: white (94% and 38%), black (88% and 24%), Hispanic (71% and 17%), and Asian (91% and 55%)
Political Representation	The Voting Rights Act of 1965 had an immediate and powerful impact on voting rights in the South; by the end of 1966 (the year I was born), 9 out of 13 southern states had more than 50% of African Americans registered to vote.	White and black Americans vote at 62% and 56% rates, respectively; Hispanics at 45% and Asians at 43%.	White (65%) and black (60%) voters still vote at higher rates than Hispanics (48%) and Asians (49%), a disparity some experts attribute to the relative youthful average age between groups (young people vote at a far lower rate than older voters).
Access to Opportunity	The median income of a white family was $5,835; median income for African American families was only 55% that of whites at $3,230. Governments and corporations such as IBM began hiring more people of color.	Median family income reached $61,715 for white Americans, $40,131 for African Americans, $44,867 for Hispanics, and $68,143 for Asians.	Asian median household income has taken a clear lead at $81,331 compared to white ($68,145), black ($40,258), and Hispanic ($50,486). Note the flat growth of black income. Median household wealth for black families is still roughly only 10% that of white families.

Whiteness in the United States, and I can only assume, in other white-dominated countries of the world, is like playing a game of Monopoly, in which a substantial amount of cash and property are dealt to you at the start of the game. Even if you're one of the white folks who didn't inherit tangible wealth, your dice are still loaded in a way that you can jump ahead of the other players with each roll. The head start that was built into the American economic and cultural system—to stack the deck in favor of white people of mostly European origin and against specific other groups of color—was and is highly effective, as demonstrated by the huge disparity in median household net worth between white, brown, and black families.

Perhaps it's true that modern-day white folks aren't to "blame" for the past perpetration of slavery, Jim Crow segregation, or the slavery-by-any-other-name practice of incarcerated workers. But if we as white people are benefiting from this system to this very day—from net worth to how we can expect the criminal justice system to deal with us—without working to dismantle it, using whatever methods we have at our disposal, what does that make us? Co-conspirators? Collaborators? Certainly, ongoing beneficiaries.

✴ ✴ ✴

Another narrative the data tells is that of immense faith in the face of crushing obstacles. To observe the steady climb of African Americans and Hispanics in education and income is a testimony to amazing perseverance and strength. Some have pointed to the role of religious faith in helping these communities maintain hope and resilience. Whatever the reason, it should be an inspiration to all of us—as well as a disgrace to those of us considered white—that Americans have had to face such unequal challenges, decade after decade. When given a real shot at opportunity, all humans, regardless of skin color or ancestry, thrive.

These aren't pleasant thoughts. I can see why the hair on the back of the neck of a white person might rise when this is discussed—especially that of one who is struggling economically. To help me more deeply grasp the personal impact, I thought about Archie and Hazel on Red Hill, and I looked through those generational statistics. What if my grandparents had been African American?

Born in 1911 and 1909, only 44 years since the Thirteenth Amendment officially abolished the legalized owning of black people, Hazel and Archie would have had many family members who had lived through slavery. Assuming in this imaginary scenario that they still lived in Wood County, West Virginia, their access to quality schooling, especially in that mostly white, very rural region, would have been nonexistent. Even if their children had been fortunate enough to have made it through high school, the opportunities for a college education and the loans to pay for it would have been severely limited in the 1940s and 1950s, when lending was highly discriminatory against black people. Until the Home Mortgage Disclosure Act of 1975, they would have faced major barriers in buying a home (98% of home loans went to white families from 1934 to 1962), the source of most white Americans' net worth.[15]

Had my grandparents been black, I may have been the first generation of the James family to attend college, instead of the second. Perhaps I, or one of my cousins, instead of those of our parents' generation, would have been the first to receive a home loan. Or not. Regardless, my theoretical African American version of the James family today would have $10.50 in net worth for every $100 that the average white family has today.

Real-world data create a dissonance between what we hope or think is true, and how things really are. I began to think a lot about numbers as it relates to my whiteness. In the case of race and the experience of nonwhite people in the United States or any region of the world, numbers can help the majority population understand just how immensely different their experience is from the experiences of those not in their race or class.

For example, what is the likelihood that a person of color in the United States will experience dealing with an individual who holds racist views and wields power over them, or controls access to resources they need for their lives? Despite the recent publicity around how our country's demographics are changing rapidly, and the projection that we will be a "non-majority" country by 2055 (meaning no one racial group will represent over 50% of the population), today those categorized as "white alone" in terms of race amount to 77% of the population. That leaves 23% as nonwhite (Hispanic Americans, as an ethnic category and not a race, can be categorized within white, black, or other races). Although the United States has made slow, somewhat steady progress, we also know that people considered white are overrepresented in most leadership and authority roles in this country. Bear with me while we knit together what that means for typical interactions in daily life.

According to a recent and extensive study on racial attitudes in the United States, approximately 15 to 20% of Americans hold what most people would consider "deeply racist views."[16] Measuring overt racial bias in surveys can be notoriously difficult, since in the latter half of the 20th century it became more socially awkward to share such sentiments, but responses to specific statements provide a pretty solid predictive framework. Here is a sampling of statements on the survey and the responses they garnered. "America must protect and preserve its White European heritage": *16% of respondents strongly agreed; another 15% somewhat agreed.* "Marriage should only be allowed between people of the same race": *10% strongly agree; 6% somewhat agree.* "All races are equal": *only 70% strongly agreed.*

"All races should be treated equally": *80% strongly agreed—leaving a concerning group of 20% who didn't.*

While racial attitudes do shift toward a more diverse worldview and a belief in equality as individuals acquire higher levels of education, a surprising number of college-educated individuals hold racist views. Many other respondents have likely learned how to react in an acceptable way to a direct question about racism—while continuing to hold racist views that are thus not reflected in the data.[17]

I decided to mathematically put myself in the shoes of a person of color in the United States. Unfortunately, as a math-challenged individual, I had to tap into the skills of my brainy sister-in-law, a college math professor, to determine the daily likelihood of a person having to deal with a person of another race or ethnicity holding power over them in basic areas of life, while also holding racist views. Assuming the strictest definition of overt racist views and holding that assumption equally across racial and ethnic groups, let's say for the sake of this exercise that 16% of any given racial group holds clear animosity or prejudice against other races. Then, factoring in the current percentage of racial and ethnic representation across various leadership roles, it becomes clear why people of color have a much different perception of the level of racism that exists in our culture than most white people do:

* If you're one of the 83.5 million people who take out some type of loan each year, chances are you'll deal with a white loan officer 84% of the time. That means if you're a white person seeking a loan, you have a 3% likelihood of running into a loan officer who is a person of color and happens to have overt anti-white feelings. If you're a black person seeking a loan, you'll have a 13% likelihood of running into an

actively racist loan officer. That means a black person is five times more likely than a white person to run into an overtly racist loan officer.

* A citizen of color is eight times more likely than a white citizen to be living under the governance of a public official with a racial bias against them. Of course, with the severe segregation of many US cities, this estimate could differ greatly with public officials, such as city councils or mayors, who may or may not reflect their community's demographics.

* In the workplace, an employee of color is nine times more likely to be working for a CEO (of any company size) who doesn't believe he or she is equal. If you work in a Fortune 500 corporation in which only 0.6% of CEOs are people of color, your chances as a person of color of working for a racist top executive stand at 16%. If you are a white person in a Fortune 500 company, your likelihood of working for someone biased against your race is 0.1%. If you consider all 17 million managerial roles, a person of color is five times more likely to work for a racist.

* A patient of color has an 11% probability of being treated by a white doctor who is biased against them; a white person has a 5% probability. While that's only about two times more likely, the wild card here is that a much higher proportion of doctors than the general population in the United States are Asian. So, if you look more specifically at African American patients, that patient population is twelve times more likely to experience a racist white or Asian doctor than a white person is. When you consider the average person visits a doctor three times a year, that's a lot of potential bias in the healthcare system.

* A K–12 student of color has a 13% probability of being taught by a teacher who holds clear racial or ethnic bias against them; a white child has only a 2% chance of encountering such a teacher.
* A citizen of color is about six times more likely to engage a white law enforcement officer who is biased against them, than a white citizen is likely to run into a biased cop or judicial official.

Of course, these are all very rough estimates. Great differences could be experienced depending on the racial makeup of a given neighborhood or region. Also, it's important to remember that the 16% racist estimate in a given racial group doesn't really do the exercise justice; that's only the number who are overt in their racism. It doesn't factor in more moderate racist tendencies, which can still factor consciously or subconsciously into how people get treated. Even with these conservative estimates, is it any wonder our perceptions are so different about racial equality in America?

Studying (and agonizing over) the implications of these statistics and historic realities wasn't enjoyable for me (nor would it likely be for any white person confronted with them). I can understand why most don't want to dive into this information and would prefer to think that everything is equal today. Then I as a white person could quite easily determine I have no responsibility to dismantle this tainted system that benefits those who look like me, but systematically limits everyone else.

It turns out that guilt doesn't sit well with happiness. And don't we all want to be happy? Embracing truth that steals my happiness has a built-in disincentive. At the same time, researchers have proven that guilt is a powerful motivator for people to take action to make things right if they see the correlation between their own actions and harm done toward others. If we deny the direct responsibility of maintaining a system that benefits "our people" to the detriment of others, we feel no motivation to fix things. Psychologists have found that after accepting responsibility, humans tend to work hard to purge guilt and seek the satisfaction of pursuing restorative action.[18]

Soothing the pain of our realities is obviously tempting. Denying the truth and blaming others are great tactics for minimizing guilt in the short-term. However, working to solve the problem is the only long-term, sustainable way to reset our inner selves to equilibrium. It's not about working off white guilt; it's about working toward equal justice and supporting other humans in their pursuit of the American Dream. That's the challenge and opportunity for all of us in our time.

I looked again at our family's journey and compared it, first, to the broader experience of white Americans, then, to the trends for people of color. Of course, all mothers and fathers and grandmas and grandpas want their own progeny to acquire the education and find the economic opportunities that our family did. Yes, my grandma and grandpa made sure their children were headed down the right path, but the path clearly led to a reward that matched the sacrifice. For so many others in American history, the path has been much steeper and the odds far lower that the risks would lead to rewards. My children and I are dually privileged: privileged to be part of the James family, but also privileged to be in the dominant racial and cultural category where those opportunities were far more tangible.

I felt proud of the one privilege, and I felt frustrated by the other.

4

Plato and Pecking Orders

The discovery of personal whiteness among the
world's peoples is a very modern thing—a nineteenth
and twentieth century matter, indeed. The ancient
world would have laughed at such a distinction.
—W. E. B. Du Bois

As I sat in my neighborhood Starbucks on July 4th beside an Arab-American gentleman wearing a Nashville Predators hockey jersey, I thought about where we were now, as a country of growing diversity. History is pretty clear that racial and ethnic tensions facing our country in the last few years are much more the norm than the exception. American heroes across the political, business, cultural, academic, and sports spectrums—the shapers of our cultural mores—have espoused and championed white supremacy. The continuity of this worldview throughout history testifies to just how deeply race penetrates and defines our society.

The late Senator Daniel Patrick Moynihan once said, "Everyone is entitled to his own opinion, but not to his own facts." These days, it seems, people are challenging that notion and making up their own facts, or at least choosing which ones they want to believe. If my mission to explore giving up whiteness was to have any credibility for myself and others, I realized I needed to understand the origins and history of this ubiquitous and peculiar notion of race—which to some is a differentiation of small, almost meaningless degree, and to others is a differentiation of a vast, essential kind that determines inherent levels of human intellect and moral superiority.

I needed to answer a key question: Is race *real*? In other words, are there real, scientifically valid differences between distinct races, and are those differences in any way significant for how we relate to ourselves and each other? Or is race just a social construct, something invented by some humans to classify those deemed as "other"? That question seemed to be at the heart of whether whiteness was something even possible for me to give up. If race is a valid physical and genetic construct, I could no easier give it up than being five feet, 11 inches tall.

The social construct argument around race was of equal interest to me. If our ideas of race have no basis in physical, measurable difference, how have we built such deep cultural identities and rules around it? If *race* isn't a real thing, how is it that *racism* so clearly is? And if the vast majority of people in our society are still firmly convinced that race is an actual physical reality, is it possible to give it up? I realized how ironic my journey seemed in contrast to the journey of an African American woman who has fought hard for decades to find pride in her race. Here I was, seeking to rid myself of the pride and privilege associated with mine. Were we supposed to meet some-where in the middle on our journeys, or should we all give up these categories?

Learning a much more comprehensive history of race and its impli-cations seemed a critical place to begin answering these questions.

It can be a little awkward studying books on the origins of race in public. Based on recommendations from friends, as well as a little Google sleuthing, I came upon incredibly helpful references, such as *The History of White People* by Dr. Nell Irvin Painter (think about how that title could be misconstrued while you hold it up to read in a coffee shop), and *Stamped from the Beginning* by Dr. Ibram X. Kendi. One elderly, overly friendly gentleman who worked at Chick-Fil-A, once stood over my table, and after asking if I wanted a drink refill, proceeded to lean over and read aloud the subtitle from Dr. Kendi's book: "The . . . Definitive . . . History . . . of . . . Racist . . . Ideas." He then proceeded to accidentally spill the tray he was holding all over my lap.

The more I read about the racist beliefs and actions of celebrated leaders across our history, the more I asked myself: How and when did these beliefs take shape in the history of humanity? What caused them to stick so perniciously to our human psyche and permeate so thoroughly our culture's institutions and systems of power? At what point were "white" people seen as superior (at least in their own minds)? Was there an era when the tables were turned, or have the ancient writings of Asian and African cultures also laced their histories with descriptions of pale-skinned inferiority? With so many amazing achievements and cultures across the span of human history and from every nook and cranny of the globe, where did this stuff come from?

✳ ✳ ✳

The interaction between science, religion, and history has always fascinated me. Not surprisingly, all these disciplines have played a significant role in inventing and shaping the ongoing concept we think of as race. Perhaps it is a marker of adult-onset awareness, but it's difficult to grasp and accept how so many forces beyond our control shape us.

The first, and probably most illuminating thing I learned, is that from the perspective of most modern scientists, race as a biological concept isn't real.[1] In fact, along my journey, I was continually surprised to learn how race seemed to be more of a legally or culturally defined concept than a scientific one. As far back as 1950, an international panel of anthropologists, geneticists, sociologists, and psychologists declared that race was not a biological reality but a myth. Decades later in June 2000, at the momentous White House announcement of the completion of the mapping of the human genome, Craig Venter, one of the scientists who supervised the mapping of 22,300 human genes, said, "The concept of race has no genetic or scientific basis." His scientific team could not tell from an individual DNA basis which human specimen was Hispanic, Asian, Caucasian, or African American.[2] Since then, a great deal of research as well as statements published by the American Anthropological Association and the American Association of Physical Anthropologists have affirmed this conclusion.

Scientists agree that all humans, despite whatever racial categories we try to slot them in, share the same set of genes. They've even pointed out that there can be more DNA similarities between two people apparently of *different* races than between members of the *same* race.[3] In fact, genetic investigation has shown that: all humans have common biological ancestors who migrated out of East Africa; humans have intermingled genetically since their beginnings; and that the 7 billion plus humans on Earth today share common ancestors who existed just 2,000 or 3,000 years ago.[4] British geneticist Adam Rutherford summarizes our current understanding of race:

> It isn't good enough to say that race doesn't exist, tempting though that might be. Race certainly does exist, because *we perceive it and racism exists because we enact it* [emphasis mine]. What is unequivocal is that the colloquial and traditional descriptions of race that are commonly used in the West are not accurately reflected by underlying genetics. Much of this disconnect is derived from the historical roots of the pseudoscience of race, founded in the so-called Age of Enlightenment, by writers and thinkers, most of whom did not visit the continents or the people they were attempting to categorize. These clumsy, erroneous and judgmental taxonomies stuck and echo into the present.[5]

Many scientists prefer to use the term *ancestry* far more regularly than *race*, because it is more precise in referring to a human's ancestral story and its impact on who they are, instead of a broad, nonbiological, socially constructed grouping such as race.

Genetic researchers have found that 99.9% of our DNA is the same across apparent racial categories. Only a tiny fraction determines the outward features that became so dominant in the development of race-based classification. Scientists now realize such features are primarily environmentally derived. We might as well have determined which races were "superior" based on clothing style, instead of skin color or hair type.[6] I had to think about that for a deep moment: just 0.1% of our DNA has formed the basis for centuries of division, chattel slavery, tens of millions of deaths, and crippling oppression.

Lots of questions come to mind in the wake of this information. When in human history did physical features—skin color, hair types, facial features—begin to differentiate humans enough for early scientists to attempt their creation of racial categories? There seems to be a surprising lack of consensus on that question. After our ancestors lost our hairy exteriors, complexion became a battle between two key vitamins, folate and Vitamin D.[7] Since the impact of the sun's ultraviolet (UV) rays varies by region, the theory is that adaptations led to variations of skin tones that balanced the need to protect folate (sunlight breaks it down) and produce more Vitamin D (UV initiates its production). These adaptations occurred as humans migrated out of Africa and warmer climates into northern climates. Those traits are still within the 0.1% of our DNA differences.[8]

In the realm of conservative Christian theology, all humans derive from two narrow human fountainheads: from Adam and Eve, and then a little later in Genesis from the descendants of Noah, the only family to survive the global flood. Considering the common vision from both scientific and religious perspectives—that humans have a shared ancestry—where did such pernicious ideas about superior versus inferior races come from? Why would such spurious ideas take shape?

With each new historic or scientific fact I came upon, my mind filled with so many questions. Who started categorizing and assigning stereotypes to groups of people? Who decided that these differences came with inherent and varying levels of worth?

Who made up white?

✸ ✸ ✸

To the consternation of white supremacist genealogy aficionados, the history of race, and therefore the history of the "white" race, is actually quite fuzzy. The definition of race and whiteness has never been very firm or linear. Who was "in" and who was "out" of preferred categorizations morphed several times. Here is how it went down.

Since we can only interpret recorded history, not observe it, we can only look back so far before the history of humanity gets extremely murky. Whether scrawled in drawings on the sides of caves or clues from the earliest written languages, the story of humans is a history of competitive division, struggle, and war. The earliest groups of people banded together around familial lines, and, for the most part, the assumption was that those not in your tight little tribe were the enemy competing for your resources. In addition to committing unspeakable violence against each other, many humans had another favorite element of warfare: slavery. Once you conquered an enemy group, you either slaughtered the people or made them your slaves.[9]

Of course, most of the time the groups of people that ancient humans fought against looked a lot like themselves. Africans fought Africans, Native Americans fought Native Americans, Asians fought Asians, Europeans fought Europeans—mostly because that's who you rubbed up against in daily life. These other people were trying to hunt in your territory or take over your little patch of land. So, people tended to enslave people who looked like themselves.

Over time, as humans began building larger cultures and kingdoms formed from local tribes, the perceived enemies began to represent larger groupings of people from more distant lands. For example, before there were "white" people, there were tribal groups in Europe: Scythians, Celts, Gauls, and Germani—which, by the way, are the names the Greeks gave them. We don't know exactly what those tribes called themselves, but those names have stuck; it's another reminder that those who write history get to shape it. Those who would now be considered "white" Romans saw other "white" Germani tribes as inferior barbarians. It wasn't until these humans consolidated, became more mobile, and began to engage other humans across far-flung regions that they noted how different-looking these new groups of people were, with their varying skin tones, hair textures, and facial features, all of which had evolved over time as homo sapiens spread out across the globe. The earliest documenters of physical and cultural differences, therefore, were explorers, traders, and conquerors. The more I learned about the history of race, the more obvious it was that the development of race and the theories of superiority or inferiority were closely tied to the economic and political goals of those doing the defining.

Much of what we in North America have assumed about the origins of race come from either European or Arabic sources; by definition, that's a limited, biased lens. However, other groups of ancient groups of people had similar prejudicial tendencies. For example, a third-century Han Dynasty historian dismissed blonde-haired, blue-eyed barbarians as resembling the monkeys from which they surely must have descended. Apparently human descent from primates was not only Darwin's idea.[10]

Greek philosophers and historians were among the first to collect observations from their explorers. They formed these observations into histories rife with assumptions and sometimes wild stories shared by the returning adventurers and traders. Most Westerners still consider Socrates, Plato, and Aristotle intellectual heroes, yet as historian Nell Irvin Painter points out in *The History of White People*, their search for "nobler races" laid a lot of groundwork for future theories on race and racism.

Hippocrates would document his thoughts on various groups and opine broadly with simple observations that, let's just say, lacked scientific rigor. He wrote that people living near stagnant water "must show protruding bellies and enlarged spleens." In areas of fertile lowlands, "the inhabitants are fleshy, ill-articulated, moist, lazy, and generally cowardly in character." (*Moist*—really?) Which terrain produced the most brave, intelligent, and strong humans, according to Hippocrates? Greece, of course. The rugged Greek countryside produced, as Painter quotes, "men who are hard, lean, well-articulated, well-braced, and hairy; such natures will be found energetic, vigilant, stubborn and independent in character and in temper, wild rather than tame, of more than average sharpness and intelligence in the arts, and in war of more than average courage."[11]

Later, Plato argued that it made no sense for Greeks to enslave other Greeks; why not focus on enslaving "barbarian" foreigners who were clearly inferior to any Greek?[12] Plato's student, Aristotle, articulated even deeper ethnocentric, proto-racist ideas that assumed some superior humans had a responsibility to rule others as slaves for their own good: "That some should rule and others be ruled is a thing not only necessary, but expedient; from the hour of their birth, some are marked out for subjection, others for rule. [T]he lower sort are by nature slaves, and it is better for them as for all inferiors that they should be under the rule of a master."[13]

The Greeks became fascinated with the Caucasus region, which brings us the term *Caucasian*. The Caucasus Mountains are found between the Black Sea and the Caspian Sea. Today this territory is governed in the north by the Russian Federation and the states of Georgia and Azerbaijan, and in the south by Turkey and Iran. Before any definitions of racial categories, this region was first referenced in historical records by Greek mythology. Jason and the Argonauts searched for the Golden Fleece in this region. Many of the Greeks' wildest myths seemed to occur in the mysterious Caucasus. It's where Odysseus's men were turned into animals in Homer's *Odyssey*. And it's where Prometheus, who stole the source of fire from Zeus, had his liver pecked out by an eagle sent from the always-grumpy god. However, it wasn't until the 18th century that German scientist Johann Friedrich Blumenbach began assigning light-skinned European people the classification of "Caucasian," based on an assessment of the beauty of the women in the region. Apparently even science can get derailed by sexual attraction.

In Europe, as Christianity became the official religion of Rome, spread across the empire, and mixed with politics and power, theological and observational theories also commingled. The curse theories of Cain and Ham (for more on this erroneous biblical interpretation, see chapter 9) were handed down, while observational theories spread that race was a result of environmental factors. As Christian and Muslim cultures clashed and traded with each other, these intermingled theories were extended. Although the notion that lighter skin was somehow inherently more valuable than darker skin was clearly taking shape among Europeans, the concepts and categories of "race" were still vague. European peoples were still more commonly classified by tribal names, such as Scythians, Celts, Gauls, and Germani. Greeks and Romans considered all of them inferior races. But as those civilizations declined and other European kingdoms arose, assumptions of stratified human value were passed to the next generation of dominant societies. As Northern European cultures and nations formed, they flipped the insult and began writing about how they viewed Southern Europeans as inferior. Those same Italians and Greeks who had called *them* barbarians now experienced the racial shoe on the other foot.

Soon enough, economic ambition and competition between cultures created a huge demand for the racist theories that supported slave trading. Slavery itself is not unique to Europeans. European slave traders were rivaled by Islamic traders in terms of who was most prolific at this dehumanizing practice. Islamic traders sent approximately 10 million Africans across the Sahara to north Africa, Arabia, Yemen, Iraq, Iran, and India. Christian and Muslim cultures jockeyed for dominance in all manner of trade, including salt- and gold-trading routes into Africa.

For years, Europeans had to work through Turkish and other Muslim cultures to source their desired goods, including the acquisition of slaves. Since the ninth century, those slaves included people captured from Slavic regions, people who today would be categorized as "white." The Greeks considered Slavic tribes inferior humans, as much as Africans or any other non-Greek peoples. (The word *slave* has its root in *slav*.) Over time, Slavic cultures banded together to build forts and fight off the slave traders, effectively closing the spigot of "white" slaves. Europeans and Arabs now began refocusing the slave trade exclusively toward Africa.

✳ ✳ ✳

In the 15th century, an ambitious prince, Henry of Portugal, decided to cut out the Muslim middlemen and find a way to procure slaves directly. In 1444, the Portuguese decided to sail around the Western Sahara's Cape Bojador and invade West Africa to capture people. The journey was documented by Gomes Eanes de Zurara in *The Chronicle of the Discovery and Conquest of Guinea*. Zurara's account, the first European book about Africans in that era, became highly influential among the economic and social elite. It held out racist observations and justifications for the slave trade, including the new theory of slave trading as a "missionary expedition" for the Christian faith, which spread rapidly to those hungry to justify their practices. The book's assertion that capturing and enslaving other humans was not just justified, but a dignified endeavor, was built on the idea that Prince Henry "reflected with great pleasure upon the salvation of those souls that before were lost." Yes, Portugal surely must be doing a favor to these people who "lived like beasts, without any custom of reasonable beings . . . without covering of clothes, or the lodgement of houses, and worse than all, they had no understanding of good, but only knew how to live in bestial sloth" as Zurara put it.

There's only one problem, of course. Well, several problems. One is that West Africa, in fact, had several well-developed cultures which

included the Mali kingdom (1230 AD–1670 AD) with its capital city
of Timbuktu, a center of Islamic education and commerce, and the
Songhai empire (1375–1591). It's quite clear from the history of those
societies that their residents wore clothing, lived in homes, and had a
well-developed sense of religiously rooted morality, despite the inaccurate descriptions from Mr. Zurara. In fact, Timbuktu maintained
extensive libraries and an Islamic university. At the same time when
Zurara published his biased, erroneous description of captured Africans living in "bestial sloth," one could find Europeans and Slavs
(aka "white" people) living in abject poverty, in small "cruck" houses
made of mud, straw, and manure, just outside of major urban centers.
"Bestial" is in the eye of the beholder.[14]

The other blindingly obvious issue is that Christian faith—or any
faith, for that matter—is only legitimate when you have free will to
adopt it. Faith is a belief. Belief is a personal decision. Forced conver-
sions are not real decisions. Most of the assumptions held by those
then in power, as heinous as these assumptions sound today, formed
the basis for the spread and defense of slavery across European colonies and into America. As race concepts and a belief in white superiority took firm hold in European culture, European states used such
paternalistic rationales as "these savages are better off this way," to
justify colonization, slavery, apartheid segregation, forced religious
conversion, reeducation propaganda to strip native people of their
culture, and widespread confiscation of land and resources. To this
day, you can hear some white racists refer to the "better off" defense.
Cliven Bundy, a US rancher who has run afoul of the government for
letting his cattle graze on public lands, speaking to his supporters,
referred to "Negroes," saying: "I've often wondered, are they better
off as slaves." That speech was delivered in 2014.[15]

Back in the 15th century, soon the Spanish, Dutch, and English were following Portugal into the West African slave trade. The

Europeans would not have been as successful in their slave-trading without the cooperation of African tribal leaders. Those leaders helped to supply them with people from deeper within the interior of the African continent. However, it is important to note that the Africans who were complicit in slave-trading lacked the philosophical race-based inferiority rationale. They operated primarily from a spoils-of-war justification. Many other people were simply kidnapped or traded as debt payment.[16] To this day, some African activists are pressuring descendants of those slave-trading Africans to acknowledge that their families benefited from this practice, just as Western activists are calling out multinational corporations and individuals for their slave-derived economic advantages.[17]

By the end of the African chattel slave trade, at least 10 to 15 million African human beings had been sent across the Atlantic. At least two million of these trafficked people (but probably more) died during what is called the Middle Passage. Traders packed people like sardines, one on top of another, in inhuman conditions aboard slave ships. It is known that before the Middle Passage, many millions more died during forced marches from deep inside the African continent to the coastal slave-trading centers. It is estimated that for every 100 Africans who made it to the "New World," another 40 died in Africa or on the Atlantic. Imagine the long-term impact on any region or continent, when tens of millions of the most able-bodied members are carted away to distant lands or die in this process.

It's no wonder that many white people aren't all that interested in this history, and that it's still not covered thoroughly by our academic curriculum. The level of genocide within the construct of the slave trade is unimaginable. It's impossible to understand how slave traders and buyers—whether European, Middle Eastern, or African; Christian or Islamic—could observe this carnage and continue participating in it. I doubt that many slave owners in Virginia or South

Carolina gave a second thought to the death toll or the impact on families, tribes, and cultures. After all, these dark-skinned people were "other," "less than," and "better off."

All told, during the period of Atlantic slave trading, as many as *60 million Africans* died or were enslaved as a result of the slave trade.[18] Sixty million human beings at a time when the population of the entire globe was under one billion and when the estimated population of Africa in 1850 was only 100 million. The trans-Atlantic slave trade has been identified as the reason that Africa's population remained flat from 1700 to about 1900; the vast forced resettlement, and the huge death rates that accompanied it, depopulated the entire continent.[19]

Of course, much of what Americans think of slavery, when the uncomfortable topic comes up, centers on the European slave trade to the shores of the American colonies, and later the United States. However, large-scale slavery practices having little or nothing to do with Europeans are well documented in China, Japan, and Korea, and as mentioned, throughout the Islamic and Arabic worlds. Native people in the Americas practiced slavery—again, often as the spoils of inter-tribe warfare, but sometimes through kidnapping. Systematic practices of slavery have been documented as early the 12th century BCE in the Shang dynasty of China.

Most if not all human tribes around the globe practiced slavery at varying degrees of scale and brutality throughout history. The generational implications for those who did the enslaving and those who were enslaved are immense, as we'll see in coming chapters. But why has the made-up categorization of race been so stubbornly attached to it? And how did the so-called white race come out on top, in a way that continues to deliver widespread, unique privileges to this day?

Observations about the various skin tones of human groups go back in recorded history to ancient Egyptians and their *Book of Gates*. These afterlife-themed writings refer to light reddish-brown

Egyptians; dark or black-skinned people from Nubia (today's Sudan region); light-skinned Semites from the Levant (modern Syria) and Canaan (modern Lebanon, Israel, and Jordan); and fair-skinned Libyans.[20] In Europe, an association of dark skin with evil, deformity, and degradation began showing up in popular culture, as it did with Shakespeare's *The Tempest* in 1611. The character Caliban, described as the offspring of a demon and African witch, represents a savage beast in need of being civilized by his colonizer.

The use of "white" to represent goodness fed into Christian notions of purity and sinlessness. This was embedded in the culture through continued repetition in songs, stories, and sermons:

Oh, for a heart whiter than snow!
Savior divine, to whom else shall I go?
Thou who didst die, loving me so,
Give me a heart that is whiter than snow![21]

The term *race* may have first appeared in a French poem in 1481. In that poem "race" referred to hunting dogs, literally meant "descent." The term didn't appear in any European dictionaries until 1606. It was then, in the 17th century, that the innovative concept of a unified "white" race description began taking full shape, often rooting itself in regions such as America, where diverse populations existed. Essentially, this was used to draw clearer delineations between those in power and those in servitude. A later term, "Caucasian," wasn't an official race description until the 18th century, when Germany's Göttingen School of History combined it with "Mongoloid" and "Negroid" to collapse a confusing array of race classifications. Those "Big Three" classifications later expanded to five, to include American Indians and Malaysians.[22]

Before the increase of race-based slavery practices, Europeans still considered distinct cultures—such as Irish, Germans, or Italians—as different racial groups that carried their own assumptions of inferiority or superiority, often depending on the origin of the "scientist" in charge of the categorization.

Yet despite the simplification of races into "red and yellow, black and white," white people are not literally white, and as history attests, neither are they any purer than any other race. Black people are likewise not literally black; neither are they more sinful than any other group of people. Those words, designated racial classifiers, were purposely chosen by their inventors—European cultural and clerical Christians—for their powerful associations.

"Scientific racism"—the attempt to place observational facts and categorizations around socially biased assumptions—became quite the rage throughout Europe through the 17th, 18th, and 19th centuries, spilling over into the European colonies. All manner of racial theories and categorizations were explored, debated, debunked, and revived in waves of scientists from Sweden (Carl Linnaeus 1707–1778), Germany (Johann Friedrich Blumenbach 1752–1840), France (Georges Cuvier 1769–1832), and Great Britain (Thomas Henry Huxley 1825–1895). A myriad of skull measurements, physical feature sketches, and behavioral and cognitive assumptions were included in publications during this era, in an attempt to classify, describe, and rank human intellectual capacity and physical characteristics. These "studies" fueled political decisions relating to colonialism, education, and economics, and their legacy reverberates powerfully, even today.

✱✱✱

To summarize, here are some key points on the history of race:

✱   Pastors, historians, and scientists agree that we all come from common ancient ancestors.

* As different groups of people migrated north from tropical to colder climates, superficial physical differences (amounting to 0.1% of DNA) appeared in response to environmental characteristics.
* Cultures and religions developed around tribes; as these cultures discovered each other, their differences were noted.
* Observers—explorers, traders, historians, and early scientists—always assumed their own culture was superior, so their observations of the "other" were biased from the beginning.
* As economic and political ambitions grew, theories of conquest were interwoven with inferiority theories, so that European colonizing could advance unfettered. These theories provided rationalizations by Christian theologians and early scientists who looked through a superiority lens. "Race" categories and their assumed characteristics were invented around these assumptions.
* Systematic policies based on these racist theories and justifications took deep root, first in European, and later in American cultures. This included, for example, the American legal novelty (detailed in the next chapter) that dictated that enslaved people could never be considered white, only black.
* Because these racial separation and domination policies supported the ongoing economic and social interests of their inventors, these policies were therefore fiercely protected.
* The wealth of several nations, including and perhaps especially the United States, was founded upon and still owes much to the economic value of the labor of enslaved people.

Even if we were able to "un-invent" race, we shouldn't be so naïve as to think that it would eliminate humans' proclivity to divide, designate, and dominate each other. Since the dawn of humankind, familial tribes have been more than willing to attack another tribe's village in the next valley, full of people who look just like them. Humans have always been able to find justifications for their self-centered purposes.

Then it finally dawned on me. The unique contribution of race and racism to human evil was one of scale. It's one thing for a self-interested malevolent tribal king to raid a neighboring village in order to capture and enslave people for himself. It's an entirely different thing to unite multiple tribes around a superficial commonality such as skin tone, provide a religious justification for your endeavors, and embark on economic-fueled injustice on a global scale that will lead to more than 60 million human deaths and the ruination of the lives of millions more for generations to come. As I learned, this scale perspective was the primary difference in how white people understood racism, compared to how people of color experienced it. People of color are acutely aware of whiteness and its systemic policies that impact their past and present. However, people who are considered white tend to fixate primarily on individual decisions within this terrifying history. An individual or family tribe issue is one thing to address; an entire global system of oppression is quite another.

It had taken me a while to begin catching up with the historic roots and realities of race, but once I did, it was time to tackle how this race-based worldview poisoned what was seen as a new entity promising equality and democracy: the United States of America.

5

We Hold These Truths to Be Self-Evident—For Some of Us

> We've been here for four hundred years and now
> [Robert Kennedy] tells us that maybe in forty years,
> if you're good, we may let you become president.
> —James Baldwin, *I Am Not Your Negro*

Wanda Battle gave me a big bear hug. It was my first (and probably my only) experience of such a thing from a guide on a historic tour. Since moving to Nashville, I'd been making a personal pilgrimage to holy sites on the Civil Rights Trail of the South. This had brought me to Montgomery, Alabama, on a hot June weekend. Here in Alabama's capital city, on Dexter Avenue—a sort of Miracle

Mile of American civil rights history—a 24-year-old pastor with wisdom, eloquence, and courage beyond his years, whose name was not yet known to millions, was voted in as the first president of the Montgomery Improvement Association. Here is where a bus boycott that black citizens persistently orchestrated for 381 days in 1955 and 1956 provided the spark in confidence and tactics that marked the beginning of the era of the civil rights movement—an era historians bookend with the assassination of Dr. Martin Luther King Jr. in 1968.

There I was, standing in Dexter Avenue King Memorial Baptist Church, as Wanda squeezed the stuffing out of me and the other participants in our small tour group. I felt overwhelmed, standing in this historic epicenter of the movement—the very same church that held the office of the man who had been my hero since my college days. Wanda led us through Dr. King's personal office. We sat in the original pews and gazed up at the same pulpit, pastor's chair, and baptistry that he used from 1954 to 1960, while serving his first full-time pastoral call. The church building's familiar layout stirred memories of my boyhood First Baptist Church of Glenville, all the way down to the "In Remembrance of Me" carving on the communion table. Baptist churches are mostly segregated on Sunday mornings, but we all seem to use the same furniture.

This church, though, was one block from the seat of Alabama power: the impressive Greek Revivalist–style state Capitol complex gleamed white from atop Goat Hill, looking down imposingly on Dexter Avenue. The church first gathered in 1877 in an old slave trader's pen. The current structure was designed and built from 1883 to 1889. White Alabamans protested allowing a black church to meet so close to their beautiful state Capitol building. But some—including Wanda—say that God's hand of protection was on this little church, with an eye toward its future role in confronting the powerful segregationists, just a stone's throw away on the avenue.

For decades, the congregation supported their community in the shadow of legislators busy devising Jim Crow laws; governors promising "segregation now, segregation tomorrow, segregation forever"; law enforcement looking the other way when folks were lynched; and courts upholding all of it. To see how closely these structures are juxtaposed on Dexter Avenue is to envision the shepherd boy David's tent set up within 100 yards of Goliath's fort. In no less a miracle, God raised up a new kind of King to take on the racist goliaths on Goat Hill.

By now I had visited several of the South's sacred civil rights sites. However, none of them felt as heavy with the oppressive legacy of slavery as Montgomery. You could almost feel it as you walked along Dexter Avenue. The city that had been a hotbed of slave trading now had a beautiful fountain sitting in the roundabout where the main slave auction site once stood. Numerous structures that housed slave pens and served as the offices of slave traders still existed.

You could feel the legacy even more deeply at the National Memorial for Peace and Justice, a haunting display of rectangular steel sculptures that hang from above, in protest and remembrance for the thousands of African American people lynched in the South. Developed by the Equal Justice Initiative, a nonprofit launched by lawyer and author Bryan Stevenson, the memorial challenges the 800 counties in which lynchings occurred to confront their brutal history. To do so, it invites each county government to claim and install its own memorial to lynching victims in their county. It is a brilliantly creative challenge for justice. Over time it will become apparent which parts of the country have reckoned with their role in racial terror and which have not.

After learning the origins of race, I couldn't help but connect the dots and ponder how the invention of whiteness itself led to the legacy of what I was now absorbing around me. To cover all the history of what some call "America's original sin" would take its own separate book, and many thorough accounts already exist. I won't attempt to recreate it here. But for my personal journey toward understanding and possibly shedding whiteness, I needed to address some gaps left unfilled by my very typical American education experience. What did I need to understand about the real history of the United States that my 40-plus years of exposure to public schools, media, and cultural celebrations had failed to teach me? And once I learned it, how would that affect my understanding of being a white person in this country?

✽ ✽ ✽

It didn't have to be this way. Throughout my deeper self-education on these topics, I have found it maddening to revisit the historic forks in the road—those moments in which we in the United States came tantalizingly close to getting it right, only to let real progress slip through our country's fingers. The early realities of race, slavery, and servitude in North America are more ambiguous and awful than many Americans realize.

In August 1619, English pirates appeared upon the shores of Virginia with goods they had stolen from a Portuguese ship. The "goods" were 20 Angolan people stolen from their native land, and they were exchanged for food in the Jamestown settlement. These enslaved people were once part of a larger group of 350 Africans stolen from their homeland, of which half died in the Middle Passage. In many US and African American history lessons, this is often referred to as the notorious "first" transaction in what would become almost two and a half centuries of slavery.

This commonly known historical date lacks some important context, however, and has rightly been criticized, much like the celebration of 1492 as the date when Columbus "discovered" America.

The indigenous people already in America and the European colonists who were seeking to take over the region were quite familiar with African people far earlier than 1619. For example, Africans were key—if unwilling—players in a Spanish attempt to establish a base settlement in South Carolina in 1526. The enslaved Africans rebelled, effectively ruining the Spanish attempt at colonizing North America at a much earlier date than what most US history students learn regarding Jamestown. Perhaps those who seek "English only" language requirements have enslaved African people to thank that we aren't speaking Spanish as our current official language.[1]

More surprising to me was the fact that some, if not all, of those early Africans who ended up in Jamestown were not necessarily assumed to be slaves in the lifetime chattel category. Cassandra Newby-Alexander, a professor of history at Norfolk State University, observes: "This first group that came survived and created a solid and growing community of people of African descent, with some of them intermingling with English and the Native peoples."[2] The initial British settlers were familiar with indentured servitude, in which an individual could work out her or his freedom over time, and some historians believe some of these early Africans may have been regarded in this way. Other historians disagree. What historians do agree on, however, is that at this point in colonial history, rules about servanthood and slavery were not as defined by racial boundaries as they soon would be. Indentured servants could be of any color. Some African settlers, such as Anthony and Mary Johnson, owned slaves and hundreds of acres of land; some Native Americans owned slaves of African descent or those from other indigenous groups of people. Some Africans of that time even won their freedom in court. Although never exactly considered equal, Africans in that brief early era weren't stamped with a lifelong sentence of being considered property instead of people.

Although the origin mythologies of the United States celebrate religious freedom and brave, pious Pilgrims, in reality, a bigger story of economic opportunity and power drove the investment to establish European domination in the Americas. The Pilgrim story of 1620 sticks in our minds more affectionately than the Virginia Company's economic motivation for the earlier Jamestown, Virginia, settlement in 1607 and the subsequent corporate forces leading to settlements in other parts of the Americas. Some faith-filled Pilgrims provided an inspiring story; some well-funded trading companies provided the bigger justification and the real resources to make it happen. As with many clashes between religion and economic forces, religious piety usually walked away the most scathed.

Soon enough, beginning in 1640, laws delineating a racial foundation for the practice of slavery crept into the General Assembly of Virginia. These laws became increasingly severe. The year 1705 is one of America's important historic inflection points. In reaction to the growth of the black population, resentment over some of their personal successes in the colony, and a few unnerving uprisings involving teamwork between European indentured servants and African slaves, European settlers established the Virginia Slave Codes. These codes solidified the notion of white supremacy into law. From that point on, the codes provided the underpinnings for race-based chattel slavery. Free men of color were denied any opportunity for public office, although in the earliest years of the colony they had been landowners, a prerequisite for suffrage. Neither free or nor enslaved African Americans were allowed to testify in court. Black, "mulatto," and Native American slaves were officially considered property with no hope of future freedom. Interracial relationships of any kind, whether social or romantic, were severely banned.[3]

Whiteness and its supremacy were now deeply embedded in the law of the land in what would become the United States of America.

What began as a European attempt to define and advance a white race over all others—draped in Christian theological justification (literally, perceived permission from God) for the purposes of economic domination—was now complete.

* * *

Living for the past few years in the South exposed me to some interesting myths that I hadn't realized persisted. I'd been aware that some modern Confederacy sympathizers denied that the Civil War was about slavery at all; it was about "states' rights and Northern aggression." After my move to Nashville, I began to realize these myths still have a fairly broad foothold in the South. The war was about states' rights, all right—a state's right to maintain a slavery-based economy and to maintain white supremacy and racial segregation. These issues were very much at the center of the United States' deadliest war, as evidenced by the seceding Confederate states' own words. South Carolina, the first to jump ship, was very clear in paragraph after paragraph of its secession document: "We affirm that these ends for which this Government was instituted have been defeated, and the Government itself has been made destructive of them by the action of the non-slaveholding States . . . they have denounced as sinful the institution of slavery. . . . They have encouraged and assisted thousands of our slaves to leave their homes; and those who remain, have been incited by emissaries, books and pictures to servile insurrection."[4]

Georgia shared similar complaints as outlined in their secession document: "For the last 10 years we have had numerous and serious causes of complaint against our non-slave-holding confederate States with reference to the subject of African slavery."

Mississippi: "Our position is thoroughly identified with the institution of slavery—the greatest material interest of the world."

We could go on. But we don't need to, do we?

Many white people these days are tempted to believe that slavery and Southern slave-based wealth disappeared with the stroke of Abraham Lincoln's pen. The Emancipation Proclamation, the Union's victory over the Confederacy, and the Thirteenth Amendment hit the reboot button and struck a blow to the value of slavery once and for all. Right?

Of course not. The post-bellum and Reconstruction Era was another one of our country's soul-crushing missed opportunities. One of the most depressing books I absorbed during this unwhitening journey was *Slavery by Any Other Name*. In it, Douglas Blackmon thoroughly documents via actual judicial, penal, and commercial records how the humiliated white elite of the post–Civil War South schemed to get their free labor back where (they believed) it belonged: under their authority. Violent vigilante mobs of whites—including, but not limited to the Ku Klux Klan, founded in 1866—began terrorizing black people from the very beginning of the post-bellum South.

Federal protections and investments of the Reconstruction Era were completely abandoned in 1877. These protections had included voting rights for former enslaved people, which led to such stunning milestones as the first African American to serve in the US Senate, Hiram Rhodes Revels of Mississippi, in 1870. (Imagine the shock and horror of the Confederates at *that* development.) At that point it became open season on African Americans. Blackmon documents in vivid detail how the highly creative officials in the South—many of them recent Rebel leaders allowed back in the leadership saddle—began to leverage the judicial system to effectively re-enslave thousands of the recently emancipated people. Shaken by their loss and desperate to regain power, a collective of law enforcement officials, judges, and corporate kingpins devised elaborate collaborations. For example, through simple nuisance laws such as vagrancy, the local sheriff would round up recently freed black citizens, send them to jail, and rent them out to companies and landowners. This essentially re-enslaved black people all over again. As long as their scheme was "lawful," white powerbrokers were free to implement it as they pleased, especially after the hated Northern "carpetbaggers" left the region after Reconstruction. In addition to that $13 trillion of free slave labor in the antebellum South, someone needs to calculate the value of the additional nine decades of unpaid labor these work crews of re-enslaved African Americans provided, both to the resurgent Southern economy and to the Northern bankers and brokers who benefited from this practice well into the 20th century.

This brings us to our next fork in the road, one in which our country yet again chose a path of white centricity. Before I began my research into giving up whiteness, I was quite aware of affirmative action as a strategy applied by the federal government during my generation, in an attempt to address inequities and injustices against people of color caused by prior discriminatory hiring practices across the private and public sectors. But I had no understanding of the scale of earlier affirmative action programs applied only to white people. These programs had been in place for decades between the Civil War and the civil rights era and gave people with my ancestry a head start. This form of affirmative action didn't have anything to do with righting past wrongs; it was about rewarding and supporting white veterans and advancing white citizens' economic prospects in the growing country. When you understand how persistently African American citizens, in particular, were left out of these prosperity-building programs, it's extremely clear that it wasn't just slavery that had held African Americans in bondage. *The force of the United States government continued to elevate and invest specifically in white citizens and squeeze out citizens of color—up to and continuing through my lifetime.*

The scope and scale of this historic investment in white upward mobility is astonishing. I felt embarrassed for not knowing the full extent of my country's ongoing, official, race-based practices and policies. For example, although granting large tracts of land to rich white men started in colonial days, beginning around the Civil War and continuing all the way through the 1970s, the United States gave away huge tracts of land to individual everyday citizens through the Homestead Act, primarily for the purposes of farming. Between 1862 and 1934, more than 270 million acres (basically the size of California and Texas combined, and yes, primarily land taken from Native Americans) were divided into 1.6 million individual homesteads and given away for the price of a small processing fee. Through a combination of racist approaches to implementing the policy and bureaucratic obstacles that made it impractical for many black citizens to complete the process, only a paltry 4,000 to 5,000 black families (0.3% of total grants) received any of this largesse.

Remember, at this time in US history, land was *the* key form of wealth. Such a head start for so many white families is a fundamental historic reason why the average household net worth—a measure of all assets including savings, investments, homes, and real estate—of a white family to this day is 10 times that of an African American family of similar education level. It's estimated that over 46 million white families in this country—*around half of all white families*—can trace their roots back to a Homestead Act land recipient.[5] Today, one in seven white families are millionaires, a number that has doubled in the past 25 years, while only one in 50 black families has reached that status.[6]

Affirmative action for white citizens continued into the 20th century. As President Franklin Roosevelt sought to push through New Deal relief legislation during the Great Depression, he often bowed to the resistance of Southern Democrats whose support he needed to pass his agenda. The National Recovery Administration consistently offered white citizens the first opportunity for new jobs and set lower pay scales for black citizens. The Federal Housing Administration, created in 1934, provided home loans with little or no down payments and very low interest rates to millions of white families, yet explicitly denied black people loans to purchase any of the new housing in the rapidly expanding suburbs. African Americans, if they received loans at all, were condemned to stay in inner-city neighborhoods redlined by the government, banks, and realtors. Redlining is the practice of literally drawing geographic lines on a map, limiting where loans can be made. Predictably, redlining doomed those neighborhoods designated as "not fit for white folks . . . or for future investment" to plummeting real estate values, making it even harder for a black family to get any kind of loan or to experience an increase in net worth. Redlining was an official practice that lasted until the 1968 Fair Housing Act, but lawsuits from the Department of Justice against banks that still practice this policy continue to be filed today.[7]

More subsidies that invested in the futures of white families and excluded people of color continued. Although more than a million African Americans served in the military during World War II, they did not receive the plethora of benefits (benefits my dad leveraged to build our family's future) provided by the Servicemen's Readjustment Act of 1944, commonly known as the "GI Bill." These benefits were designed to help the 16 million Americans—one-eighth of the US population—involved in the war to rebuild their lives after the conflict and included school loans, low-interest mortgages, job training, and unemployment benefits.[8] About half of white veterans took the government up on the offer to extend their education for free, with 2.2 million attending college and 5.6 million gaining vocational training.[9] Unfortunately, since many of these programs were locally administered, the racist practices of local officials—much like the decisions made for home loans—provided an insurmountable barrier for most veterans of color.[10]

All these practices predictably led to unprecedented wealth creation, but almost exclusively for white families. What amazed me was that the extent of these investments (albeit in white American life) rivals many of the controversial ideas of politicians like Bernie Sanders or Alexandria Ocasio-Cortez. Millions of white Americans not only got their college tuition paid in full; they received small stipends to live on and next-to-free home loans. It reminded me of the utopia sung about in Big Rock Candy Mountain by Harry McClintock in 1928: "In the Big Rock Candy Mountains, / there's a land that's fair and bright, / where the handouts grow on bushes, / and you sleep out every night." Meanwhile, African Americans watched from the sidelines, struggling to break through barriers to even some of the most basic jobs, while white wealth and opportunities skyrocketed.

The total measurable economic impact of the GI Bill is difficult to determine, but historians and economists believe it has generated billions, if not trillions, in Gross Domestic Product (GDP) since its inception. Author and historian Ed Hughes notes, "The scientists and engineers and teachers and thinkers who brought in the information age, who took us to the moon, who waged the cold war, you name it—all those men and women were educated through the GI Bill." The GI Bill, according to Hughes, "provided the education for 14 Nobel Prize winners, three Supreme Court justices, three presidents, a dozen senators, and two dozen Pulitzer Prize winners."[11]

These programs, among others, helped lift up multiple generations of white Americans in the 20th century—a century in which the United States established its current dominance. Yet the official, systematic, and long-term exclusion of people of color remained constant. This was white supremacy and white national identity baked into official policy and practice, far beyond slavery and Jim Crow segregation in the South. It's demoralizing to ponder the fact that it didn't have to be this way. What if all Americans had had access to these programs? How much more Gross Domestic Product could have been generated? How many more Nobel Prize or Pulitzer Prize winners? How many more stable, thriving families? How much less money spent on prisons and entitlement programs because more people would have had the opportunity to thrive?

I was finally learning the ugly, unavoidable, and unfiltered history of the Foot.

＊＊

Understanding race in America, without touching on immigration policy as both a feeder and inhibitor of diversity, would be nearly impossible. Many people are surprised to learn that for the first 100 years of the United States, no immigration laws existed at all; we literally had open borders. So if you are of European descent and your ancestors migrated to the United States from 1787 to 1887, they had no need to worry about coming here "illegally." There wasn't such a category.

There was, however, the naturalization process, or the process of becoming a citizen eligible to vote, and it was here that white centricity was embedded. The Naturalization Act of 1790 provided for a process allowing "free white persons" of "good moral character" who lived in one of the US states for at least two years (later, five years) to apply for citizenship. When the writers and signers of the founding documents wrote that "all men are created equal," these later naturalization laws filled in the blanks on who they assumed were qualified (white men) for this Creator-derived equality.

As the country pushed westward over the lands of Native Americans in the 19th century, indigenous people, along with Hispanics and

Asians, make their first appearance in the census reports in very small numbers (all less than 1% each). Hispanic population growth doesn't show signs of surging in the records until the late 20th century, even though the spoils of the Mexican-American War (1846–1848) included more than 500,000 square miles of formerly Mexican land that is now New Mexico, Utah, Nevada, Arizona, California, Texas, and western Colorado. The Treaty of Guadalupe Hidalgo guaranteed the former Mexican citizens in those territories citizenship in the United States if they wanted it; this was the first time people other than those considered white were offered that designation. Soon enough, though, like a racial broken record, their rights and lands began slipping away as more white settlers made their way West. Mexican American land was either confiscated or otherwise forced for sale under unfair legal conditions and loopholes that violated the original treaty.

I also soaked up history about Asian Americans and their long presence in what is now the West. Chinese immigrants migrated to Western shores to fill the demand for cheap labor left open after legal slavery was abolished, including famously providing the bulk of human effort to build the transcontinental railroads in the mid-19th century. After the railroad barons—who, it must be noted, were also the beneficiaries of corporate welfare in the form of free land grants in exchange for building their product—were no longer in need of their services, the Chinese became the "Yellow Peril" in the minds of white citizens and our government. The Chinese Exclusion Act of 1882 was the first law specifically banning an entire racial and ethnic group from the country; it and its variants effectively shut out Chinese immigration for 61 years. Just as Southern states banned miscegenation between blacks and whites, Western states banned marriage between Chinese and Euro-American citizens.

Once again, the nation had reached a fork in the road and made its choice. By applying racial and immigration policies, the government had chosen to support the economic goals of white entrepreneurs and their supportive politicians.

It can be dangerous to look backward through history and judge participants through our own biases and standards. It's also dangerous to allow hero worship to fog our understanding. Celebrated leaders were still broken humans, just like us. Thomas Jefferson wrote the soaring words of liberty in the Declaration of Independence—all while owning people and impregnating at least one of them. Elizabeth Cady Stanton launched the women's suffrage movement with others like Susan B. Anthony—but championed the vote for white women over the voting rights of people of color. Charles Lindbergh accomplished an amazing feat by completing the first solo, nonstop trans-Atlantic flight—while being an advocate of the early 20th-century eugenics movement, an effort to "keep pure" what he and others thought of as the superior white race. Henry Ford was a manufacturing production genius—but he also really hated Jewish people to the point of purchasing a local newspaper, *The Dearborn Independent*, to spew out his anti-Semitic accusations that Jews were behind almost every societal ill imaginable. (This included 91 articles that he later compiled into a volume entitled *The International Jew* that was distributed through Ford dealerships.)

With these mindsets representing the depth of our country's racist ideology for most of its existence, I guess I shouldn't have been surprised to learn the detailed histories about American leaders and institutions. But like most of us educated in American schools, I had been taught the heroic, not the horrific.

We were taught that the Nazis were the epitome of evil because they fought for an Aryan-dominated world rule and killed six million Jews. What we weren't taught was that most of their racial theories, and even many of their racial separation strategies, were mirrored by conventional racial wisdom right here in the United States. The Nazis weren't really that unique in their racial superiority beliefs. They were unique in their clinical savagery and the scope of their genocidal ambitions. Do you know what book Nazi leader Adolf Hitler referred to as his "Bible"? *The Passing of the Great Race*, a 1916 booklet published by a prominent New York conservationist and lawyer that outlined the eugenics movement's assertions. The eugenics movement championed policies based on the belief that character traits like intelligence and bravery were embedded in racial categories, inherited through generations, and could be improved with proper human breeding strategies. The booklet sold more than a million copies from 1916 through the 1930s. It was quoted openly in legislative deliberations that shaped laws restricting immigration from Southern Europe's "lesser races" and those "blacks, browns, and yellows."[12] Congress soon passed the Emergency Quota Act of 1921 and the Immigration Restriction Act of 1924, which limited or completely banned Africans, Arabs, and Asians.

And what did Hitler study for inspiration in how to segregate the Jews into ghettos, for their systematic extermination? The American Jim Crow system and the US government's annihilation of Native Americans.[13] The United States of America, which we see as the fount of liberty and inspiration for freedom fighters around the world, was an inspiration for the greatest fascist and genocidal racist in history. For those still in an American history fog (like the one I had for much of my middle-class American white life): Does that not give you the chills?

Often, when these horrible truths are shared, the reaction among many proud Americans, especially white ones, is one of defensiveness and denial. These truths prick our pride, burst our patriotic balloons, and threaten our sacred belief that the United States is the greatest country God ever created. Surely anyone who would spread such unseemly historical observations is un-American.

But what if our understanding of the origins and progression of America were updated with a more accurate telling? The filmmakers who produced *Gone with the Wind* could have shown a more holistic view of African American characters in the Reconstruction Era beyond the house servant, Mammy; they could have included a black doctor, or even a black Senator, and it would have been historically accurate. Of course, they didn't. How would more truthful expressions of history have influenced the assumption of white superiority stamped on our country, a stamping that haunts us to this day? How would this have changed the paths we chose as a nation through these momentous forks in the road of history? Are we afraid that America would not be great if it were also honest?

Surely, though, it's never too late to be honest. If I had left my understanding of US history at the point where my public schools dropped me off, I would never have known the full stories of our origins and the foundations of our country, such as how the US Constitution has its roots in the ideas founding fathers learned from the Iroquois Confederacy. I wouldn't have known the role that African American soldiers played in winning the Civil War, or how hundreds of Navajo "code talkers" played such a critical role in World War II in delivering top-secret messages, or how Cherokee and Choctaw people pioneered the practice during World War I. I would have had no idea that NASA wouldn't have made it to the moon without the contributions of African American mathematician Katherine Johnson, until the movie *Hidden Figures* came out; I would have continued assuming it was all those white guys with buzz cuts wearing starched shirts and ties and horned-rimmed glasses, the ones you see in the newsreel footage. They were the ones allowed in the control room, but they weren't the only ones doing the critical work.

I wouldn't have known about Tulsa, Oklahoma's "Black Wall Street"—the nickname for the Greenwood community of thriving middle- and upper-class African American entrepreneurs. "Black Wall Street" was so successful that it attracted the ire of surrounding white citizens, who burned down more than 1,200 black-owned homes and businesses and killed hundreds of black people in 1921. This—and numerous other examples of retribution against African Americans who prospered when left alone to do so—flew in the face of the historical narrative I had been taught.

Once I learned not to settle for the white lens of American history, but instead to twist the kaleidoscope to see all the colorful lenses that illuminated a deeper, richer origin and development story for America, a veil was lifted. We are, in fact, not a "white" country at all. We never were. We are a country with a European-dominated historical narrative and white power structures, but with a much more diverse reality. Our story is a lot more than white men achieving great feats of exploration and advancement, with a few side stories of Sacagaweas assisting along the way.

Our founders and shapers were not just the guys in wigs sweating through their colonial garb in the Pennsylvania State House during a hot summer in 1787. Those men should be praised for their revolutionary ideas on democracy, equality, individual rights, and a brilliant government of checks and balances. But we should also call out their immense, hypocritical blindness in failing to associate these rights with women and people of color. We must also equally hold up those who were here first, those who contributed massively against their will, and those who continually demanded a more genuine and complete application of these rights to all. The white guys in wigs may have written the founding words, and some may have even died for them. But others made life in this part of the world possible, while still others made those words come to life with each passing generation, written into history with their own blood and sweat.

✱ ✱ ✱

Wanda was on a person-by-person redemption mission. Each hug, each smile, each mini-sermon of love shared during her Dexter Avenue King Memorial Baptist Church tours was a jolt of the same spirit Dr. King preached from that old pulpit. She and the aging members of the church still lived and breathed the revolutionary idea developed on the most intense fields of resistance: that love and nonviolence are more powerful than hate and brutality. Her hugs were so welcoming, her love so authentic, that we took her up on her invitation to attend worship at the church the next morning.

Sitting in the pews that morning felt surreal. Althea Thomas, the same organist hired by Dr. King more than 50 years ago, was still at the keys. Wanda had shared on the tour that 12 veterans of the Montgomery Bus Boycott of 1955 were still attending. No offense to the very capable current pastor, but at certain times during the service my mind would flash imaginary images of Dr. King behind the pulpit. It was right here that King and others began to guide American history ever-so-slowly down a different fork in the road.

What made the experience come back to present-day reality for me were the people. Member after member came to greet us, several with a long, warm series of questions to get to know us and repeated expressions of gratitude that we had visited them. These everyday people had committed themselves to revolutionary love that had changed our country. This little church played an outsized role in redirecting American history, with the same spirit I experienced that morning. At Dexter Avenue King Memorial Baptist Church, love was still conquering division. You couldn't help but walk out of the church doors on a bright sunny June day like I did and not feel more hopeful. It gave me enthusiasm to continue my journey.

6

This Is My Brain on Race

We are all cognitive misers. Our brains do not
expend mental resources thoroughly examining
problems when snap judgments will do.
—Kyle Hill, MythBusters host and science communicator

Do I belong here? That's a question that I imagine every human has asked themselves at various points in their lives; perhaps even a few times a day. As the brain processes input at a rate of thirteen milliseconds per image, one of its key outputs is an answer to that question. Should I flee, fight, or feel safe?

I was certainly asking myself that question as I stood as the only white person in front of several hundred African American delegates to the 2004 National Association for the Advancement of Colored

People (NAACP) convention. We were crammed into the Pennsylvania Convention Center hallway, waiting to get into the main ballroom. To my right was then-president Kweisi Mfume and his staff; to my left was then Philadelphia Mayor John Street and civil rights legend Julian Bond, an early leader in the Student Nonviolent Coordinating Committee, who also helped form and lead the Southern Poverty Law Center, and a former chairman of the NAACP. Looking over my shoulder was Omarosa Manigault. Yes, that Omarosa: the reality TV star from *The Apprentice* and future short-lived political appointee in President Donald Trump's administration.

Did I belong there? Somehow, I had ended up as the designated convention ribbon-cutter. It wasn't as if I had been signed up for the job against my will. As part of the convention sponsorship, in which my then-employer Microsoft had invested as part of a diversity and community giving initiative, one of our executives was supposed to provide a brief welcome message and officially open the 105th NAACP annual convention. The event coincided with Microsoft's global sales conference, so no executives were available. Word came down to our local district office that someone needed to fill the role. As the local marketing manager for Microsoft, I found that the task had ultimately fallen on me, and I took it on with some nervous excitement. The NAACP's fight for equality was one I supported wholeheartedly.

It also wasn't as if the organizers and leaders of the conference weren't welcoming to my presence. In fact, they made me feel warmly welcomed and expressed their appreciation for Microsoft's support. I wasn't expecting to meet Omarosa, who was the guest celebrity invited to the conference, but even the world's most feared confrontational schemer in all of reality television (that was her persona, anyway) was extremely friendly. She even gave me her cell number.

No, it's just that my white-trained brain wasn't entirely prepared for the experience. An ad hoc ceremonial area had been set up with the little red ribbon to cut. I thought: *No problem; when they quiet the crowd and turn it over to me to cut the ribbon, that's exactly what I'll do.* Despite my enthusiasm for the gig, my brain was already racing as I looked out into the entirely African American crowd. What were they thinking about me? Would I flub my welcome lines or screw up the ribbon-cutting? Would anyone be offended that Microsoft sent this low-level white dude to open the conference? You name an insecurity, and I can guarantee you my brain was soaking it in cortisol and adrenaline.

Why was it doing that? If I was speaking to a large, mostly white crowd, which I had done many times in the past, I wouldn't have been so worried. I had African American friends. I had even lived in a largely African American community for a time. So why was my brain sending off so many alarm bells? It really lit up when Mr. Mfume turned to me, just as the crowd's eagerness to get the ball rolling grew louder. "Okay, Jeff, you're on."

I was "on"? What did *that* mean?

"Go ahead and get their attention, make your comments, and we'll cut the ribbon," said the CEO.

I didn't say it, but I thought to myself, "Doesn't Omarosa have better qualifications for quieting the crowd? They'll listen to her."

When I agreed to represent our company, I had no idea my role was to "get their attention" and make some comments; I thought my job was to wave, cut the ribbon, and proclaim, "Welcome to the 2004 NAACP Convention!" after they introduced me. I looked out over the crowd and said . . . honestly, I have no idea what I said. I just started talking. I think the distinguished leaders standing beside me made a few arm waves to help quiet the crowd on my behalf, and I think I may have stammered a few words about Philadelphia being the home of liberty. With that, the ribbon was cut, and the doors flung open, and I had an interesting story to tell about Omarosa for the rest of my life.

✻ ✻ ✻

The implicit bias test is an online test from a team of researchers at Harvard University and other schools that seeks to uncover "thoughts and feelings outside of conscious awareness and control."[1] Their first bias test was centered on race, but they now have many other bias categories to choose from, including Arab-Muslim, Gender, Sexuality, Age, and Disability. To prepare you from getting too rattled by the results, the test asks you to affirm the likelihood that you might find out something about your subconscious that you may not want to hear: "I am aware of the possibility of encountering interpretations of my IAT test performance with which I may not agree. Knowing this, I wish to proceed."

The testing process is simple; users are shown two photos—for example, an African American male face and a white male face—and then asked to rapidly categorize them with a term that flashes on the screen. Some terms are positive, some negative. After lulling you into associating white or black images with positive or negative characteristics, it randomizes the process and quickens the pace so your brain is forced to react without thinking consciously. Since most people will try very hard to not seem like a racist on the test, it essentially measures not only whether a person assigns positive or negative word associations but also the hesitation, or lack thereof, when associating negative and positive terms. The time lapses are analyzed as evidence for bias.

Taking this controversial test is a little like being drawn to look at a car accident in which you're in the wreckage, because you know before taking the test how this is going to turn out. But people take it anyway, perhaps rooted in the desire to find scientific evidence that, hey, I'm not racist! (If you'd like to try your hand at it, visit www. implicit.harvard.edu/implicit.)

I took the racial bias test a few years ago and scored "Slight automatic preference for Euro-American compared to African American." I joined the 68% of test-takers in the car wreck who carry unconscious favorable bias toward European-Americans over African Americans (that includes people of all races who took the test, including African Americans).

Is it inherently natural, embedded in our DNA and our innate intellectual wiring, to self-select into preferring those in our racial category?

Pre-K kids can be delightfully oblivious to many of the subversive social slotting cues, but our social norms get embedded quickly. Psychologists have observed the various phases of self-awareness in small children. For example, prior to 18 months of age, children don't realize that an image they see in the mirror is of themselves. Later, through higher levels of awareness of their individuality and through the power of language, they begin to differentiate themselves as "me" or "I."

The moment children become aware of differences—in skin tone, hair texture, or income level as observed through clothing styles, how the teacher allocates favorable comments, or who gets a pony at their birthday party—the demons of pecking order and stratification stand ready to pounce into their psyches. Awareness of racial differences, and the corresponding value that one's culture explicitly or implicitly assigns to those differences, takes shape as early as nine months, something called "own-race effect."[2] Many mortified parents in grocery checkout lines can attest to the awkward moments this can create ("Mommy, why is that woman over there so brown?"). Studies have shown that even if parents make no mention of racial differences or preferences, children pick up on powerful clues all around them. In one study, children aged three and four began to show preferences for playing with those of their own skin tone.[3] In addition, it's been demonstrated that our brains don't seem to differentiate much between what we see in "real life" and what we absorb from movies and television, so all those casting decisions really do affect how we see ourselves and others.[4]

Are we helpless in fashioning an environment where we can raise a generation who truly responds equally to others regardless of skin tone? Perhaps not. An additional study of four- and five-year-olds provided clear evidence that parents whose daily lives brought interaction with more diverse friends and colleagues—which sets the stage for what their children were observing as "normal" around them—produced children who showed less racial bias or preference. Evidence of this lack of bias in children raised in diverse environments showed up as early as three months old.[5] Another study demonstrated that the other-race effect—the tendency to more easily recognize faces from the race that surrounds us most—was highly pliable.[6]

Apparently, we humans do like to stick to our tribe, but who we perceive as belonging in our tribe can be very fluid and not dependent on race or outward physical characteristics. When we're exposed to diversity from the beginning, diversity is what we embrace. This reminded me of my early childhood years in the diverse college apartment building with my playmates from around the globe. Playing in the clay pit, taking in those amazing food aromas, and observing my parents interact with their Afghani best friends in Morgantown may have wired my brain differently than many of my small-town peers, at least partially.

✳ ✳ ✳

I had learned a great deal about the history of race and racism. But I wanted to go deeper. *Why* has it been so easy for humans to use superficial external characteristics as triggers of division and hate? And is it possible to retrain my brain to see through a lens that isn't limited to a white tint?

It seemed as though understanding the human brain and how it makes decisions would be highly relevant to these questions. I didn't have to research very long to see how the latest science delivers several "aha!" moments when it comes to race. No matter what exactly you believe about human origins, you have to marvel at these supercomputers made of meat that reside in our heads. Our brain has 2,500,000 gigabytes of storage space available, compared to a lowly 256 gigs in an iPhone 7.[7] Our 86 to 100 billion neurons are constantly reprogramming and growing, slowing down to focus on new or complex tasks, and zapping through things we perceive as routine. And yes, we can consciously play a part in reshaping how our brain works, for better or worse.[8]

The difference between the "lazier" habits of the brain (scientists would describe them as "efficient") and our willingness to change them lie at the heart of racism and its cure. It turns out that as finely tuned as our brains are for survival or sending humans to the moon, they are quite prone to some serious mistakes because of specific heuristics, or decision-making processes. Physical characteristics that get processed with fear through cultural conditioning—race-based prejudice—can trick what otherwise can be useful triggers in our brain. Unfortunately, these tricks can make it extremely difficult to rewire what we've been taught to fear. Fortunately, when we understand what's going on, we can change. Self-awareness is an important beginning to the process of addressing racist thoughts and behaviors.

Take the concept of *availability*. This mental shortcut leads us to make decisions based on how easy it is to recall prior examples of similar objects or circumstances at the point we're making a decision. For example, many Americans are of the mindset that violent crime has been going up in the United States for the last few years, or even decades. In fact, FBI statistics have shown that violent crime rates have been steadily declining since the early 1990s.[9] So why do our brains trigger us to believe otherwise? Perhaps the dramatic, non-stop manner in which mass shootings and other violent attacks are pumped into our brains via 24-7 cable news shows and the internet makes these scary crimes more available to our memories. The images of violence are easier to recall, even though the actual facts show that overall violent trends are going down.

What about terrorism? Scary, right? Fear of Americans being harmed by terrorists has driven pushes for travel bans targeting certain Muslim-majority nations and has even influenced immigration policies for countries such as Mexico that have no association with terrorism. Since 9/11, how many Americans have been killed by foreign-born terrorists? An average of one per year. We are more than five times more likely to be shot by our own local police; 10 times more likely to die from riding a bike; 68 times more likely to die from having an accident while walking down the street; and 184 times more likely to be killed by a US citizen.[10] And lately, with a recent flurry of mass shootings by native-born murderers, we are far more likely to be hurt or killed by homegrown killers.

So yes, science backs up what many have pointed out as the negative effects of an overactive, often very selective news media, which can make certain fears far more available to our minds when it comes time to decide what to be afraid of. We're afraid of terrorism and school shootings at a far higher rate than we are fearful of getting in our car to drive to work. Given what we know, we should probably flip those fears.

How does the availability heuristic play tricks on us when a disproportionate number of media stories involving African Americans or Hispanics are alarmingly negative? When a presidential candidate claims, regarding Mexican immigrants, "They're bringing drugs. They're bringing crime. They're rapists. And some, I assume, are good people," it can, unfortunately, resonate in the minds of people with few other available interactions or images from which to judge. The truth—as documented extensively by even the right-leaning Cato Institute, which gathered all available research going back as far as 1911—is that both illegal and legal immigrants commit far less crime than native-born citizens of this country.[11]

The *representative* heuristic is another brain shortcut that can lead to bias. Our brains often quickly form a mental map of people or things based on only a few experiences. Certain facts cling in our minds to form a prototype so that our brains don't have to exert much energy the next time we run into a similar scenario. For example, what job would you deem more likely to project on a young man with a conservative haircut, with no tattoos, who is wearing a business suit and a tie? What about a young man with dreadlocks and several tattoos, who is wearing skater shorts? Which one is the attorney, and which one is the coffee shop barista?

This brain trick can wield enormous power, and assumptions about who represents "respectable" or "safe" citizens can be deadly wrong. Do we really think this subconscious trick hasn't led some law enforcement officials to be quicker on the trigger with young African American males? Or that hiring managers in our workplaces haven't been deceived into erroneously and disproportionately hiring who they thought represented a successful candidate, without factoring in all the relevant information?

Finally, the *base-rate fallacy* is the decision-making gaffe in which our brains zero in on an irrelevant piece of information that distracts us from focusing on the actual probability data most relevant to the situation. Here's an example: Sierra is a 26-year-old African American woman with braided hair who loves hip-hop music, lives in the urban core of Philadelphia, and has one child out of wedlock. Do you think Sierra is more likely to be: a) on public assistance; b) attending college; or c) holding a full-time job?

According to the most recent data from the US Census, an African American female of Sierra's age is more likely to be advancing herself with higher education than a white or Hispanic female (and almost as likely as an Asian female). For each subsequent step up in age range, African American women lead all racial categories in terms of participating in higher education.[12] In addition, African American women had the highest workforce participation rate among all female demographic categories.[13] Among part-time college students, African American women were at the top of the chart of those who were employed and attended school at the same time.[14] Thus, Sierra is among the most statistically likely to be attending college and/or holding down a job. The distracting details of her taste in music, where she may reside, or her single-parenthood status may lead many to the wrong conclusion about her life status.

By the way, female black-owned entrepreneurship grew 164% from 2007 to 2018. So, Sierra may also be hiring soon. (She could also likely use some startup funding; businesses led by African American women received, on average, only 0.06% of the venture capital funding that white women–owned startups garnered.)

What begins as understandable human nature—preferring the comfort of supportive humans who seem to be like us—can quickly turn into overblown fear and hateful bias. At the most benign levels, these brain tricks may keep us from visiting a church where the members don't look exactly like us, avoiding small talk in the grocery store line, walking a little more briskly to the car when we see someone whose appearance doesn't map to our norms, not taking a chance on a job candidate, or neglecting to invite someone from work to lunch. At their most malicious, these tricks, especially when cloaked in cultural, economic, and spiritual justification, have led to terror: lynching, shooting innocent people, and the enslavement and mass slaughter of millions.

✦ ✦ ✦

So, what moral responsibility do we have to modify our brains' seemingly natural responses? Should we give up, like the white supremacists preach, and keep everyone as separate as possible—however ridiculous that sounds in an ever-shrinking world? It's one thing to know why our brains work the way they do; it's another to address unhealthy patterns of conscious and subconscious thought.

If we missed the opportunity to get comfortable with diversity in childhood, are our brains still malleable later in life? Is it possible to retrain our brains to the point where subconscious bias could be reduced or eliminated?

Sharon Begley claims in *The Plastic Mind*, "We are not stuck with the brain we were born with." Researchers at Brown University studied a small area of the brain called the cingulate cortex, which is associated with attention, emotional stimuli, and memories. After specific brain exercises, researchers were able to measure a change in subjects' emotional reactions when certain faces were shown: those previously rated "negative" or "neutral" were rated "positive" more often. Another study at Northwestern University in 2015 measured whether "counterbias training" could be delivered during sleep. The answer? It sure can.

This research is very much at the beginning stages, and it also has potentially negative implications; that is, these same techniques could be used to instill racist emotions. But the research does beg the question of whether we could help solve, or at least dramatically improve, the problems we've already discussed in terms of bias within academia, law enforcement, healthcare, government, and business. Based on early promising results, the US Justice Department has in fact been seeking to install racial bias training at various levels of law enforcement.[15]

Psychologist and economist Daniel Kahneman describes two internal decision-making systems that manage our lives. System 1 is involuntary and automatic; it responds rapidly and efficiently, so no brain energy is wasted on what you already "know." System 1 is very helpful for survival and is great at evaluating facial expressions, filling in the blank for a known formula or verbal expression, or driving a car in a normal environment. System 2 focuses mental energy on decisions that require it—things like making distinct choices that need concentration. Concentrating on one voice in a group, sharing your email address, making a decision between two pieces of fruit, charting a course on a map, and evaluating the logic of a complex statement are all examples of System 2 thinking. System 2 requires real concentration, so it sucks more energy from the brain.

Psychologists have had a lot of fun devising experiments demonstrating how these systems work, and how they can be tricked. They are especially interested in how Systems 1 and 2 work together. Mental handoffs between systems can often lead to comical misunderstandings or miscalculations. One of the most famous experiments is the video in which two teams wearing different-colored shirts are shown passing a basketball back and forth. Viewers of the video are asked to count how many passes are made between members of just one of the teams and to ignore the other team. Meanwhile, someone wearing a gorilla suit meanders into the scene for nine seconds and then wanders off. Of the thousands of people who have viewed the video experiment, about half did not notice the gorilla at all.

Our brains really like System 1 tasks because they are designed to conserve energy. If we don't have to think hard about something, we won't. The problem comes when what our brains *think* are System 1 tasks are actually erroneous assumptions requiring more complex System 2 processing. Are those two teen boys walking toward me on the street a threat? System 1 sees them wearing hoodies, remembers a media image of a black teen wearing a hoodie involved in a violent crime, and says, "Yes; cross the street immediately." This response, sadly, could be embedded even in the mind of an African American adult whose brain has been trained by media to cement that connection.

Overriding System 1 requires intention and energy, something we humans are often not willing to invest, especially if we're high on the scale of impulsiveness, impatience, and immediate gratification. In other words, if our brains are not disciplined, they are more easily susceptible to making System 1 errors instead of questioning them.

One of the most unnerving discoveries about our brains and psychology is the effect of *priming*. It's scary because our brains can be so eager to categorize our experiences as a System 1 decision that a simple associative suggestion can trick our minds into error. Study after study has proven that humans can be primed to make certain kinds of decisions when they are fed a piece of information that their minds associate with one of the options.

For example, one study demonstrated that voting patterns for a state ballot proposition to increase funding for schools were much stronger in favor of the initiative when voters cast their ballots in a polling station *in* or *near* a school. In another study, participants primed to think of money demonstrated less willingness to help others. (Some of the studies are just downright bizarre, such as the study that asked participants to fill in the missing letters in these words: W_ _ H and S_ _P. Those in the study who were asked to think of something that made them feel ashamed were more likely to fill in WASH and SOAP, while those not exposed to the shame priming were more likely to fill in WISH and SOUP.[16])

Most of us would like to believe that we're in more control of our decisions than we really are. But science is pretty consistent about the fact that we are highly influenced by prompts all around us, in addition to System 1 assumptions embedded in our brains from birth. Why was I more nervous in front of an all-black NAACP audience, than when I was in front of mostly white audiences? Subconscious System 1 associations flooded my mind: There aren't any other white people here. I'm white. Therefore, I should not be here. The NAACP is about fighting inequality and injustice. White culture and white leaders are primarily responsible for the inequality and injustice black people have experienced. Therefore, this audience sees me as part of the problem.

These thoughts may be illogical, but they frequently guide how we feel and react. This immediately begs the question: If our brains are that susceptible to adjustments from some of the subtlest influences, could we adjust how they work on complex societal issues like race? If our minds are already so heavily influenced by negative and erroneous inputs that lead to terrible outputs—police shooting innocent unarmed black people at a higher rate than white people, hiring managers ignoring resumés with "ethnic"-sounding names—would creating a flood of more positive associations solve some of race-related problems? Since racism has a subconscious component, perhaps brain science can help give us the tools we need to make progress.

We already discussed how the images that infants and toddlers take in can dramatically shape their acceptance and even preference for diversity. Do the images we absorb as adults have the same power to reduce our racial biases? They sure do. For example, one study exposed a group of people to an empathy-inducing clip from *The Joy Luck Club*, a movie about an Asian-American family based on a book by novelist Amy Tan.[17] Then both the exposed group and control group were given one of those computer-based tests mentioned earlier, in which they had to quickly associate good or bad adjectives to various "in groups" (their own race) and "out groups" (other races). Those exposed to the movie clip demonstrated no bias in the test, while the control group exhibited measurable bias.

✳ ✳ ✳

Would undertaking Crystal's challenge to set aside whiteness require a full-scale brain reboot? It was beginning to look like it. Understanding how my brain worked—or often didn't work—the way I wanted it to forced me to deeply evaluate everything about my life. The weight of history, biology, and media was against me, but armed with this knowledge, I felt I may have a fighting chance.

I took the implicit bias test again to see if my subconscious bias had subsided since I had first taken it in the late 1990s. My result this time? "Your data suggest no automatic preference between Black people and White people." Whether the test is completely trustworthy or not, you let out a little sigh of relief when that result appears. Could it be that several years of purposeful education and effort to rid myself of bias was paying off? With all the discouraging patterns of oppression and racist thinking my study of history had revealed, it was encouraging to think that human brains aren't necessarily doomed for ongoing bias. But it was time to delve deeper into one of the most powerful forces keeping us stuck in the mud: identity.

7

British Isles and Country Roads

Without the presence of black people in America,
European-Americans would not be "white"—they would
be Irish, Italians, Poles, Welsh, and other engaged in class,
ethnic, and gender struggles over resources and identity.
—Cornel West, *Race Matters*

After studying how and why whiteness had come to be, I wondered
what an accurate definition of white identity would entail. Was
it defined in most people's minds by skin color? Religion? European
ancestry? Affinity for pumpkin spice lattes?

After the scientific pushback on the existence of any "real" under-standing of race, dictionaries seemed to be having a hard time provid-ing a definition. The US Census Bureau goes for the ancestry angle: "A person having origins in any of the original peoples of Europe, the Middle East, or North Africa." The Free Dictionary online provided the lame "a light-skinned race" definition for the terms *white people* and *caucasoid race*. The virtual volunteer contributors over at Wiki-pedia gave a typical caveat-laden, long-winded description that nods to the modern ambiguities on race. What was relatively clear was that the popular simplistic definitions of the "white" race hadn't caught up with the scientific community's position that there was no such thing as a biological basis for it and that whiteness as I had begun to understand it was a social construct.

So what *is* a good working definition for the social construct of whiteness? An outside observer's definition of the so-called white race—namely, a person of color—could be illuminating. Novelist, playwright, and activist James Baldwin described white identity as attached to an American myth that "their ancestors were all freedom-loving heroes, that they were born in the greatest country the world has ever seen, or that Americans are invincible in battle and wise in peace, that Americans have always dealt honorably with Mexicans and Indians and all other neighbors or inferiors, that American men are the world's most direct and virile, that American women are pure."[1]

If you consider yourself white, you may find that description downright unsettling and maybe infuriating. But does Baldwin nail the definition of white identity? People who assume a superior purity, intelligence, goodness, and invincibility compared to darker-skinned people? I had to admit: I, and others who are considered white, who grew up in humbler circumstances than the folks Baldwin seemed to describe would have a hard time identifying with such a confident self-perception. Yet when I looked again at his quote and how it intertwined "white" and "American," I considered how defensive we white folks can be when that notion of America—white America—was challenged.

How are our identities formed? Until this journey I hadn't thought much about what shaped my own identity. What role did whiteness play in it, consciously or subconsciously, and how did it lay the groundwork for who I really am?

✢ ✢ ✢

I moved to Nashville just after the Charleston, South Carolina, shooting at Emanuel African Methodist Episcopal Church. Much of the country was zeroing in on the role the Confederate flag played as an icon of the shooter's racist ideologies. South Carolina's then-governor Nikki Haley, who is ethnically half-Indian and politically Republican, announced the decision to take down the flag from the state Capitol grounds. Pro golfer Bubba Watson, the owner of the original General Lee, the venerable red muscle car from the 1970s television show *The Dukes of Hazzard*, said he would paint over the flag image on the roof of the car.

These actions only seemed to entrench the position of Confederate flag-wavers, however. The men in their pickup trucks cruising around Tennessee and other parts of the South seemed resolute in their defiance as they flew the Stars and Bars from the beds of their pickup trucks. I wondered to myself, how could these people be so calloused as to fly that flag—proudly—in the face of what had just happened? How could they cling to such a symbol with the world watching and the country in such pain over the church shooting?

Identity is a concept explored by social psychologists and other academics but rarely discussed in depth at the coffee shop, dinner table, or church foyer. Basically, identity is how we make sense of ourselves and our place in this world in relation to others. The role that race and ethnicity play in our identity is really what my journey was all about.

I couldn't honestly recall anyone other than Crystal even suggest-
ing that race could be discarded as an identity marker, but it was clear
that most people haven't been aware or motivated to do so. To some,
even within progressive-minded circles, it might sound like a horrible
thing to even try. It explained why most of my white friends resisted
the very premise of this journey; "Would Crystal give up *her* race?
Why are you being asked to give up *yours*?"

These pickup drivers of various social classes were united in
their white Southern identity. They perceived that their identity was
under attack. So, they reacted as most of us would if the core of our
being was being impugned or threatened: with defensiveness, anger,
or pride. As a native West Virginian, a state that often attracts deri-
sion and unflattering jokes, I could somewhat relate to those feelings.
Nothing seems to prick our identity more than when we have placed
our eggs in a certain basket that is perceived to be eroding in value
relative to others, especially when that basket historically was on the
top shelf of society.

I began to feel the need to understand identity a little deeper. What
determines who we are, or who we think we are? All this research into
history during evenings and weekends along my journey was somewhat exhausting, and I wasn't thrilled with the prospect of diving into
philosophy books and their head-spinning existential perspectives.
But I was hungry to learn more about what seemed like a fundamental issue as it related to race.

What I was really looking for was a more practical explanation
of those elements—such as physical traits, mental constructs, and
personal experiences—that most shape who we are. Only then could
I begin to understand where race—whiteness, in my case—played a
role. Not being a psychology or sociology major, however, I needed
sources more like *Psychology Today*, and less like *Philosophy & Phe-
nomenological Research*. What characteristics are embedded in our

understanding of who we are and how worthwhile we are? What elements are changeable (or fungible, as academics refer to it), and which are we stuck with, regardless of our desire to shift our identity? Where does race fit in that cascade of identity markers?

As I feared, even the *Psychology Today* explanations weren't that simple. The authors of various articles and books on the subject outlined many elements that we don't get to choose, or think we don't get to choose, and others that we feel free to embrace for ourselves. As technological advances have shrunk our world, and as interactions across communities, countries, and cultures have increased, the rigidity of our identity alignments have softened and there are more opportunities to shift.

I made a list of the many categories I could think of that have some impact on our identity, in no particular order:

Religion
Gender
Sexual Orientation
Economic or Social Class
Political Affiliation
Nationality
Ethnicity or Tribe
Body Type
Physical Attractiveness
High School Clique
Profession or Employer
Sports Team Affinity
College Attended
Hobbies and Interests
Habits and Addictions
Race

I looked at my list of identity markers again. How many were ones that we could choose, and how many were ones chosen for us? What elements of the markers chosen for me—Appalachian, male, white—brought positive reactions from those around me, and which brought negative reactions? And why, if this country was so oriented toward positive reactions to lighter skin and European features, was I feeling ready to shed my given race marker? I began to realize that how tightly one clings to any identity marker, including race, has a lot to do with reactions to it. Positive reactions, not surprisingly, built positive associations, but not necessarily ones that felt like life or death. Negative reactions, to race or any other identity marker, seemed to have a more extreme effect, driving people either to intense loyalty to that marker (as in my case with West Virginia) or a desire to cast it off (as in my case with whiteness).

In order to learn about the clutches of identity, and especially white identity, I had to take another step. I needed to sit and talk with someone from the world of Confederate flag-wavers. The question the pickup truck flag-wavers sparked in me was: Why after all these years is the Confederate flag still so core to the identity of certain folks? Is it a Southern thing, really? A white superiority thing? Or "just" a white pride thing? Perhaps those were just all synonyms of the same identity?

As it turns out, I didn't have to find a flag-waving friend. I just needed to go shopping.

✳ ✳ ✳

One sunny Saturday afternoon, my daughter Shelby and I caught the bug for a leisurely drive. Since moving to Nashville, we hadn't really explored Tennessee beyond the metro areas of Nashville, Knoxville, Chattanooga, and Memphis. After Googling "Best Tennessee small towns," we locked Lynchburg into our phone GPS.

Lynchburg, Tennessee, is best known as the home of Jack Daniel's whiskey, the best-selling American whiskey brand in the world and the first registered distillery in the country. After enjoying a few tilts on the rocking chairs offered by the Jack Daniel's Visitor Center porch, my daughter and I walked into the anticipated quaintness of a historic small town full of shops and restaurants. After giving in to the temptation of the Moonpie General Store and enjoying a small sample of those gooey marshmallow and chocolate snacks, we continued meandering down Main Street.

As we walked, Shelby stopped in her tracks in front of a storefront with a showcase window full of Confederate-themed Stars and Bars products. We were used to seeing a smattering of Dixie-themed products in a few souvenir stores in the South, but this one was full-blown dedicated to all things Confederate. With a mix of curiosity and that anxiety of knowing you're about to regret what you're going to see, we felt compelled to explore further.

As in all the stores we entered in Lynchburg that day, we were greeted by a sweet-voiced, friendly woman who looked to be in her 40s. After the normal pleasantries such as, "Where y'all from?" we awkwardly eased our way around the store.

The product line, I'll have to say, was impressive. I hadn't even remotely imagined how a Rebel flag might look on a toddler's bathing suit, but there it was. Flags, mugs, license plates, belt buckles, mirror dice, T-shirts, spare tire covers: you name it, they had it with a Confederate flag emblazoned on it. It was a full-throated celebration of all things white, Southern, rebel.

The requisite bumper sticker rack captured the special mix of cornball wordsmithing and in-your-face defiance that are the specialties of the bumper sticker industry. Some were an attempt at educating the ignorant non-Confederates: *260,000 Southern Men, Women & Children Died for This Flag!* (We tried but failed to find a sticker with any reference to the millions of Africans who died during the Middle Passage, or thousands upon thousands who died via lynching or other heinous methods.) Some were ironic: *Defiance of Tyranny— A Southern Tradition*. Some came with a counter-protest: *Confederate Lives Matter*. Some came with violent racist double entendres: *Coon Hunter*. Some were head-scratching: *Careful! You Might Have a Black Confederate Ancestor!* Some were persistently hopeful: *Waiting till the Day the South Will Rise Again*.

Being in the publishing business, I naturally gravitated to the book display. Beyond humor titles such as, *How to Speak Southern*, and the cookbooks, there were several titles seeking to recast history from a Southern Confederate's perspective, such as *The Great Impersonator* (about Abraham Lincoln) and *Everything You Were Taught about the Civil War Is Wrong*. It was like perusing a library from an alternate universe.

A biography of Nathan Bedford Forrest caught my eye, and I just had to ask the polite store attendant about it. "Wasn't this guy the first leader of the Ku Klux Klan?"

"Yes, briefly, he was. But when he realized what the Klan was about, he immediately resigned," she asserted. "There are a lot of misconceptions about Forrest, and that book does a good job of correcting them." I immediately wondered how General Forrest got the job without understanding what the Klan stood for.

Our friendly shopkeeper's take on Forrest was historically erroneous, and it was strongly aligned with a particular identity associated with the Confederate version of history. I mean, you must have your identity deeply immersed in the Confederacy, and what it stood for, to have your toddler frolicking at the beach in that Stars and Bars one-piece, right? Our identities are the colanders that determine which nuances of history get filtered out to elevate heroes, scorn the right bad guys, and cloak ourselves in worth and meaning. The Dixie shopkeeper was trained by her culture to filter out the full perspective of General Forrest and the nature of the Confederate "way of life" that he and others fought for.

But what had I been trained to filter out? Until recently I hadn't questioned the appropriateness of having George Washington or Thomas Jefferson, two Virginia slaveowners, up on Mount Rushmore. If I were looking through any lens other than whiteness, wouldn't the sin of Washington, Jefferson, and the other founding fathers— who had left out African Americans and women from the bounty of freedom—disqualify them for such hero worship?

✦ ✦ ✦

Although admittedly more complex than this, I began to think of whiteness, like many elements of identity, as residing on a continuum. On one end is an extreme view that strongly and overtly intertwines elements of white identity into heroic, static cultural markers that Baldwin described. People on this end of the spectrum feel a deep anxiety when the association is threatened by the visible presence of diversity that seems to challenge it. This level of white identity provides a powerful sense of worth; it is seen as needing protection, possibly through violence.

Somewhere in the middle of the whiteness continuum are people who feel a similar anxiety, perhaps with a little more security and a sincere love of others in their heart, regardless of skin color. Many of my evangelical Christian friends fall into this category. They also deeply associate whiteness with America and certain values that they feel are being threatened, consciously or subconsciously; those with brown skin tones trigger a fear that their presence, and the different religions and values they may bring with them, will somehow diminish my friends' perception of the United States as the greatest country

God has ever blessed. These are folks who would tell my friend, Soni, who was born in India, that when they posted anti-immigrant posts on Facebook, "We aren't talking about *you*, Soni."

Even further on the whiteness spectrum are white folks who consider themselves very open-minded, accepting champions of equality, but harboring an underlying feeling that "We know best; let us help the poor brown folks." I've realized over the years, uncomfortably, that this one was closest to my own identity, and it's a perspective I've had to confess and overcome with each layer of awareness. The "white savior" point on the whiteness continuum embraces a collective approach to righting wrongs and creating opportunity, but with a foundation of white standards and expectations (and therefore white leadership) still firmly in place.

Not surprisingly, this continuum maps to what author and academic Ibram X. Kendi describes as segregationist, assimilationist, and anti-racist approaches to race.[2] Segregationists have an underlying belief that people in race categories other than white will never achieve the same level of human excellence as white people (whether God-given or through evolution), and mixing races at any level can only bring down the status of whiteness. Therefore, separation through immigration policies, Jim Crow laws, laws against interracial marriage, resistance to desegregating schools, setting up immigration policies to favor Europeans, or simply fleeing from neighborhoods and schools that are beginning to integrate, are all logical actions in segregationists' minds.

Blatant, overt, segregationist beliefs and policies—especially enforced by vigilante violence through the Klan or official violence via the local sheriff's office—became abhorrent to many Americans during and after the civil rights era. These are the images that come to mind when white folks hear or get called "racist." But segregationist beliefs and policies that seek to build a wall, virtual or physical, between races continue today. This occurs through more subversive methods such as: a criminal justice system that sends more African Americans to jail than white folks, under cover of "tough on crime" rhetoric; or backlash to low-income housing initiatives in expensive suburbs; or resistance to education spending that doesn't rely primarily on local property taxes to fund schools equally. Segregation lives; you can see it in the numbers. It was implemented a bit more politely from the 1970s to the 2000s, but recently segregation has been reverting to its uglier, overt ways.

According to Kendi and other observers, the assimilationist position has been the most pernicious to understand and address because it poses as good intentions—a mindset that many kind, loving individuals align with. People holding this position have a belief that white culture (also often described as "Western culture" or "American culture") is in fact superior—the greatest culture the world has ever experienced, and one uniquely blessed by God. With the right benevolent attitudes and programs, however, white people can help "lift up" other races to their level of education, success, and morality; people of color can "advance" if they cooperate and play by white cultural rules. Assimilationists want to keep the white systems and assumptions in place, but they take great joy when an individual "makes it" out of the "ghetto"; when a saintly (usually white) teacher inspires a class full of minorities to believe in themselves and achieve new academic heights; or when a middle-class (usually white) family adopts a black or brown kid and gives them a shot at a better life.

When you think of those examples, how many movies come to mind?

The anti-racist position, in contrast, is having none of the underlying assumptions of segregationist or assimilationist positions. To be anti-racist, you would adhere to an entirely different worldview in which human beings of all kinds, regardless of assumed race, are already equal. Every human population has the same innate levels of intelligence, talent, character, and opportunity. What accounts for any discrepancies in measurements of "success" are the racist policies that have been built—through history and in modern times—to elevate the inventors of race. Those who dominate others can exploit the labor and resources of those same people. Anti-racists see the inequality in the rules of the game—not in the players.

The continuum of whiteness, and its alignment with Kendi's categories of race-oriented worldviews, was a game-changer for me. I can recall moments of red-faced defensiveness when I would hear challenges to what I now understand as white cultural standards, and I can hear defenders of segregation and assimilation howl when confronted with them. Honestly, though, I couldn't see how Trump's "Make America Great Again" slogan could be interpreted any other way than through this type of white identity continuum. After hearing some white friends' views on individual love, combined with a profound mistrust, and even resentment of a collective perspective on racial justice and opportunity, I could understand more clearly the difference between looking at racism as an individual problem, and racism as a systemic one (remember the Foot?). Folks with a strong white identity prefer a one-to-one relational approach to solving racial issues, because they fear a shift coming in where the Foot lands. These "good" white folks, many of them my Christian peers, may love a specific person of color, but still fear the broader changes they represent. This represents a commitment to, at best, an assimilationist position, and at worst, a "soft" segregationist position.

The fog began to clear for me. Race was invented by its creators to exert power over others for their own gain (such as free labor and unfettered access to land and resources), under the guise of altruistic motivations: advancement of economics, education, religion, "civilization" on European terms. White identity—*whiteness*—provided air cover for otherwise kind, Jesus-loving folks to keep resisting change that would dismantle the Foot on the necks of our neighbors of color who became the target of all this "advancement."

This was why America wasn't getting much beyond the lowest levels of racial tolerance, and why I was continually struggling in my own life to make sense of it all. We—I—are addicted to white identity.

Maybe there was hope for my journey, and for all of us, if we understood and elevated the other elements that made up our personal and shared identities. Maybe we could elevate those that create self-worth without requiring the demotion of others. Perhaps we could develop healthier ways to form affiliations—some local, some national, some global—that weren't based on superiority and were therefore less easily threatened. I understood deeply from my West Virginia upbringing and recent stint there, that you can't necessarily fight off a negative identity; you must replace it with something more powerful and more positive.

During all this exploration on the very concept of race, I began to wonder how much of my own identity was based on being white without me even being aware of it. Where did I sit on the white continuum, and was I ready to get rid of the continuum altogether?

It was time to dive deep into what made me, *me*. Along this more recent journey to understand myself, the role of race in my identity and country, and the possibility of shedding race as an identity marker, the nagging question of who I really am emerged more strongly than ever. My friend, Soni, was intrigued and supportive of my journey. During one of our conversations, I noted that I wasn't entirely sure what my ethnicity was, outside of a vague awareness that I may be some Euro-mix of English, Irish, maybe German, and perhaps a little French. I had no idea.

The next Christmas, my generous new friend gave me a DNA kit as a gift. The thought of identifying my exact ancestry seemed thrilling. From those who didn't know my origins, I would sometimes get surprising questions about my ethnicity. I have very dark black (now graying) wavy hair and dark brown eyes. Several people have asked me if I am Hispanic or Italian. A few people have asked me if I am biracial (which I assume meant a mix of white and black). Maybe there were some surprises in my genealogy I didn't know about? Stranger things have happened in the isolated hills of West Virginia.

As soon as I got home, I unpacked the kit and read the directions. I'm not one to follow directions closely, but I forced myself to pay attention this time, because I didn't want to screw up the results. I cautiously opened the little sample kit, took out the swab stick, and carefully scraped the insides of my cheeks three times as directed. That was it. I took the self-mailer package off to the post office and pondered what I would find out about myself in six to eight weeks.

✦ ✦ ✦

West Virginia's tightly packed hills, and the sharp valleys they create, foster a more intense sense of community and belonging than I've experienced in any other region of the United States. Perhaps Texas is right up there with West Virginia in state pride, but where Texas pride rides on notable assets such as wealth and sheer size, West Virginia's seems to form around a deep attachment to the land that nurtured us in its womb—along with a defensive response to all those hillbilly jokes.

Like many young people who tend to look forward in life, instead of backward, for many years, I had no idea or much interest in who I was or where I came from. My identity as a West Virginian was being shaped during my youth through association with West Virginia University sports teams and the occasional hillbilly ribbing from Ohio relatives. Like many young people, throughout my high school years,

I felt a deep anxiety leading to an eagerness to get the heck out of my small town and state. After leaving West Virginia to work in Pittsburgh and Philadelphia, I met and engaged with people from other parts of the country who identified very strongly with their Italian or Irish roots and seemed to have a far stronger sense of cultural identity than I felt. They wore their "hyphens" (Italian-American, Irish-American) very proudly, and I remember feeling a little jealous. Not only did my family not celebrate similar ethnic cultural traditions, I wasn't even sure what ethnic cultural tradition I came from. What was I? West Virginian? Appalachian? With a last name like James, was I Anglo-American? My cultural association went back as far as visiting Grandpa and Grandma James on Red Hill outside of Parkersburg, West Virginia, or Nana and Papa Allen in Crooksville, Ohio. While I valued my family relationships, we seemed bland and boring compared to my new Italian and Irish co-workers. I felt like a generic American in a new land of hyphenated friends.

I wasn't sure then, nor am I now, but I wonder if the void of positive cultural identity at the time drove my interest in soaking up diverse new friends, cultures, and experiences. To be honest, what little cultural identity I did have as a West Virginian seemed to come with more than a little baggage. Although I had far less of an Appalachian accent than many of my peers from Gilmer County, the moment it was discovered that I was from West Virginia, the predictable "good-natured" hillbilly jokes would follow. Many people who otherwise would never even think of telling a racial or ethnic joke felt very free to demean Appalachians.

✳ ✳ ✳

After seven weeks, I finally saw the email hit my inbox: New DNA Test Results Posted.

As I logged into the DNA testing service website for my results, I found some of the scientific language difficult to decipher. I didn't want to learn much about mitochondrial DNA and all its amazing secrets; I just wanted a simple explanation of my genealogical lineage. Exactly how "white" was I?

The simplest chart I could find in the report showed 100% European, with 86% British Isles and 14% from southeastern Europe— Italy and Greece, mostly. That's pretty darn white based on all the definitions the culture around me had invented and propagated. I supposed the Italian and Greek influences accounted for my dark hair and other features, although I remembered from the pseudo-scientific history of race definitions that southern Europeans had to fight their way into "whiteness." But there it was, all scientifically laid out, with a helpful map of Europe with blue and green overlays of where my ancestors were concentrated.

As it turns out, researching one's ancestry can become quite an addictive habit. Spurred by the adrenaline of seeing in living DNA color codes where my ancestors hailed, combined with the research my dad had furnished in a binder years earlier, I decided to take the plunge and created an Ancestry.com account. Within a few weeks of sleuthing at home after work, I hit an ancestral hot streak and made it all the way back to a James Tyrell, born 1290 in Heron, Essex, England.

I excitedly reported my findings to Soni, my Spanish-Indian friend, who had given me the DNA kit. "Do you know the names of any of your ancestors?" I asked. "You should see if your parents can help you identify a few names to get started."

"The British didn't keep records like that on Indians," she replied. "We weren't worth that kind of bother to them."

✸ ✸ ✸

Thinking back to my research on the origin of the concept of race, I realized I had followed my documented lineage back to the same era in which race theories were being developed by European academics to account for their assumptions and biases. These academics' "findings" were reinforced by religious interpretations and a merchant class eager to exploit whatever theories they could find to justify their lucrative slave-trading enterprises. The ancestors I had found were living in the historic petri dish of racist thought and the very devastating actions that emanated from them.

Now, more than 500 years later, I was attempting to undo the race virus from my own identity. I had boned up on the roots of racism, its terrorizing reign through history, its continuing impact on today's world, and why it can so easily trick our brains. I had carefully dissected my own identity. But now the hard work would begin. Could I reorient my life in a way that was no longer dominated by the framework of whiteness?

PART II

Getting the White Out

8

Sharp Knife and
Una Starbucks

Which of these three do you think was a neighbor
to the man who fell into the hands of robbers?
—Jesus (Luke 10:36)

Despite not being a coffee drinker, I have been a coffee shop nomad ever since the rise of wi-fi internet. There I can nurse my attention deficit tendencies with the background stimulation of sounds from espresso machines, private conversations between people who seem to think there is a soundproof bubble around them, and baristas' shouts of customer names.

The Starbucks in my Una neighborhood in Nashville often seems to hold at least one person to represent each of the 30 or more countries from which it sources its coffee beans. Many evenings the coffee shop is filled with immigrants or second-generation children of immigrants from almost every continent: Ethiopians and Egyptians, Venezuelans and Mexicans, Lithuanians and Ukrainians, Cambodians, Indians, and Vietnamese. A large percentage of my fellow coffee-shop squatters seem to be college students, studiously taking notes or taking an online class on their laptops. Often a mother or father has a brood of children gathered around them in a corner, some doing homework, some playing videogames. At other tables, men talk to each other in their native tongues or in their second or third language, English. The occasional Euro-American, like me, or recent immigrants from the United Kingdom, Spain, or Eastern European countries, can be found typing away on a laptop.

On one evening, the weekend after Thanksgiving, I was still weary from the drive home from West Virginia after visiting my family. At one time, during the early 20th century, my home state was one of the most diverse regions in the country, due to the draw of coal-mining jobs. After the post–World War II coal bust settled in and mechanization rapidly replaced human labor, the diversity of the coalfields, and thus much of West Virginia, vanished almost as rapidly as it had arisen. Now, according to the American Community Survey, West Virginia has the smallest proportion of workers who were born abroad, at just 1.4%.[1]

On nights like this at my local Starbucks, especially after returning home from my very homogenous home state, I couldn't help but wonder: What would my more conservative and rural friends think and feel if they sat here with me with such diversity all around them? Growing up in West Virginia, and even during my more recent 10-year stint there, I often felt like a fish out of water. Even though ethnically,

I looked like everyone else, I didn't quite fit. Here in Una, I felt like I was in an aquarium with tropical fish from around the world, and I felt at home. But I knew that many friends from Appalachia would feel immense anxiety here, in what I considered a little slice of Starbucks utopia.

I recalled a comment from a friend's wife upon visiting me here in Nashville, soon after I moved. The couple's cab driver was apparently of Arab descent, or at least had an accent she perceived as Arab. "After I got in that cab, I kept thinking, 'Dear God, please don't let him blow us up or shoot us,'" she said. I bit my tongue, hard, for my friend's sake and to get through the visit. (After the visit, I pondered how too much tongue-biting from the friends of people with these fears is why they feel free to share such sentiments openly.)

Is that what certain friends from my home would be thinking as they sat here in Starbucks with me? Would otherwise nice, Jesus-loving people be scanning this gentle, peaceful, family-oriented Starbucks scene, trying to pick out the terrorists? The thought depressed me greatly. After hearing more from Soni about the hostility and feelings of isolation that confronted her after the Trump campaign, I started thinking about our sense of community in this country, and about what it means to be a part of America these days—or in the past, for that matter.

✦ ✦ ✦

The term *community* has evolved over the years. It used to be fairly straightforward; it was the area in which you physically lived. Now it can mean many things. In the modern church, the term indicates close relationships within the body of believers. Some more radical Christians live in community by sharing a house and belongings, like some of the young people at my old church in Philadelphia, Circle of Hope. There are references to the black community, or the Asian community, which can sometimes lead to claims of homogeneity and oversimplified characteristics within a race that doesn't really exist. There is the Gator Nation community of University of Florida fans and the Packer Nation community of Green Bay fans. *Community* has become a catchall term for any particular grouping of people that align around a common cause, characteristic, or shared experience. Its corollary, *tribe*, is used ad nauseam these days in my marketing profession, often in reference to an online community.

A sense of community is core to human existence and health. As an introvert, I often struggle with connecting with others deeply enough to consider my relationships true community. During those adult years when I felt I had experienced true community, it had almost always been sourced from two arenas: church and work.

Community, usually a positive term, can be fraught with unseen boundaries and land mines. Who gets to join a community? Who gets to *decide* who gets to join a community? Who are the gatekeepers? What are the criteria for belonging?

During our family's three-year stay in West Philadelphia in the late 1990s, my then-wife and I experienced a bit of what it feels like to be in the minority, both racially and economically (in our case, at a far higher income level than those around us). This was a purposeful move, partially motivated by the ethos of the Circle of Hope church we attended and partially from a desire to save money after a failed business startup. For a fraction of our previous rent, we moved from a one-bedroom trendy loft in Center City to a gigantic, three-story rowhome beside a sprawling park in West Philly. We had become gentrifiers.

Our entire lives, my wife and I had lived in primarily white neighborhoods, attended vastly white schools, gone to white churches, and had a white circle of friends. Sharing memories of what went through our minds when exploring whether to purposely move our young family into a completely different socioeconomic and racial environment feels awkward. I was probably driven more by a combination of that white savior complex explained earlier, and a desire for the cultural excitement of diversity. My wife was perhaps more eager to save money and pay off debts from my recently failed business. We certainly held some anxiety in common over how we would be accepted in the neighborhood.

Currently, researchers calculating US Census data show that 64% of African Americans still live in neighborhoods almost entirely made up of people with the same skin color, although this has been steadily dropping since the 1960s. Hispanics have been stuck at around a 50% segregation rate over the last several decades, while Asian-Americans display a 41% rate of segregated living. Of the 658 housing markets tracked, 522 of them displayed a decline in housing segregation.[2]

Perhaps most encouraging is that the number of white people who indicated they would plan to move if an African American moved next door to them dropped from 44% to 1% between 1958 and 1997. Cynics might point out that the percentage of white people who would *admit* planning to leave is what has dropped; but perhaps that should even still count as progress.[3]

People of color in America are forced to interact with white citizens far more often than white people must interact with people of color simply based on the math of white dominance in leadership roles, healthcare, education, and other required societal touchpoints. Therefore, people of color have a lifetime of experiences dealing with cross-racial interactions, more than most white people. My wife and I encountered those realities for the first time upon moving to West Philadelphia. Questions we never had to face before flooded our minds: Is it okay that we're here? Are we accepted? Are we safe? Are people looking at us because we're different?

Motivated by what we considered a positive desire to live in a more diverse community, as well as simple economics, we could make an unfettered choice on where to live. Whatever trepidation we may have been dealing with from the almost instantaneous hyper-awareness of our whiteness, the perceived benefits pushed us to make the choice. We decided with relative ease to live in a majority African American neighborhood in West Philadelphia.

People who study this sort of thing have found an interesting trend. As mentioned, although patterns of neighborhood segregation have been going down since the 1970s, they are still quite high. Notably, white families and black families who make the same level of income show different patterns. Black families with middle to high incomes are far more likely to remain in predominantly lower-income neighborhoods, while white families of the same income level have a higher tendency to migrate to high-income neighborhoods.[4] Perhaps people of color, even those armed with equal income to purchase property in a "better" neighborhood, don't feel the same sense of welcome—or entitlement—as white families? Or perhaps redlining at some level is alive and well.

Let's be honest. There is a certain level of self-congratulation involved when a white person with the means to live in any neighborhood environment proactively chooses to live in a lower-income neighborhood, especially one where minorities are the majority. Back in 1990s church circles, it was considered "brave" and "missional." (Or perhaps "irrational," based on some of the comments we heard from our friends back in the suburbs where we used to live.)

Today, moving into a distressed neighborhood is considered hip. The influx of young educated white folks (in some cases older empty nesters) has driven a notable spike in population and housing values in many urban areas. The phenomenon of white flight, in which white families fled urban neighborhoods en masse, as minorities purchased homes in or near their neighborhoods, has reversed in many cities. Now white folks are flooding back into urban areas, designating them the "next cool neighborhood" . . . and pushing a lot of lower-income, largely people of color who have lived there for generations out to the aging outer rings of urban and suburban areas. Gentrification has become one of today's most serious economic justice issues.

I'm not sure I had even heard of the word *gentrification* when we moved into West Philadelphia. Whatever negative impact the macro trend we were participating in had on lower-income people in the neighborhood, we were blissfully unaware—that is, until a talk by Ewuare X. Osayande at our church made us, well, aware.

✷ ✷ ✷

One Sunday evening in 1999, I and other mostly 20-something white people, along with a few boundary-crossing people of color, sauntered up the dusty stairs to a newly planted church called Circle of Hope in Center City Philadelphia. Founded a year earlier by a minister from central Pennsylvania who had moved back to the area with his family after a period of church-planting in California, the church was located one floor above a convenience store on Locust Street, a site strategically chosen for its location near the city's hip South Street neighborhood. Energized by a Jesus-loving, anti-racist, pro-justice mission, Circle of Hope brimmed with idealism and a faith stripped of many barnacles of modern white, Western evangelical assumptions.

I was immediately drawn to the church when I learned about it from a flyer hung on the campus of Eastern University, where my wife at the time attended. In fact, the church's existence became a basis for my suggestion to her that we should move from the suburbs into the city to be a part of it. Many young Christians (the vast majority of them white), had adopted the church's challenge to reconsider materialism and live in community; some shared homes and even income, and our attendees included members of The Simple Way, an intentional Christian community based in North Philadelphia. Several moved into struggling, mostly African American or Hispanic neighborhoods in West and North Philadelphia. A loft apartment near the art museum was about as radical as my wife was willing to embrace at the time, so we eased into the "living in community" aspect of things.

As a small-town, traditional Baptist, white kid from West Virginia, I found Circle of Hope exhilarating and slightly irritating. Most days I was thrilled to be rubbing shoulders with people more radical than I, even while I perceived underlying hostility from certain congregants when they learned I worked at Microsoft, the evil-empire, corporate success story of the 1990s. On this particularly hot Philly summer evening, in the un–air conditioned, sparsely decorated room we rented as our church, we settled into folding chairs after singing bluesy-style worship songs. That evening our pastor had arranged a guest speaker: Ewuare X. Osayande. Other than the whir of the large window fans, the room was silent as we waited in anticipation for his message on anti-racism. I think most of us felt confident we would be agreeing with the points of view about to be shared.

I can't recall his exact words, but this paraphrase of his message is pretty close: "Why are you moving into our neighborhoods?"

Our brows collectively furrowed; they must have betrayed how this question was being received: "Sir, you must be mistaken; we get this issue. We're on your side! We're down with the cause."

But Mr. Osayande hadn't mixed up his words. He was very clear. For the next 45 minutes, he articulated in great detail how it was the height of ill-informed arrogance, enabled by white privilege, to assume that simply by plopping ourselves down in African American or Hispanic neighborhoods we would somehow "help." In fact, we often did the opposite, by driving up housing prices and pushing out current residents of color. And if some of us were honest, how many of the preexisting residents did we befriend and hang out with, once there?

Ouch. Osayande had just sprayed a garden hose onto the do-gooding embers in our naïve hearts. "Do you *really* want to help?" he asked. "Go back to your white neighborhoods, your white friends, your white family members. Go back to the places where you work. Educate them on institutional, structural racism that has destroyed these very neighborhoods you want to move into to 'help.' Educating and dismantling the white power structure is the single most helpful thing you can do."

✳ ✳ ✳

Like a naïve participant on a mission trip to Haiti (yes, I've participated in one of those, too), I became more aware of changes in my daily thinking from the experience of being in a racial subgroup.

For example, after perhaps a year of frequenting grocery stores where the majority of shoppers were African American, walking our new baby girl in a stroller through nearby Clark Park, or even pumping gas at the corner convenience store, I began to lose the hyper-awareness of being white in a black neighborhood. It was becoming simply my neighborhood. To be sure, there were moments when racial anxiety reared its head again, such as when my wife was called "cracker" by an older lady a couple of times on the trolley to work. But by and large, my System 1 mind trick of flagging "You're different!" settled down.

Economists often view the world through the lens of value trade-offs and theorize that humans make decisions that they perceive will benefit them the most. What was the value I was seeking in placing our family in surroundings where we would feel awkward at first, and indeed experience occasional hostility, however slight? What was the payoff for seeking a more diverse community?

Years later, when my daughters and I moved to Nashville for my new job in 2015, we were thrust into a situation that most people moving to a city enter into: a relatively uninformed, quite anxious scramble for a place to live. A lot of online resources these days are designed to help people make informed choices about which neighborhood to choose, based on any number of factors—school district ratings, crime rate, median home cost—but really, who has the time when your new job starts in three weeks? By default, we had to entrust our new living arrangements to a real estate professional. My company offered to pay for a real-estate consultant to guide us, so we took them up on that.

In our first interview with the consultant, we gave the requisite information: price range; type of living space that would work for the three of us, our cat, and our rambunctious chocolate lab, Tuck; and our desired type of neighborhood. Before meeting in person, I had made the misstep of driving around town and showing the girls the various neighborhoods near downtown Nashville that we knew fit our tastes, including the uber-hip East Nashville. Big mistake. East Nashville had become a burgeoning hipster community, and gentrification had pushed prices for even smaller, run-down apartments through the roof—or at least through the upper limits of our budget.

Without a lot of purposeful planning, we settled on renting a home in Hermitage, Tennessee, a suburb near my new office. Our new community was named for President Andrew Jackson's historic home. Roads such as Old Hickory (Jackson's nickname), and Andrew Jackson Parkway crisscrossed the community, which we were told had been farmland only a few short years ago. Now it and the neighboring communities had all the staples of an American Dream community: Best Buy, Target, Starbucks, cul-de-sacs. You can fill in the rest.

This was the same community in which we noticed a lot of Confederate flags waving from pickups during the summer we moved—the summer of the Charleston, South Carolina, church shooting. My American history knowledge being as sketchy as it was, I thought it would be interesting to learn about this Andrew Jackson, who was so honored here in Hermitage.

Jackson was the seventh president of the United States and considered the founder of the Democratic Party after being, as he figured it, robbed of the presidency in a deal between John Quincy Adams and Henry Clay in 1824. In the 1828 election, running as his newly founded party's candidate, he won in a landslide. At first, I was pleased to learn he was the first president of Appalachian heritage; one of my people! During his presidency, he faced a secession threat by South Carolina, a harbinger of things to come in the coming Civil War.[5]

Then I learned more. Jackson had signed the Indian Removal Act in 1830, which forced more than 45,000 Native Americans from numerous tribes to leave their indigenous lands in the southern states, particularly Georgia, and relocate to Oklahoma. This policy was especially popular with white officials after gold was discovered on Cherokee lands. This forced relocation initiative became known as the Trail of Tears, after more than 4,000 Cherokees died during the grueling journey. Somehow, though, one 2015 ranking of presidents slotted Andrew Jackson as the number nine best president in history.[6] *Indian Country Today* had a different opinion, as expressed in a 2012 article: "Indian-Killer Andrew Jackson Deserves Top Spot on List of Worst US Presidents."[7]

After learning about this painful history, I thought of it often as I drove home each day on the road honoring the man the Cherokee nicknamed "Sharp Knife" and "Indian Killer." To the victors go the spoils, as they say, as well as the road signs; in my new neighborhood they were labeled Andrew Jackson Parkway, not Indian Killer

Boulevard. On one drive home, my mind drifted to the thought of what a Native American would be forced to think about when driving on this road. Imagine the rage and pain felt by future Americans if they were somehow forced to drive on Osama Bin Laden Highway? I could only assume the Cherokees of the time and Native Americans of today would feel no less rage and pain.

After a year of living in our Hermitage housing development, and with a desire to move closer to the city and my office, we decided to move again. Sonora used her internet search skills to find a nice, affordable apartment complex in the Una-Antioch neighborhood of Nashville, just minutes from the airport and from my office.

The Una community of Nashville, snuggled between Interstate 40 and Interstate 24 and settled mostly around Murfreesboro Pike, immediately signaled to us that this was a different neighborhood than Hermitage, which was just 15 minutes up the highway. We noticed a major difference in the level of diversity. I also noticed something that I had not felt since the move to West Philly 15 years ago, something that embarrassed me: anxiety.

We toured the apartment complex and noticed the clean, sparkling swimming pool and well-kept grounds. The buildings were painted in earthy green; we also noticed many more brown faces, including African Americans, Latinos, and immigrants from around the world. I noticed a feeling of difference within me. Flashes of "Do we belong here?" and "Is it safe here?" entered my mind once again, seemingly without warning. Having started my "unwhitening" journey just a year earlier, I was disappointed and concerned about these thoughts. Surely, after living in black neighborhoods such as West Philadelphia and Mount Airy, I should now be cured of such race-conscious anxiety. Yet apparently, our brief time in Hermitage, and 10 years in my very white Charleston, West Virginia, neighborhood, had reprogrammed my brain again. System 1 brain told me again that being surrounded by lighter skin tones was "safe"; being surrounded by browner skin tones raised red flags.

I beat myself up over these concerns for a few days. I found myself purposefully willing my mind to question these feelings. Why did they spring up? Why was race once again wreaking havoc on a state of mind I had worked so hard over my lifetime to cultivate? Was I going to let these unfounded triggers dictate where I chose to live with my daughters? I know many white folks would hightail it out of the Una neighborhood after experiencing this dissonance. Indeed, when I mentioned we were looking at apartments in the Una-Antioch area of the city, a co-worker's response was: "Don't get shot."

✳ ✳ ✳

It is quite easy to view the detailed crime statistics in a city or neighborhood using today's modern tools, and it can feel disconcerting. We may hear sirens now and then, but most of us rarely see the actual crimes. The Nashville Metro Police Department's web-based visual tool made it easy to determine what exactly was going on in every neighborhood. I did a quick search for the half-mile radius around our targeted apartment complex: 27 reported crime incidents in the past four weeks.

I picked some other half-mile radiuses, including our prior location in Hermitage: two incidents. Advantage, suburbs.

What about the hip 12 South shopping area of Nashville, where so many young people were moving? Twelve incidents in the same time period. The hip East Nashville neighborhood we wanted to live in earlier? Nine records.

So, there you have it. Una, at least the area around the apartment complex, was thirteen times more crime-ridden than Hermitage, and three times more dangerous than our desired hipster neighborhood of

East Nashville. If you were the parent of two teenage daughters, what would you do?

"I love this area," said Sonora, my oldest, about Una. "Me, too," said Shelby, my youngest. We visited a few more times before deciding on the move. My data-loving brain cut the numbers this way and that, both criminally and financially. Financially, and in other ways, it was a no-brainer. Safety-wise, I needed to assuage the "dad as protector" element of my mind, and I needed to purposely push through the racist grooves that had been reformatting my subconscious in the last ten years of living almost exclusively among white people in West Virginia.

It turns out that when looking at crime statistics, everything is relative. So many people, from the media to real estate agents, are incentivized to turn crime statistics into major freak-out headlines, but they often lack perspective. For example, you may have heard that airplane travel is far safer than riding in a car, but few people have auto phobias; lots of people have a fear of flying.

Even with a crime rate in Una 13 times higher than where we currently lived, what did that mean in terms of likelihood that we would be victims of crime? And what influence should that likelihood have on our decision on which community to live in?

In Una, our likelihood of being a victim of a crime of violence or property was 1 in 37. In East Nashville, 1 in 111. In Hermitage, 1 in 500. Judging from those numbers, if our only concern was safety, we should have stayed put. However, compared to the odds of dying in a car accident (1 in 77), by poison (1 in 53), or of any accident in general (1 in 20)—all things I didn't spend many brain cells worrying about—the odds seemed just fine.

In the end, the practical desire to save some money with more affordable housing, along with a System 2 desire to live in a more diverse neighborhood, settled our decision. I was surprised how much emotional effort it took for me to overcome those initial involuntary concerns, however. My reaction to the area wasn't much different from the way my friend's wife reacted at the sight of an Arab-American cab driver; it was simply a difference of degree, not kind. System 2 often must work overtime to overcome System 1.

Sitting in my new Una neighborhood Starbucks, I watched as a group of young Middle Eastern men, mostly 20-somethings or late teenagers, gathered chairs in a circle to drink their lattes and laugh uproariously at each other's stories. A real estate website I was exploring at that moment to learn more about Una let me know that my new community has a higher percentage of residents with Arab and Lithuanian ancestry than 99.6% of the neighborhoods in America.[8]

I glanced over at a table of young Ethiopians, male and female, entranced with each other, and an Ethiopian mother dressed in bright colors tutoring her two children. I observed three Lithuanian young men sitting by the window. I realized that throughout this latest struggle to wrestle away the racist triggers in my brain, not once had I thought about how *my* presence may trigger *them.*

The voices combined into the comforting background noise I so often cherished during my coffee shop evenings. I closed my laptop and headed to my car, feeling a deep sense that we all belonged here.

✢ ✢ ✢

Twice in my life I have made conscious commitments to move into a more diverse neighborhood, to place myself in a community in which I was not in the racial majority. I wasn't sure exactly why; but the more I thought and prayed about it, the more I realized how the desire for diversity was planted in me during those early years in Morgantown, surrounded by children of different colors and faiths who went home to their mothers' kitchens to eat tasty food from their home countries. I wasn't consciously aware of my tendencies until adulthood, but I began to yearn for a diverse circle of friends and neighbors for the rest of my life.

I thought back on the friendships my then-wife and I developed fairly easily in the diverse areas of Philadelphia in which we lived. Thanks mostly to the gregarious nature of my wife, we easily connected with neighbors and traded dinner nights at each other's apartments or went to movies together. Diverse neighbors seemed to easily translate into diverse friendships, many of which stand strong to this day. My children played with a diverse group of children from their preschools and in our neighborhood, which I hoped planted seeds of desiring diversity in their own lives.

To me, the value tradeoff of living in a diverse community compared to a homogenous one is so one-sided that the benefits of living in a multiracial neighborhood more than make up for any initial anxieties over belonging or misperceived risks placed on our psyches by media. In fact, it's a no-brainer. But it can unfortunately be a System 2 no-brainer, not System 1. Although I had once again successfully resisted the tendency to let whiteness play a lazy, short-sighted, dominant role in where my family and I lived, I was frustrated how my own subconscious race-based concerns had bubbled to the surface again.

I realized even more deeply that race programming wouldn't be defeated so easily. Now it was time to move on to the next hurdle in eradicating race from my identity and decision-making: church.

9

Ham's Curse and
Hipster Church

The contemporary church is so often a weak, ineffectual
voice with an uncertain sound. It is so often the
arch supporter of the status quo. Far from being
disturbed by the presence of the church, the power
structure of the average community is consoled by the
church's often vocal sanction of things as they are.
—Martin Luther King Jr., "Letter
from the Birmingham Jail"

Attending Cross Point Church in Nashville can be somewhat daunting when you're 50 years old. It's a bit like walking into an alt country or indie rock video. Whatever the latest research shows about millennial and post-millennial generations giving up on church, the ones who remain congregate at places like this. Set in a refurbished downtown industrial building in the shadows of Nashville's gleaming modern skyscrapers, Cross Point is everything you would picture when envisioning the hippest environment possible to attract young people: exposed ceilings, creative directional signage (including a lighted marquee pointing to children's worship, for those ancient 30-somethings old enough to bring along some young ones), and pulsing club lighting in the main auditorium. The church's mission statement—Everyone's Welcome, Nobody's Perfect, Anything's Possible—is frequently reinforced on walls, in programs, and in pre-service videos that roll on the gigantic dual screens on either side of the stage.

The dominant demographic at the main church campus in the city's industrial warehouse district represents the energy and youth of modern hipster Nashville: young, beautiful, and stylish. Did all these people just step out of a Taylor Swift or Sam Hunt video? The standard Sunday uniform here includes casual jeans (ripped in the right places, of course), designer boots (more of the Italian variety than cowboy, unlike the touristy, country music–themed parts of town), long tunics for the women, designer tees for the guys. And tattoos. Lots of I'm-hip-but-not-dangerous tattoos.

Unlike many churches, where you strain to find a young person, at Cross Point you struggle to find a Generation Xer (my demographic, by a hair) or, even rarer, a Baby Boomer. Maybe it's just too darn loud.

The first time my daughters and I visited Cross Point, we felt right at home. My daughters loved it because these are their people and this is their music; me, because I still hold vain visions that I trend hip, at least mentally if not demographically. Maybe I could become the cool dad figure? When we heard a 21 Pilots song mixed in with the contemporary Christian songs playing over the loudspeakers in the lobby, we knew this was the place. After a pulsing music video featuring quick-edit images of urban Nashville and young people at work in the city the rave—I'm sorry, I mean the *service*—launched.

With my enhanced race-conscious lenses, I looked around for people of color. Ah, there is an African American person. There's an Asian person. Both young, beautiful, and stylish. On the hipster criteria, at least, they clearly fit here. Perhaps one out of 250 people were people of color. In the crowd of 2,500, that makes 10 or so. Sadly, even with those ratios, Cross Point may be among the upper percentile in church diversity.

My teenage daughters and I felt drawn to Cross Point church. Culturally, it seemed to fit us. But what implications might giving up whiteness have for my patterns and preferences of worship? And, more importantly, what would a person of color have to give up to feel comfortable here?

✳ ✳ ✳

I grew up in the warm cocoon of small-town faith at First Baptist Church of Glenville. Since the mid-19th century, the church sat in a prominent Main Street location, with worship and Sunday school disrupted only by the occasional flooding of the Little Kanawha River that flowed directly behind it. My dad was a deacon and my Sunday school teacher for years; my mom was an active participant in many women's and children's ministry roles. Both were always on boards or committees of this, that, or the other thing. Mom and Dad sang together in the Billy Graham Evangelism Crusade while dating in the 1960s in Columbus, Ohio, and after my dad took a professor position at his alma mater, Glenville State College, the James family took root in this little town and church in central West Virginia.

First Baptist was the only community of faith I knew from age two to 18. Honestly, for a white kid in a small, white town, it was pretty great. Older ladies or my friends' mothers were Sunday school teachers for the kids, all of them warm and friendly. We had cute older teen girls volunteer at our vacation Bible school sessions, which increased the enthusiastic attendance of the middle-school boys. The men, including my dad, served as deacons, took the offering, and kept up the grounds. The pastors during my childhood were mostly educated men with divinity degrees, although I do recall an occasional female guest speaker or two. Only later did I learn that among some churches, a woman speaking from the pulpit was a major taboo and that my church was considered liberal by pastors who led the small Independent Baptist churches that dotted our region's hillsides. We even read a modern translation of the Bible instead of the King James Version; so clearly, we were on the wild side.

My hometown Baptist church was one in which the issue of race, so volatile and forefront in the '60s and '70s generation in which I grew up, was never mentioned. As referenced earlier, to the best of my ability to observe such things as a white kid in that era, the occasional African American visitors or international students were welcomed in our church when they appeared. I also have a vague recollection of three African American young women whom our pastor must have invited one Sunday to give the "special music" (that's Baptist-speak for anything not sung by the choir). After they sang a few black gospel tunes that were clearly beyond the hymnal selections we were used to, our tall, learned, white pastor said, "I don't know about you, but when I get to heaven, that's the kind of music I want to hear."

In other words, I did not grow up in a church environment filled with fire and brimstone preaching or racist paranoia. I learned through example and indirect teaching that being mean or hateful to anyone was not how Jesus would act, and that we accept whomever

God sends to us at First Baptist. Yet with all that warm and fuzzy influence, replicated across thousands of churches to sincere believers each week, Dr. Martin Luther King Jr., accurately noted that, "Everyone knows that 11 o'clock on Sunday morning is the most segregated hour in American life."

Recent studies have found that is still the case.[1] Driven in various parts by persistent neighborhood segregation, inflexible cultural preferences, and deeply held assumptions of what the "right" way to do church really is, the studies found that 86% of churches are of one predominant race (usually categorized as such based on whether there are less than 20% non-majority attendees). Only about one-third of Americans have ever attended a church where they were the racial subgroup. The majority of white respondents to the surveys felt that was just fine, and their churches had done enough to diversify, thank you very much. Not surprisingly, nonwhite respondents to the survey felt more could be done.[2]

The Apostle Paul's great statement on the diversity of God's kingdom remains more prophecy than reality, at least in how it plays out on Sunday mornings: "There is no longer Jew or Gentile, slave or free, male and female. For you are all one in Christ Jesus" (Galatians 3:28 NLT). It's interesting to note that Paul didn't mention race in this affirmation of cross-cultural unity; the concept of race categories as we now understand them wasn't invented or widely adopted until centuries later.

✱ ✱ ✱

I've been reading the Bible since my early youth in Sunday school and vacation Bible school, first in those children's versions with Precious Moments–style Bible scenes (which made the global flood that destroyed everyone but Noah's family less terrifying), and later through my own personal study time. I could never remember a reference to skin color or race. It turns out there is one, in the prophetic book of Jeremiah, where God asks the question, "Can the Ethiopian change his skin or the leopard his spots?" (Jeremiah 13:23 ESV). In the New Testament, there are verses translated into English such as 1 Peter 2:9: "But you are a chosen race, a royal priesthood, a holy nation, a people for his own possession." However, a quick review of various translations makes it pretty clear that the word *race* is not understood as a physical racial category; the root concept is translated as "generation" in the King James Version, or "people" in the New International Version, New Living Translation, and other versions. God's adoption was based on faith, not biological distinction. In addition, the earliest Christians were, of course, Middle Eastern Jews, so you would think that would have discouraged the early racist interpretations.

Overall, the Bible refers to people as nations and tribes, not by race or skin color. I knew that somewhere down through history, revisionist interpretations of the Bible had entered the picture, such as the idea that God created the races when scattering ancient people at the Tower of Babel. That story is told in Genesis 11, but there is only a reference of "confusing their language," not creating different physical features such as skin tone.

God put a curse on Cain after he killed his brother, as told in Genesis 4, which refers to a "mark" put on Cain by God. Some later read into the text that this mark indicated a change in skin color, despite no support for that anywhere in the text. Often these cultural and religious assumptions don't get thought out very well; it's quite odd that the Cain-based racial curse myth was assumed to have taken root at the beginning of human origins. If God created dark skin as the "mark" of Cain's curse in Genesis 4, yet all humans except Noah's family were wiped from the face of the earth in Genesis 7, wasn't Cain's line—and therefore their theoretically dark skin—wiped out?

Later in the book of Genesis, we find what some have called the "Curse of Ham," a misnomer for Noah's curse on Canaan, Ham's son. After realizing Ham saw him naked in his tent and that he did nothing to cover him, Noah calls out, "Cursed be Canaan! The lowest of slaves will he be to his brothers" (Genesis 9:24). Some white Christians have misunderstood and misapplied this as a reference to race and a supposed divine mandate that darker people are to be servants of lighter people.[3] Once again, those seeking justification for racial stratification and subjectification read into the passage what they wanted it to mean. There is no reference whatsoever to race or color, and no suggestion that the implications of Noah's curse beyond Canaan, and certainly not to an entire group of dark-skinned people. In fact, later in the Bible, references to interactions by Israelites with people of darker skin, such as Abraham with Egyptians or Moses's marriage to a Cushite (or Ethiopian) wife, reflect no sense of supposed superiority or assumption of servitude based on skin color. Once again, our modern notion of race wasn't even invented yet in that period of history. Scientists have wielded the power of DNA analysis on Canaanite history, and found no genetic connection to dark-skinned African peoples.[4]

So much for the "Curse of Ham" (or Canaan) theory. Whatever you think of the Bible as an accurate source of history, its paucity of reference to skin color and race as we understand it is telling. White Christians (and members of other religious groups) may have been guilty of collaborating or perhaps even creating racial division, but the Bible didn't lead them to do so; their own twisted, unrepentant hearts and minds deserve the blame.

✷ ✷ ✷

The Christian church has much to confess and repent of, when it comes to its role in racial separation and subjugation. This is true across Catholic, Orthodox, and Protestant branches. In my conversations with white Christians, not many are fully aware of the laundry list of injustices played out under the banner of Christ's church, what the Apostle Paul describes as Jesus's "body" here on earth (1 Corinthians 12:27) as lived out in our world and America. Here are just a few of the lowlights.

* Erroneous Christian theology that cast darker-skinned people as destined for servitude was conveniently on the rise in the same historical moment in which the slavers and their financial supporters were encouraging colonialism, all in the name of expanding economic power. When theology is subservient to economics, all kinds of verses can get twisted.

* Entire Christian denominations have been formed, in large part, to provide safe haven for racial stratification and the institution of slavery. Northern and Southern Baptists split in 1845 over the issue of slavery, with the newly formed Southern Baptist Convention—now the largest Protestant denomination in America—clinging to a specious interpretation of the Bible's endorsement of slavery. The denomination finally apologized and forcefully renounced such a stance in 1995. The Assemblies of God split in 1917 over an incident in which the denomination refused to confirm an African American missionary who wanted to serve, and a new black denomination was formed in 1920. Nearly 100 years later, the two Pentecostal relatives mended their rift and announced a partnership in 2014.

* In the 1960s, many Southern and even Northern pastors resisted integration of their churches and communities. Southern Baptist historian Mark Hall states that "white evangelicals

throughout the South were overwhelmingly opposed to the civil rights movement. And that's the cruelest historical irony of it all: those who loved the 'old rugged cross' were often also those who torched crosses in protest of desegregation."[5]

+ Many pastors and denominations resisted interracial marriages. Bob Jones University, a fundamentalist Christian college in South Carolina, banned nonwhite students until 1971, when it was threatened with losing federal funding. Only as recently as the year 2000 did the university begin allowing people of different races to date. Just two years earlier, in 1998, the school's spokesperson had claimed, "God has separated people for his own purposes. He has erected barriers between the nations, not only land and sea barriers, but also ethnic, cultural, and language barriers. God has made people different from one another and intends those differences to remain. Bob Jones University is opposed to intermarriage of the races because it breaks down the barriers God has established." Finally, in 2008, the great-great-grandson of Bob Jones and president of the university at the time, Stephen Jones, reversed the claim. Better late than never, I suppose.

+ The Catholic Church certainly isn't off the hook as concerns racist practices, ranging from centuries ago in Europe to its more recent history in America. Many of the earliest slave traders in America were Catholic, as French and Spanish colonists introduced a distorted concoction of Catholicism and race-based slavery to the Mississippi Valley. The Catholic Church was one of the largest slaveholding institutions in Louisiana; despite Pope Gregory XVI's 1839 apostolic letter strongly condemning the slave trade, local Catholic leaders such as Bishop Auguste Marie Martin of Natchitoches claimed that slavery was "the manifest will of God" and put forth the curse

of Ham theory described above as justification.[6] Racism is so
powerful it can cause a local religious leader to oppose his
own Pope, who by Catholic theology is perceived as infallible
in teaching a doctrine.

✳ I don't even know how to measure the effect of countless
images of a white, blonde-haired, blue-eyed Jesus that cir-
culated through Sunday school materials, children's books,
paintings, and movies, many to this day. Edward J. Blum and
Paul Harvey, authors of *The Color of Christ: The Son of God
and the Saga of Race in America*, observe, "Deep down in
their psyches, many American children learn to associate the
divine with the white race. This is crucial because it allows
white people to see whiteness and racial categories as ever-
lasting. Even though science, history, and anthropology has
[sic] shown that races are cultural and social constructions,
Americans can continue to believe that a 'white race' has
always been."

It's more than disheartening how blinded Jesus-followers can be
on this issue. When confronted with these historic realities, too many
white American Christians that I've interacted with react with a superficial dismissal, "Well, that was *then*." Few want to contemplate the
implications of history on today's world, and even fewer are interested
in dealing with the problem as an extension of personal and community life in the church. We can't redeem what we won't acknowledge.

Malcolm X observed in a 1962 speech, "The white man never
has separated Christianity from white, nor has he separated the white
man from Christianity. When you hear the white man bragging, 'I'm
a Christian,' he's bragging about being a white man."[7] Is it true? Is
Christianity inherently a "white man's religion"? How could this
be, given that it was founded by a resurrected Jewish rabbi and his

Middle Eastern Jewish followers? How could this be when the fastest-growing percentage of the world's 2.5 billion Christians are Asian, African, and Hispanic?[8] If I could give up being white, how would that change my understanding of being Christian?

＊ ＊ ＊

It was clear that my recent journey to unwhiten myself wouldn't have a lot of guidance or support within the dominant white Christian church. With the exception of my experience at Circle of Hope, I could recall just one sermon, in any of the predominantly white churches I attended in my five decades of churchgoing, that had to do with the evils of racial discrimination—and that includes Martin Luther King's birthday weekend, a built-in excuse for a pastor to say *something*. How could I go about naming and then excising race as a primary pillar of my identity if I couldn't rely on my faith community to help me?

This is a particularly sad failure of the modern church because of the diverse nature of the early Christian communities that took root as the Apostle Paul and others spread the gospel into Asia Minor and beyond. And it's not as if this hypocrisy hasn't been continually called out through centuries of cries from African American brothers and sisters in the faith. Frederick Douglass minced no words: "I love the pure, peaceable, and impartial Christianity of Christ; I therefore hate the corrupt, slaveholding, women-whipping, cradle-plundering, partial, and hypocritical Christianity of this land. Indeed, I can see no reason, but the most deceitful one, for calling the religion of this land Christianity. I look upon it as the climax of all misnomers, the boldest of all frauds, and the grossest of all libels."

Modern prophets and preachers have kept the flame of truth-telling on this issue brightly and consistently lit. Jemar Tisby, in his powerful book, *The Color of Compromise: The Truth about the American Church's Complicity in Racism*, describes the modern signs of the white church's role in maintaining white supremacy and injustice: "It looks like Christians responding to 'black lives matter' with the phrase 'all lives matter.' It looks like Christians consistently supporting a president whose racism has been on display for decades. It looks like Christians telling black people and their allies that their attempts to bring up racial concerns are 'divisive.'"

Circle of Hope, with a passion and commitment for social justice and equality far beyond any other church I have attended, still had its struggles. At one point during my time there, the church hired an African American associate pastor, a huge step for a largely white church. I remember excitement over this development . . . and then disappointment as the new pastor and his wife shared deep frustrations with me about how inflexible our church was about making changes they'd suggested in order to attract more people of color. They left within a year. It became clear, even at a church so progressively minded on issues of race and reconciliation, that it's one thing to seek diversity and equality; it's another thing entirely to be willing to collaborate, compromise, and communicate on equal levels to make it stick.

For quite a while after that, I gave up on finding or participating in a church where diversity was a deeply rooted reality. As God impressed on me that I should get more serious about this journey, it dawned on me that there was one important part of my faith experience that I had not fully explored—one that put me in the same category as all those white Christians who agree with racial reconciliation and equality in theory, but often not in practice. I had never belonged to a faith community where I wasn't of the dominant race and culture. I had never submitted my own spiritual growth to a mentor or leader of color.

Sure, I had visited a black church or two. But on my current journey toward shedding whiteness, it was clear to me that to discard any racial assumptions or privileges when it came to religious practice within my Christian worldview, I had to be willing to let myself be stripped of 50 years of religious tradition and community assumptions. I had to immerse myself in a more meaningful way in churches where my culture and race were not dominant.

***

It's not easy for anyone of any racial and cultural classification to find a safe, welcoming church. That's a sad statement and a perception that many churches have worked hard to overcome, but it's still true. Church-shopping is weird. You never know what you might walk into. Am I entering a Terracotta Army kind of church where people sit stiffly in the pews, or a wild and rambunctious cluster of tongue-speakers? When do I stand and when do I sit? First visits require a sharp eye and quick responses to follow the established pattern of worship. Layer on the prospect of being in a racial subgroup—maybe the *only* one—in a church, and you can begin to understand why churches are intractably less diverse than the population around them.

I didn't yet know any African American friends in Nashville who could guide me through the local, nonwhite church options, so I had to cross that barrier as well. One church in my Una-Antioch neighborhood was an option. The Mt. Zion Baptist Church of Nashville was established in 1866, just three years after Lincoln's Emancipation Proclamation. Today, more than 22,000 people at eight weekly services in three locations call the church home. The church's history page on its website notes that the grandchildren of founding member Sister Mary Cole, who once hosted the fledgling church in her living room, still attend.

It just so happened that one of the largest of Mt. Zion's venues was located just across the street from our apartment. My daughters and I had noticed a large billboard of Bishop Walker and First Lady Dr. Stephanie Walker, a former Harvard Medical faculty member and neonatologist, beside the highway as we drove to services at Cross Point.

First, though, I had learned enough by now that I needed to check my motivations. Was this a book report project so I could tell this story? Was my white paternalistic tendency influencing me, or white guilt kicking in to make me think I was visiting to "help" the cause? Or was I genuinely seeking community and spiritual growth from a mindset of equality, or more importantly, submission? Beyond a motivation check, I also had to wonder about the effect of a lone white man walking into a black church after the deadly Emmanuel A.M.E. attack in Charleston, South Carolina, which was the basis of my original text to Crystal.

On a beautiful, late-October Sunday, I prayed about it and felt a peace to make the short trek across the street to the shopping center— the Mt. Zion Shopping Center, mind you; the church had purchased the property and essentially took up the whole strip mall—where the Una neighborhood campus was located. Tamping down my anxiety by reminding myself that this would be an exploratory visit, I entered the church with the stream of thousands of other churchgoers.

I had dressed a little nicer than usual, but I noticed everyone seemed to be attired in purple. Did I miss that it was "dress in purple day" on the website, or was this the normal Sunday dress code? The greeter handed me off to an usher, who at my request sat me near the back. I scanned the crowd. I was the only white person in a sea of brown people dressed in purple, but I noticed no side glances or "what's he doing here?" looks. After a few minutes, I spotted another white person several rows over. I thought to myself, is this what people of color do when they visit Cross Point or any other mostly white church: try to find a signal, in the form of someone of the same race, to reassure themselves that it's okay to be here?

The service started with a burst of music. The praise band launched into a fast-paced gospel song and the 40-member choir stood and joined in with a beautiful power. The bass, the saxophone, the drums, and the other instruments blended with the electrifying voices. For years after my divorce, worship time during church services had become much more emotional than in my prior churchgoing years. Worship songs were cathartic, and after the emotional mayhem of my 40s, it was hard to keep tears from streaming when certain songs were sung. My conservative, small-town Baptist shell had cracked, and I had even started raising my hands in those years. It was as if the pain had fractured the self-conscious layers of my heart. I was able to connect with God during worship in a way I never could before.

But here, as this choir sang, this band played, and the people around me lifted their voices, I felt something that was hard for me to describe at first. Eventually I realized what it was: it was joy. It dawned on me that I hadn't felt this kind of peaceful joy in so long, even during the hundreds of church services I had attended in my lifetime. Emotion, yes. Overwhelming awe and gratitude, yes. But this feeling? It was new.

At that moment, my self-protective persona as observer turned into that of a true worshipper. I lost my self-consciousness and just basked in the joy of connecting with God, with these people in purple. The music became mine, too. There were praise dancers on stage, doing their thing, with colorful flags flying around them. There was no expectation or pressure to do so, but most people waved their hands, swayed, and sang. Some stood stoically, but most expressed a freedom in worship that seemed liberating. I swayed a little. I lifted my hands a little. I did what I felt comfortable doing, but probably more so here than at my prior white churches. The cues of freedom in worship were already influencing me.

Later, after church, I thought about the cultural norms embedded in my small-town Baptist church experience. We stood when prompted by the pastor. We opened our hymnals and sang. We didn't sway or dance or raise our hands. We stood, sang, and sat down. Even in the more contemporary nondenominational churches I had been attending for most of my adult life, where the soft rock worship music was radical compared to the centuries-old hymns sung in my hometown church, it was an exercise in conformity within certain boundaries. Here, at Mt. Zion Baptist, worship was freer, more expressive, and yes, more extended. No three stanzas and you're done. One praise song seemed to go on forever, but that felt just fine.

Did that make those prior churches "white"? If so, why? Why was a certain service structure, music experience, and audience participation level identified with a race tag? I knew that certain Pentecostal churches, even mostly white ones, were much less structured and exhibited more freedom in worship. I knew that there were certain African American denominations that were far more conservative in their worship style than others. So, what made a church "white" or "black," other than the color of the majority of people who attended it?

I decided to come back the next week. On my second visit, I observed another indication of the deep hunger for Jesus's bread and water of life at Mt. Zion, not just for heavenly blessing but for daily rescue. On this Sunday, the church held a baptismal service. For any of you not well-versed in various Christian denominational practices, Baptists and some other churches fully immerse a convert in water for baptism. It's a symbol of that individual dying to their old life and being raised up out of the baptismal waters victoriously into new life in Christ.

Two young men entered the water in the baptismal above the choir loft. As soon as they entered, a woman began to shriek, "Thank you, Jesus! Thank you, thank you, thank you, Jesus! Oh, dear God!" She wailed and cried over and over. After that portion of the service concluded, an assistant pastor took the stage as the energy from the baptisms still crackled in the audience. "You hear, now, a sister—these boys' mother—was becoming overwhelmed, didn't you? Let me tell you! When every day—every day!—our young people are gunned down on the streets, or taken away from us, how can we not become overwhelmed over the salvation of these two young men!" The church erupted in praise.

I felt inundated with emotion. No church I had ever attended had such a large percentage of its people attending services with this type of shared experience, with this hunger for help from God for themselves and their children. Church here wasn't an activity like attending a movie or a ballgame; it wasn't a place just to come to get cheered up for the week. Church was *life*. I felt humbled before God and the people surrounding me. I realized that perhaps the reason I felt joy here was that my heart, so damaged from the pain of my divorce, was desperate for God also. I shouted along with that woman in my heart. Perhaps before long, if I continued attending Mt. Zion, I could relearn some norms and would feel the freedom to shriek my praise out loud as well.

My experience with Mt. Zion was early in my unwhitening journey. Was this the church I was supposed to belong to and serve in? Doubts and racial baggage still weighed on me. At times, I could still hear some taunts from my youth precipitated by my preference for "black" music and perhaps my love for basketball. "You wish you were black, don't you?" "I'll bet you're really black!" Was it wrong or weird for me to be drawn to this church? What would attending Mt. Zion on a regular basis, and attempting to be a full member of the community there, be like? I felt accepted during my visit. But would I truly belong?

I'd grown so tired of racial labels. I didn't want to be black. I didn't want to be white. I just wanted to be with people who accepted me, who shared a hunger for God, and with whom I could soak up God's grace with deep and lasting joy.

10

Bad Justice for Good Jobs

Never forget that justice is what love looks like in public.
—Cornel West

In my younger years, I was a bit of a lead foot. Once in the mid-2000s, I was pulled over twice in one day for speeding. Both times I received a warning from white police officers and went on my way. At the time I felt lucky, like I should have purchased a lottery ticket that day. After sharing that story a few times with friends of color, who buckled over laughing at the thought of what would have happened to *them* in a similar situation, I began to realize there was some pretty thick privilege involved.

How does one interpret these types of experiences? I'm a sample of one. Other white people have their own personal samples of life experiences. Rarely, if ever, do any of them lead us to believe that conscious or subconscious bias may enter into how police operate under stressful conditions.

Most white folks I know aren't motivated to go looking for it, but there is a body of evidence that in the realm of criminal justice, the "privilege" in "white privilege" is both frequent and high stakes. The benefit of policing that is *for* me and not out to *get* me is an essential element of white privilege.

Relative to a black person, as a white man I am:

* Less likely to be charged with a crime, even if I commit one.
* Less likely to be convicted by a jury of my peers. (One of the biggest discrepancies between white and black defendants is how infrequently African Americans actually receive a jury of their peers, at least racially and economically.)
* Less likely to be given jail time, if I am convicted.
* Less likely to receive as long of a sentence for the same crime.

Here's the evidence. All other factors being equal, black offenders are 75% more likely to face a charge carrying a mandatory minimum sentence than a white offender who committed the same crime. That's according to a 2014 University of Michigan Law School study.[1] If you are a black man who committed a crime, you will, on average, receive a federal sentence that is 20% longer than a white criminal, according to the United States Sentencing Commission. This disparity has shot up in the last few years, as judges have been given more leeway in sentencing. It seems the more flexibility judges are given in sentencing, the more racial bias jacks up the sentences given to black criminals.

The United States, although representing only 5% of the world's population, houses almost 25% of the world's prisoner population. Within our prison-first culture, white folks face an incarceration rate of 450 inmates per 100,000 people. The black community faces an incarceration rate that is *five times greater*, or 2,306 inmates per 100,000 people. If our country wanted to save $232 million a year, simply assigning black folks who happen to have been convicted of a crime the *same* sentence as a white perpetrator of the same crime would reduce the black incarceration rate by 9%. Because of this disparity in policing and sentencing even among petty crimes or low-level drug offenses, as compared to white defendants, one in nine African American children have a parent in prison.[2]

This aspect of the Foot I had learned about in my Damascus Road session was brutal and far more devastating. It is racism expressed not through a sneer or a snub, but with publicly authorized force. As Ta-Nehisi Coates wrote in a letter to his son, published in *The Atlantic* and adapted from his book *Between the World and Me*: "All you need to understand is that the officer carries with him the power of the American state and the weight of an American legacy, and they necessitate that of the bodies destroyed every year, some wild and disproportionate number of them will be black." The negative cycle of losing a family member to prison had so many long-term implications for keeping people of color poor and outside of the mainstream economy that it boggled my mind.

I knew from my days at West Virginia University, perennially named in the top 10 party schools in the nation, that a whole lot of white kids were using and dealing drugs. I couldn't recall that any of them went to jail. My roommates and I once received a visit from the Morgantown, West Virginia, police for stealing cable service one year (I didn't participate in the cable splicing, but I didn't exactly protest the free service, either). The officer didn't cuff us or pull a weapon. He simply told us to report to the downtown precinct, where they took our fingerprints and politely charged us with cable theft. My anxiety was soon assuaged when a roommate's father, who was an attorney, wrote a letter and made a few calls. Within hours the charges were dropped.

Just within the brief window of my unwhitening journey, equal
or lesser crimes had led to the deaths of African American citizens
through engagements with law enforcement. Sandra Bland, pulled
over for a minor traffic violation, was later found dead in her jail cell.
Michael Brown was killed after allegedly stealing cigars. Eric Garner
was killed in front of everyone on a Staten Island street after selling
loose cigarettes. My body was preserved; theirs were destroyed.

✷ ✷ ✷

During those impatient, wistful months of my final year at my small
high school, a rumor undulated through our county. The rumor was
that a developer was considering building a federal prison in our
county. Jobs!

Everyone was abuzz. Was this real? Would a significant new
source of jobs, beyond the limited number of oil and gas drilling service jobs that existed in the region, really come to fruition? This was
the most exciting thing to hit Gilmer County since the discovery of
pockets of oil and natural gas in the region in 1859, or Glenville State
College's founding in 1872. I was only 18 at the time, but I felt the
possibilities for my community.

A public meeting was set up at the county recreation center building near our home on Mineral Road. I remember car after car driving
by our house that evening. My parents didn't seem particularly interested in attending, but even at that young age, I was excited by the
concept of economic development and growth. The county seemed
equally divided between those with visions of growth and new pros-
perity and those with visions of danger and dread. "So, you're saying
the federal prison would house prisoners from Washington, DC, and
some of the DC employees might move here?" they would say. Left
unsaid: "Wouldn't that mean inner-city people (*black people!*) would

be coming into our county, both to visit their family members in jail and—gasp—even to follow their newly relocated jobs and *live* here? Is that what we want for Gilmer County?"

At that time, the prison project was too good—or bad, depending on your point of view—to be true. Like so many Appalachian dreams of opportunity, the buzz and the jobs that were expected to come with its construction dissipated after several months. The prison never materialized. Excitement over. Back to regular life, tending wells or working at Go-Mart, and nursing our fatalistic tendencies. Nothing much good ever happens to us here in small-town Appalachia; why did we expect otherwise?

Later, after I had carried on with my adult life, far away from Appalachia for several years, a prison did come to fruition with the help of the local oil and gas baron who donated land to the cause. The miracle had come true. A new source of "good jobs with benefits" (the slogan of every politician in Appalachia) had been realized. I was excited for my old home, from afar. Such growth, with potential to draw in at least some diverse new citizens, seemed downright progressive for my small home county. During a visit home one summer, I even drove past a new hotel, put up to ensure prisoners' visitors had a place to stay, and continued across the bridge and up the road (which the local oil and gas man had donated to lure the prison developer) to take a gander at the great new source of good jobs with benefits.

It looked modern and impressive, as much as any cement building with barbed wire fence around it can. I learned from that visit to my hometown that the good jobs with benefits inside paid in the high $20,000s to mid-$30,000s range. Perhaps lower middle-class wages for a family, if both partners worked. Unfortunately, I learned that most of the people who landed jobs at the prison, or followed their old jobs' relocation, decided not to live in Gilmer County, but to commute from nearby towns that offered more housing, a Wal-Mart, and better fast food options. Only a handful of prior DC employees—including one or two African American families—had migrated from urban DC to life in small-town West Virginia.

I learned that this was a medium-security prison, which, in the language of the modern-day prison industry, largely meant that nonviolent offenders caught with drugs were stored here. This was somewhere between the country club white-collar criminal prison environment and the yikes-these-guys-are-dangerous setup. Hence the fence, but without the need for a county-wide siren if someone escaped.

Yes, that meant that most of the prisoners housed in Gilmer County—prisoners who now counted toward Gilmer County's population statistics but couldn't vote or have any role in the community—were black. I was surprised one day long after my visit when I looked up Gilmer County's census demographics and found that it had shot up to top of the list for having one of West Virginia's largest African American populations. Now 11% of the county's "citizens" were black compared to 0.03% before. It's just that they lived behind bars up on the hill.[3]

Black people from the metro areas of Washington, DC, Baltimore, and Philadelphia who had loved ones housed in this prison now had to drive six to eight hours away to Gilmer County, West Virginia, and stay in a Best Western at the foot of the mountain where their family members were held.

Only recently did my mind grasp the situation. Black people were snatched by law enforcement from their home neighborhoods for drug offenses that, in many cases, were equal in severity to what some local Gilmer Countians were doing on any given weekend: drinking illegal moonshine, smoking weed, or taking pills. The prisoners—these mostly black and brown prisoners—were hauled from their homes off to West Virginia so that rural, mostly white West Virginians could have $30,000-a-year jobs with health benefits.

Welcome to what passes for economic development in Appalachia. During my repatriation years back in the state, which I spent championing new forms of innovation economy development, I learned that several counties had gladly accepted shiny new prisons to provide those good jobs with benefits. So many, in fact, that West Virginia now led the nation in federal prison cells per capita. Almost one out of every 200 people who reside in the state do so against their will with a forced stay in a federal prison.[4] I suppose that's one way to address West Virginia's declining population problem; we'll just force you to live with us for a while.

Only during my recent unwhitening experiment did I consider: What if rural white Appalachians were arrested and convicted for their moonshine stills, backwoods weed growing, and prescription pill-trading at the same rate and for the same long-term sentences? What if rural white people were shipped to urban prisons so that black folks could have good jobs with benefits?

✳ ✳ ✳

As a student and younger man watching documentaries about the 1960s, I felt a certain eerie spookiness while absorbing the intensity of the political and social turmoil of those times. Having been born in 1966, I remained unaware of the chaos of those days until later in teen life. The urban riots, the political assassinations, the antiwar protests: it all seemed completely foreign through the lens of my bucolic, small-town, white upbringing.

But now racialized turmoil has been erupting again all around the country. A few flare-ups seemed like anomalies—at least to white people—in the otherwise peaceful coexistence between the races through most of the 1980s through 2000s. There were the occasional Bernie Goetz vigilante subway murders; the Central Park Five, kids who were accused of raping a white female jogger and then later exonerated when it was proven the police coerced their confessions; and the police beating of Rodney King, the acquittal of the officers, and the LA riots. But to my white mind somehow our country didn't seem so deeply frayed as it is now. Then again, maybe I just wasn't paying attention.

During the last five years, as outrage grew over what seemed like weekly shootings of unarmed black people, a volunteer website called MappingPoliceViolence.org popped up that provided clear visuals for the trend. Data have a way of cutting through the emotions and clarifying what's really going on. The site, put together by a data scientist and public education official in Minneapolis, and an activist from the Ferguson, Missouri, movement, was illuminating. The team found:

* Black people are three times more likely to be killed by police, per capita, than white people.
* 30% of black victims who were shot by police were unarmed, compared to 19% of white victims of police shootings.
* 99% of officers in 2015 involved in shooting unarmed black people were never convicted of any wrongdoing. Only a tiny fraction of officers was even charged with any wrongdoing at all.

Those are a lot of anomalies. When does a long string of anomalies turn into, well, a normality?

Before the days of the internet, smartphone cameras, social media, and 24-hour cable news, these patterns were often either completely ignored or only studied by academics. Today, footage of incidents is uploaded almost immediately, and data patterns are shared for the world to judge on their own.

Can I be considered a supporter for equality and justice if all I do is post my outrage online? Do I need to march to truly align? Is a letter to the governor entry into the cause? What action would a formerly white man take if he could see "them" as "us"?

Most white people have no frame of reference for the recent spate of black citizens slain by law enforcement, much less the impact of generations of this phenomenon. For many of my white friends and colleagues, especially in West Virginia, black people were invisible to their grandparents; to their parents, African Americans may be thought of as people from far-off cities who protest a lot and sometimes riot; and to our current generation, at best superficial acquaintances from school or work.

To white people, those who fill the role of law enforcement are almost unquestionably good. According to a Pew Research Center study in late 2016, 75% of white people agreed that "police in my community use the right amount of force for each situation." Seventy-five percent also agreed that they "treat racial and ethnic groups equally." Black folks weren't so high on those statements; only 33 and 31% agreed to each statement, respectively.[5]

What I found amazing among some of those in my white circles was the inability, or unwillingness, to consider those numbers. What could account for such a low confidence rate among people of color? Do white folks think black people are just making this stuff up? The actual police shooting statistics justify a lack of confidence among people of color; why is it so hard for white people to accept these numbers? Clearly, the lens of race was inhibiting some obvious interpretations.

Those in blue are the ones who put their lives on the line every day to protect "us." Most white people I know are happy to include people of color in their definition of "us"—as long as they dress properly (i.e., by white European formal standards), do things the right way (defined again by white cultural standards), and have a decent job with an intact family. Middle-class black folks who play by these rules are assumed by white folks to basically experience the same life as "we" do. Lower-income black people, or anyone who doesn't fit these related norms? Well, if they got stopped, the police probably had a good reason, right?

Throughout my life, hearing story after story from my growing circle of African American friends, I learned that a police run-in for them could get ugly, really quickly. Still, while that registered as unfair to me, a subconscious opinion had formed in my mind, perhaps growing from my lack of direct witness of such ugly incidents and the morbid humor with which my black friends shared their stories. That is, while it agitated me that my black friends may experience more skepticism or even racist disrespect from police, I still assumed as long as they "kept themselves out of trouble" or avoided acting suspicious, they could expect to exist without much anxiety of running afoul with the law.

I was not yet fully woke on this topic, as I was about to find out.

✲ ✲ ✲

I'm fascinated by what people think and why. What shaped someone to be conservative, liberal, or middle-of-the-road in their political views? What mix of family environment and assumptions, mashed up with life experiences and media influences, led someone to make a certain public statement of their affirmations and agitations on Twitter or Facebook? What's the story behind their tweet?

Social media's rise to prominence occurred around the time I had moved back to West Virginia. Now, since I only recently left West Virginia after living there 10 years, most of my social media friends and followers are from that region. Church friends and acquaintances, people who heard me speak on economic development topics around the state, and old high school friends make up a lot of my social media community. I had to understand them better, at least the ones who were the most agitated by the Black Lives Matter movement or my posts about racial justice. Even though we seemed light-years away from each other in terms of worldview, at least on topics like these, most of them were still "my people": Appalachians.

Did my friends who shared anti–Black Lives Matter image memes from conservative bloggers really think this was all just a conjured-up movement to take away rights from white people? Surely they didn't believe that all the protestors "didn't have jobs" or "were paid to protest by George Soros"?

I went home to Charleston to meet with some of the most frequent dissenters against my pro-BLM posts. Some were from my old church—kind and upstanding church folk with whom I had often met in living rooms to pray and study the Bible. My kids had watched their kids. And yet their lenses were much different from the ones I had donned after interacting with so many other friends of color during my lifetime. What I heard during these individual discussions were mostly common between each of them.

"I suppose Black Lives Matter has honorable positions; I'm not fully educated on them enough to have a legitimate opinion. But it seems like their protests exacerbate things and hurt more than they help."

"Why can't they work peacefully through the system like everyone else to get what they want?"

"I'm opposed to Black Lives Matter because of their name. It highlights race and divides us more than unifies us."

"Most tensions are just tensions; then race gets layered over them. The media just blows all this stuff up and causes dissension. They overreact and seek to get people fighting against each other. The media is creating more racists than there used to be."

"These protesters aren't like Gandhi or Martin Luther King Jr. They're not about civil disobedience and peace; they cause riots and destruction."

"Maybe there are 1 to 2% bad white folks, but probably a lot of black people have to interact with them." (As we learned earlier, more like 15 to 20% of white folks have overt racist beliefs.)

I was struck by the tendency to attempt to delegitimize the underlying concerns of the BLM movement. In the minds of most of the people I interviewed, it wasn't because there were real issues that led to the creation of BLM; it was "the media," "the violent protestors," or "it goes both ways."

One final question I asked them: Do you have any close friends who are black? You know, people who you hang out with outside of work?

"Not really."

A quick review of their Facebook friends list, as I had recently done to review my own level of friend diversity, proved the accuracy of their responses. Hardly any had even one person of color who was close enough to them to follow on social media, or if they did, showed among their most active friends. This didn't make me any better than any of those friends of mine, because without the blessing of diverse relationships derived from my life experiences, I would probably have similar views. It's through the portal of relationship that our eyes and hearts are opened, making change possible.

The turmoil of police shootings of unarmed black men over the last two to three years finally broke my heart enough to ask my African American friends: What has been your experience with police? Black male friends, in particular, shared detailed, gut-wrenching run-ins that ranged from open disrespect—including frequent use of the n-word by officers—to outright threats by law enforcement officers toward them personally. Not every interaction with police officers was this way, of course. But the vast majority of African American male friends shared at least one example, and several more than one. Female African American friends had fewer direct incidents with police to share, but all had a family member with incidents that affected them, and some had their own. After hearing their stories, some of which I detail in a later chapter, my heart broke even deeper. I finally had to question myself: Why did it take me so long to ask?

What blew my mind the most about this discovery was that most or all my friends who are African American are highly educated, successful professionals and solidly middle class to upper middle class. That says a lot to me about how far I must go to understand the experiences of the vast majority of Americans who do not have college degrees or professional jobs. The amplification of these incidents of harassment and violence among those in lower-income neighborhoods is almost too great to imagine without developing real relationships with people in those environments. Yet if I'm truly to give up the privilege of my race and class in America, I must commit to the class journey as well, in order to advocate for a different reality.

Next, I polled my closest 20 white friends. Had they experienced any negative experiences? Pulled over for odd or suspicious reasons? Asked to keep their hands where they could be seen when pulled over for a minor traffic stop? Asked to get out of the car slowly (unless they were under suspicion of drunken driving)? Did they have a friend or family member who had been unjustly victimized by the police?

Zero.

Granted, my personal circle does not constitute a scientifically valid number of interviews. Still, actual national surveys and studies say the same thing my anecdotal research would suggest. The reason that a higher percentage of African Americans are harmed by police per capita is that they are *stopped* by police at a much higher rate than white people.[6] Conscious and unconscious bias kicks in during the interaction from there, leading to the disparity in full-blown tragedies.

Personally, I could not recall one moment in my personal life when, after being engaged by a law enforcement officer for a traffic stop or even an interaction on the street, I thought to myself, "I better keep my hands where he can see them." I have never once feared a police officer misinterpreting my words or physical movements in a way that would lead her or him to cause me harm or even to express a tense word toward me. Not once.

To shed whiteness and its privileges—which seemed more and more daunting, particularly after studying this aspect of its impact—would mean voluntarily tossing myself into a new life of daily anxiety. Not the anxiety that comes when a police cruiser pulls behind you and your mind immediately races to "I hope I wasn't speeding," or "I hope I remembered to renew my tags." The kind of anxiety that would introduce far more disturbing fears that African American families have managed for generations: "I hope I make it home."

But even if I could somehow give up whiteness emotionally or mentally, I couldn't give up the fact that the agreed-upon societal value placed on the color of my skin gives me a pass in interactions with law enforcement. I also couldn't just cloak myself in that kind of fear. I couldn't conjure it up naturally, in some white guilt sign of solidarity. And why would any sane person of any race-assigned group want to?

All fear, regardless of its focus, is a mix of rational and irrational. Rational, because something very real happened to plant a seed of thought that terrible things can happen, or happen more severely, because of the color of skin. Irrational, because how often does that bad thing actually happen, especially if a person plays by certain understood rules? Fear is rooted in a lack of control and predictability and amplified by frequency.

African American and Hispanic folks have a different set of experiences, both direct and indirect, through their own families and circle of friends. This justifiably gives them a massively different level of anxiety due to the experiences of discrimination, disrespect, and violence done to them by representatives powerfully equipped to enforce the laws of the society they live in. That doesn't mean that a majority of law enforcement officers are racist or excessively violent. It doesn't even mean that a majority of minorities have been mistreated in their lifetimes. But it does mean that a significantly higher level of experiences enabled by conscious or subconscious biases within law enforcement has done great harm to many Americans; great harm to my friends, and yours, too, if you have even one friend of color.

To give up whiteness as it relates to justice and law enforcement in America: What would that look like for me? And would I be willing to trade my safe, oblivious assumption about criminal justice and what it currently means for me as a white person for a different state of being?

Clearly, I lacked the power to change how a police officer or a judge viewed me upon seeing me in person. I could not change their use of race as a lens in which they made split-second judgments. What should I do the next time I am pulled over—say to the officer, "If you were likely to give an African American a ticket or ask him to place his hands on the wheel where you can see them, you should go ahead and ask me to do that right now also"? Should I go out looking to be pulled over so I could make a personal protest statement each time?

As in other areas of life that I was attempting to unwhiten, I thought of some analogies. What would I do if, for some odd reason, police were pulling over people who drove Jeeps at a higher rate? I would be annoyed, post on Facebook about how ridiculous that policy was, and would probably avoid buying a Jeep; but doubtful much else. Bad analogy, as it's possible to avoid driving a Jeep but not really to change my skin color. But my erroneous analogy did make me realize something sobering: the same level of protest that I would launch for a Jeep-related injustice is about the level of protest I had to this point in my life levied against the racial disparities in America's criminal justice system.

What if Appalachians, "my people," were for some reason being harassed and jailed at a significantly higher rate for no other discernible reason than being Appalachian? What if members of my own Appalachian family were being pulled over when they drove into Maryland or Pennsylvania simply because of their West Virginia license plates? What would I do then?

I realized that if there were no longer to be a "them" defined by falsely constructed racial boundaries, and the boundaries were simply set by friendship, religion, or even more broadly by national community, then my responsibility to act would be the same. To give up whiteness would demand that I act and advocate in meaningful ways for equal application of justice under the law.

11

Facebook and Affirmative Action Friendship

Amicus certus in re incerta cenitur. [Earliest known
version of "A friend in need is a friend indeed."]
—Quintus Ennius, 2nd-century BCE poet and playwright

As a data nerd, I love sorting and analyzing and finding trends. Don't judge me, but I also like to compare my experiences and habits with those of others. How normal am I? How weird am I? Dozens of click-bait online comparison surveys promise to size me up each week on social media, and I'm a sucker for them.

An old clichéd defense expressed by many white folks when confronted with their own racism has been, "Some of my best friends are black." Unfortunately, when you look under the covers of that cliché, the reality is that hardly any white people have friends who aren't white; in fact, according to the Public Religion Research Institute, 75% of white people in the United States have zero nonwhite people in their friendship networks. Zero. African Americans aren't that different in this regard; slightly less than two-thirds have no white friends in their network.

When looked at as an overall average, white America's friend network consisted of 91% white friends, 1% black friends, 1% Latino friends, 1% Asian friends, 1% mixed-race friends, 1% "other" race, and 3% "friends of unknown race." Again, African Americans weren't that much different; their average consisted of 83% black friends and 8% white friends, zero Asian friends, and 2% Latino friends. However, the study made a point of noting that although 8% white friends isn't a lot, it's still eight times more than white people have black friends.[1]

That's fairly depressing, but it explains a lot about those large divergences in how we see the world around us, doesn't it?

Back to my data-nerdiness and susceptibility to comparing myself with others. I decided to see how my life compared with most Americans as it relates to friendships across racial lines. For better or worse, social media seemed like the easiest way to analyze my own friendship network. For all the criticisms against it, social media looked like a pretty good representation of my friends from the past (high school, college, previous jobs and communities) and present.

As of this writing, I have 984 "friends" on Facebook. For some, that may seem like a lot, but of course some are close friends, and some are acquaintances. I tend not to accept friend requests from friends of friends or random people that I've never even met, so, for the most part, I do know those 984 people enough to call them friends at some level.

Facebook's algorithms list your friends in order of how recently and frequently they've engaged with you on the network, so the first

100 friends listed on my "friend" tab seemed like a good place to start. How many of those friends that I engage with the most are white, Asian, African American, or Hispanic?

Stick with me and my data-loving brain for a moment. I placed my top 100 friends into an Excel spreadsheet and counted them up: 85 white friends, 12 African American, 2 Asian, and 1 Latina. Those tallies surprised me a tiny bit. In my mind, I had imagined myself with a more diverse set of friends than I apparently had. I scrolled through the rest of my Facebook friends list and identified other nonwhite friends, but the ratio seemed to hold true through all 984 faces.

I suppose I could celebrate the fact that, if I were competing against other white folks in a "some of my best friends are black" contest, I could probably win; I had twelve times more black friends than the average white person. But the average white person is so woefully low in nonwhite friends—having an average of one, with 75% of white people having *none*—that it seemed like a hollow and, well, ridiculous bragging point.

As noted earlier, my life experience seemed to have opened my mind to nonwhite friendships more than the average white person. But even with that advantage and emotional tilt toward an openness— even a desire—for diversity, my friendship network wasn't really that diverse. A lifetime of going to schools, living in neighborhoods (my brief stint living in the very diverse West Philadelphia, notwithstanding), going to church, and working at companies whose workforce was vastly white had formed my largely white circle of friends. In fact, to take my analysis even further, I estimated that 26% of my friends had derived from church, 24% from work, and 21% from my volunteer and nonprofit work. The rest originated from family, college, high school, and my neighborhoods. All these, with the noted exception of living in that diverse Philadelphia neighborhood, were vastly white environments. In that context, the fact that 15% of my closest friends were nonwhite seemed quite amazing. It was clear that the communities and institutions that I chose, or perhaps that society guided me into, were dictating who I cared most about.

***

Without an authentic friendship with someone from within a different background from us—such as race, religion, class—we are basically doomed to judge others' experiences from the outside, using a lens developed strictly through our own limited experiences. "Cops are trustworthy and almost always treat others fairly," report white folks, because that's their experience. The level of confidence you have in various American Dream-isms—such as "People who stay out of trouble, get an education, and work hard will get ahead"—is based on whether that has been true for you and those around you. Without a deep friendship with someone of another race who we trust and to whom we listen, we are likely to experience dissonance when we hear reports of persistent inequity. "What? That person is complaining about being pulled over? They must have been doing *something* wrong. Cops don't pull people over without a reason."

Friendships create empathy and understanding that broaden our willingness to see through new eyes. The seismic shift in how Americans are deciding which sources of news to trust is confusing things even more. Even reliable academic studies on race get summarily dismissed by many people with closed hearts and minds who have no trusted personal friends to validate them.

If I were to give up my whiteness, how would that change my friendship network? How would it change my perspective on the hopes and realities of living in America?

***

Sometimes when I travel to New York or some other highly diverse metro area, I'm encouraged by the sight of people from different races and ethnicities walking, laughing, and working with each other. I'm certainly encouraged by the diversity in my local Starbucks, in the Una neighborhood, where I tend to write. Yet as I look around the coffee shop, I also notice that most of the tables where people have gathered aren't actually diverse. Ethiopians are talking to their Ethiopian friends; Syrian family members cluster together; a couple of white friends of unknown ethnicity study together. The room is diverse, but the tables are not. If we are a melting pot, we tend to stay clustered in pockets of ingredients instead of blending our flavors.

Why is this? Psychologist Beverly Daniel Tatum's groundbreaking book *Why Are All the Black Kids Sitting Together in the Cafeteria? And Other Conversations About Race* pointed out that the anxieties and experiences that occur as we develop our identities (there's that word again) push us toward "safe" places, where we perceive the highest likelihood of acceptance and support. The combination of nature and nurture is a difficult force to overcome when forming meaningful relationships, which are difficult enough regardless of the racial barriers. Makes sense to me.

I thought about some of my cross-racial friendships, from that first preschool friendship in Morgantown with my African American playmate to some of my current work and church friends. I began to cringe at some of the foibles and frustrations involved in some of the earliest adventures in cross-racial friend-making. Exposure to more diversity in college and career environments dramatically lowered my anxiety over friendships with people of other races. I thought of my first real experiences with friendships with people of color in Glenville. Speedy, an extremely extroverted African American college student at Glenville State, took an interest in me after watching me play high school basketball. Racial barriers were no match for his extroversion, and he gave me confidence I didn't often have in myself when we played hoops together and hung out at my house for dinner. Closer friendships with my biracial roommate Steve and my African American classmate Shelby opened deeper connections and insights. But often it didn't eliminate cases of extreme foot-in-mouth.

One such experience still causes my blood pressure to rise in embarrassment and regret. As I've mentioned, Circle of Hope church in Philadelphia was an interesting source of diverse experiences. Despite very purposeful and proactive efforts to diversify, the church was still more than 90% white. Rachel was one of the few nonwhite attendees of our prayer and Bible discussion group in our Mount Airy neighborhood home. She was a young biracial woman who was generally quiet, warm, and friendly, and who contributed to the discussion and prayer time.

One evening during a game night, our small group divided up into males versus females in a battle of Scattergories, and as usual, the women were crushing the men. To this day I don't know why I said it or where it came from, but I blurted out, as a joke, "The guys are going to need some affirmative action to help us catch up."

I don't know if you've ever experienced the phenomenon of words flowing in slow motion out of your mouth but being completely unable to stop them—even as you're becoming aware how stupid they are sounding. It's a horrible feeling, kind of like being in a bad dream in which someone is chasing you and you can't run away. I felt sick in my stomach the moment the words left my mouth, and the stunned silence and wide-eyed faces of everyone else in the room only amplified my desire to crawl into the cubby space under our stairs.

"What did you say?" said Rachel. Her tone didn't sound angry; more shocked or stunned. Everyone else in the group was silent, but the looks on their faces made it clear that they really couldn't believe what I had just said.

I can't remember what I stammered as an explanation. I had meant it as a joke among a group of friends whom I assumed knew that personally I very much supported affirmative action. I had learned the reasoning for it in my college equal employment opportunity class, and I believed it was a just method for deconstructing continuing workplace discrimination and equalizing generations of white affirmative action in the form of biased hiring practices, government programs, and educational policies. I harbored no feelings of malice toward affirmative action and did not see it as "reverse racism," as some critics called it. Didn't everyone in the room know that about me? I can honestly say there was no malice of any kind behind the joke, but the effect made it clear that it didn't matter. I uttered it from a place of cultural dominance and privilege, disregarding the context in which Rachel would have heard the words. She left our house soon after the comment and didn't stick around for the snacks. The members of our group were clearly upset about what transpired that evening. I felt horrible.

Some would dismiss the statement as nothing and suggest that anyone who took it the wrong way as just being overly sensitive or politically correct. But in a room full of white people and one person of color, all of whom were still getting to know each other, it was a stupid and insensitive comment. Rachel didn't know my heart for or understanding of affirmative action. My ham-handed attempt at humor poured a bucket of water on an ember of potential friendship. I called her the next day to apologize, but the damage was done. She never returned to our group.

Such are the risks of cross-racial—or cross-anything—friendships. I think that fear of making a dumb joke that comes across the wrong way, or a dimwitted comment that offends, keeps a lot of us from inviting a friend of a different race or religious background out to lunch, or to our house for dinner, or to our church. Taking a risk on any kind of friendship at work or in the neighborhood can often seem fraught, regardless of the cultural dynamics, so few take on that added pressure for a cross-racial connection. It makes me appreciate even further those courageous souls like Speedy who are willing to put themselves out there for the benefits of new friendships.

Even though I developed treasured lifelong friends in Philadelphia, Seattle, and West Virginia, introverts must be very purposeful and focused if we want to make friends, so I knew I had my work cut out for me. In the middle of my unwhitening journey, I had to consider what strategy I would take if race wasn't going to be a powerful force in shaping me back into mostly white friendships. I didn't want to target people of color for friendships in some awkward science experiment; I wanted to develop genuine, authentic relationships. Would openness be enough?

As documented by the watchful eye of Facebook, my biggest sources of friends other than my communities and schools were work and church. My workplace, with the exception of the Spanish-language publishing team and a few African Americans, was lily white, and I still hadn't really settled on a church to commit myself to. It was clear that developing some new friends, especially friends with any sort of diversity, would have to go hand-in-hand, together with my search for a diverse community of faith.

✦ ✦ ✦

I knew that to deeply understand the implications whiteness was having on my friends of color and on me—especially the dynamics of our friendships that I was most likely unaware of—I would have to ask for help with the very thing I knew many of them were weary of doing: explaining things to a white person. All I could do was humbly ask, but at least it was with the promise that I would share their experience with others. Maybe, just maybe, it would lead to one less time they had to explain it again themselves. I began reaching out to friends one by one: Would you be willing to let me interview you about your experience as a person of color in our culture?

Either I have extraordinary friends or else, as many explained during our discussions, it was the way I asked. Perhaps it was both, but many friends agreed to be interviewed. As I quickly learned from them, the weariness often expressed by people of color in explaining things to white people is similar to the weariness you feel when talking to someone on a cell phone with a bad connection: you keep repeating yourself but you get the sense the other person can't—or won't— really hear you. When I asked my friends if I could interview them and explained the journey I was on, several of them said the same thing: "None of my white friends has ever asked me these questions."

The questions were direct and deeply personal: What is it like living as an African American (or Asian American, or Hispanic American) in the United States? What incidents of racial bias or violence have you experienced, or has a family member experienced? How often do you "code switch" in a work environment, and how does that extra behavioral tax weigh on your mindset and energy each day? How self-consciously aware of your racial category are you in any given day, or hour, or minute?

The interviews with these friends were deeply emotional for both of us. It seemed cathartic for many of them, and it generated a range of reactions for me as well: shock, illumination, sadness, encouragement, solemnity. They let me into some of the most vulnerable experiences and emotions of their lives, and I was floored by their generosity and courage in doing so. Jonathan, Crystal, MJ, Jessica, Maurice, Deonta', and others led me to a depth of understanding that would have been impossible without their trust and openheartedness.

Mind you, these are friends from professional and middle- to upper-middle-class backgrounds. They are highly educated people who, by any "American Dream" standards, have done what any "good American" would be expected to do. And yet the painful stories poured out.

An African American male friend, who happens to be an advertising professional and entrepreneur, was living in Kansas City and walking home in a "nice" neighborhood after an evening out with friends. He was well-dressed in his Abercrombie & Fitch clothing. Some rowdy white teens in a passing car began racing back and forth through the neighborhood streets, slowing down and looking menacingly out the window at him. Minutes later, a police car screeched to a stop beside him. Cops jumped out and yelled "Hands up!" with their guns drawn. As they put handcuffs on him, one of the officers warned, "Don't be a smartass, n******." He was told he fit a profile from a complaint of rowdy people in the neighborhood. The police officers then made him sit on the sidewalk for four and a half hours, from 12:30 am to 5:00 am. They kept entering and exiting their police cruiser, each time asking him the same questions, "Why are you walking through this neighborhood? Who do you know here?" Each time he explained this was his route to his home, the address of which clearly matched his ID. At one point a white woman from the neighborhood came out of her house to tell the police that my friend was not the one acting rowdy in the neighborhood; it was the white teens racing back and forth in their car. Still the police held my friend, sitting uncomfortably and humiliatingly handcuffed on the sidewalk, for hours before finally letting him go.

The next day, still shaken and feeling a mixture of anger and relief that the incident hadn't ended in an even worse manner, my friend went to work. After he had shared what had happened to him, a colleague commented, "You know, I'm tired of you talking about this black sh** all the time. If you don't like it here, you should move." He soon did.

An African American female friend in the tech industry shared her experience at one of the world's largest and most respected software companies. After watching her white peers on the team receive promotions, she learned from other employees of color about similar experiences: being moved from position to position after receiving feedback for being "difficult"; receiving no advancement while watching more aggressive and temperamental white peers receive promotions; observing how white managers and executives got away with racist and sexist comments, with no perceivable implications for their careers. Finally, a large group of these diverse team members filed a lawsuit. She was not allowed to talk about the resulting settlement. After leaving that company, she joined another software company with a more diverse group of executives, including an African American CEO. She was promoted from director to vice president in just three years and enjoys a successful career to this day.

An Asian-American friend, with ancestry from Hong Kong and Taiwan but born in the United States, shared that she is consistently asked "Where are you from?" and "How is your English so good?" by white acquaintances and colleagues who assume she is an immigrant, not a US-born citizen. Once, after being laid off by her employer during the 2008 recession, she requested unemployment from her local state office. Despite showing the required social security card, passport, and other documentation, the clerk refused to believe she wasn't a foreign national and required that she show up in person for a hearing to prove she was a citizen—a demand not required of other, white applicants. My friend felt a lot of pain from this unnecessary hassle and decided to give up her pursuit of this benefit, which may have been the goal of the clerk in the first place.

An African American male friend shared his experiences growing up in Ohio, Michigan, and New York as the son of a successful Dow Chemical sales manager. He was often the only student of color in his classes, and his ability to adapt to these intimidating environments was quite amazing. He ran for class president in middle school with the help of some white friends and won. Later, however, he experienced an ugly incident of racial harassment with his white friends present; they neither defended him nor comforted him afterward, acting as though it had never happened. Although they would often eat dinner at each other's houses before this incident, a rift of hurt and disappointment drove a deep wedge through their friendship.

Stories ranged from frequent "minor" frustrations or microaggressions (such as my affirmative action joke) to major incidents of harassment by the police, work supervisors, or salesclerks. As I listened, any subconscious hope that I may have still held—that race-themed abuses happened infrequently or only to people of color who didn't conform to the norms of white middle-class America—was forever shattered. These were all friends who *had* conformed, at least to educational and economic standards of the American culture. I could hear the weight of pain from these experiences in their voices—voices of those who have followed the "respectable" path in our culture of mythological meritocracy. If this is how people of color who have "made it" are treated on a regular basis, I could only imagine what those living in lower-middle or impoverished environments faced.

I could think of not one time I or any of my close white friends had ever experienced the same. Any incident of rudeness or unfair treatment I had experienced in life could easily be dismissed as the other person's problem, or perhaps in a rare spout of humility, accepted as valid feedback on something I should change about myself. But if I had faced a lifetime pattern of these incidents from those in power who had a different skin tone or racial category than me, how would that have affected my self-perception? My hopes and dreams for the future? My understanding of where I fit in this society? More than likely, I would have been desperate to retreat to a place where I felt safe, within a community of those who shared my experience.

This led me to one of the most surprising outcomes of my interviews. In the back of my mind, I was preparing to hear some difficult stories from my friends. I knew enough to expect that their experiences were going to be different and more difficult than my own. What I didn't expect was to hear the hopefulness at the end of the conversation. While the weariness was palpable, the flame of faith and anticipation for a better future was still flickering in them. That amazed me. Perhaps, as people of color facing challenges like these every single day, they had no other choice. Still, I would understand if anyone just couldn't do it anymore and checked out in resentment. I'm not sure I would have maintained their strength and positivity after knowing what they've experienced.

I thought again about the dynamics of friendship across racial categories and the seemingly insurmountable forces that work against them. Trying to feel what others are experiencing is a foundation of intimacy and friendship. Yet what I learned even more deeply through the interviews with my friends—for I interviewed some white friends too—is how individualistically people who consider themselves white approach friendships with people of color. Many are friendships of convenience through work, school, or sports; rarely do they extend into each other's living rooms, churches, or weekend cookouts. They also seem to tend to cut off the moment a friend of color needs support to remove barriers that are keeping them looking from the outside in or facing harassment that their white friends aren't willing to admit exist. I didn't hear a lot of testimonials from my friends of color about white colleagues who stepped in to confront an abusive manager or serve as an eyewitness advocate to HR, or about any classmates who stepped in to defend them from harassment. To be sure, such white friends and advocates exist; but through observation and these interviews, it appears that more often white friends scatter in uncomfortable situations that test the limits of their cross-racial friendship.

I started to think about my own record. In my better moments, I like to think that I have stepped in and advocated at important times for a friend of color, but I realize it has not been nearly enough. Worse, when I considered the patterns of obstacles my friends faced by the Foot I learned about in the Damascus Road training, I realized that my unwillingness to get involved in political efforts to remove these barriers was a loud signal that my friendship and advocacy had a bright line that I wasn't willing to inconvenience myself to cross. After all, political action is about influencing who makes up the Foot and how it works, or doesn't work, for all people in our country. What had I done to advocate for more equitable policing in communities of color, or in my own work environments to grow a diverse workforce, or in my daughters' schools to shine light on injustices they reported observing? And what was my lack of involvement teaching my daughters?

In the end, I had to admit to myself: Knowing what I now know, and having heard what I've personally heard from numerous friends of color, if I do nothing to dismantle the Foot, what kind of friend am I, really? Personal expressions of empathy and support are one level of friendship; getting into the trenches is an entirely different level. My conscious or subconscious identification as a white American was inhibiting me from being the kind of friend a person of color would ultimately care to have. What was I ready to do about it?

12

Open Hearts and
Oreo Cookies

Almighty God created the races white, black, yellow,
malay and red, and he placed them on separate
continents. And but for the interference with his
arrangement there would be no cause for such
marriages. The fact that he separated the races
shows that he did not intend for the races to mix.
—Circuit Court of Caroline County, Virginia, 1958

The Fourteenth Amendment requires that the freedom
of choice to marry not be restricted by invidious racial
discriminations. Under our Constitution, the freedom

to marry, or not marry, a person of another race resides
with the individual and cannot be infringed by the State.
These convictions must be reversed. It is so ordered.

—United States Supreme Court, in

Loving v. Virginia, 1967

L eading up to my first marriage, my hometown Baptist church in
Glenville did what small-town churches do when there is a death,
crisis, or marriage. They held a reception and brought loads of food:
casseroles, fried chicken, pies, and various dishes that made otherwise
healthy vegetables become fattening and delicious.

Even though my first wife, of German and other European ancestry, was from Pittsburgh, the sweet old ladies of First Baptist Church
embraced her warmly and made her the star of the show. Since my
fiancée didn't know anyone there other than my mom, I bit down on
the guy bullet and attended as the only male participant. Traditional
wedding shower gifts were shared, with Anna doing a good job of
reacting as she was expected: "Oh, we'll need this potholder! Thank
you soooooo much!" "You know, my grandmother has an apron like
this, and now I'll be able to show mine off!" It was a perfectly pleasant Saturday afternoon reception and I felt cared for, as I often did, by
my little hometown church.

As we stood at the door in an ad hoc reception line after the eating and cleanup came to a close, the husband of one of the bridal
shower attendees sauntered up to me. He was one of the prominent
businessmen in the community, the kind that serve as a de facto cultural norms enforcement squad in a small town like Glenville. He
came to shake my hand heartily.

"Jeff, we're just glad you found a white woman to marry."

✻ ✻ ✻

Years earlier, during the spring semester of my first year of college at Glenville State, I had met two new female friends in an Introduction to Business class. Kim was a South Korean exchange student, and Sandra was a young African American woman from southern West Virginia. Classroom friendship turned into occasional cafeteria table–sitting friendship. Spring semester ended, and I learned that Kim and Sandra would be staying in Glenville over the summer to take classes. Almost any description of the intense boredom a 19-year-old can experience in a small town like Glenville, during the summer when most students are gone, would be an understatement. I was thrilled to have new friends to hang out with.

Sandra happened to have a second-floor apartment above the insurance agency office on Main Street. My job that summer was as distant as you could possibly get from the oil and gas fields; I worked in the college library. I hid in the stacks of books as often as I could to steal some time to read—anything to help my mind escape from my small prison made of bookshelves. The boredom hammered me, and I looked forward to the evenings hanging out with my new friends. I soon noticed, however, that "friends" turned into "friend"; soon it was just Sandra and me hanging out. I could tell Sandra was beginning to have feelings for me. I wasn't sure how I felt, exactly, but I knew I enjoyed hanging out with her.

In Glenville, the third week of June is Folk Festival season. The West Virginia State Folk Festival celebrates Appalachian folklife through food, music, crafts, and Lions Club hot dogs. My new friend, Sandra, and I strode back and forth through town together, a loop that took all of ten minutes. We weren't holding hands or anything that would suggest romantic involvement; just eating caramel apples, walking up and down Main Street, and sitting on the sidewalk edge to watch people.

The next day was Sunday. After church, my family—Mom, Dad, and brother—sat down for our normal post-church meal. It ended with one of the most disappointing conversations in my life.

I need to back up a minute. I've mentioned that my parents, relatively speaking, seemed positively enlightened and open-minded when it came to relationships with people of other races, religions, and cultures. For people of their peer group, they certainly were. Which made the conversation that happened next even more surprising to me.

"Who were you running around with last night?" my father asked me quietly as we sat at the table for Sunday dinner. My dad was not a stern man and rarely if ever raised his voice. It was odd for his voice to have an anxious, accusatory tone. I hardly ever got reprimanded or scolded by him, much to my mother's chagrin.

"What do you mean?" I responded. This was a very strange question indeed, and it threw me off guard.

"Mr. Henry came and told me you were running around town with a black girl," he said.

I could feel my face turning flush; I could tell from the tone where this was headed, and I immediately resented it. The combination of disappointment and embarrassment intertwined like a hand grenade within me. "I was with my friend Sandra. So what?" My tone was less than respectful.

"Mr. Henry was giving me a lot of grief after seeing you two. I'm not sure it's a good idea to be seen around town with her." He went on to share how this man was chastising him about my behavior.

I wasn't furious at Mr. Henry, since I had always taken him for an old racist crank. But I was absolutely beside myself to hear these words coming out of my father's mouth. This man, who I saw as a virtual saint, was clearly agitated and embarrassed that someone from town was making fun and complaining to him that his son was being seen with a black girl. *Heaven forbid, perhaps they are dating!*

"Are you telling me you didn't tell that guy to go jump off a bridge when he said that?" I raged. "Are you serious? What is wrong with hanging out with Sandra?" I had never felt such anger and disappointment, certainly not against my father. Embarrassed and hurt, I screamed "Racist!" combined with other words that I now regret and bounded from the table.

It took me a few days to calm down from that interaction. It was unsettling. Not long after this incident, I was hanging out in Sandra's apartment. Certainly no racist pinhead from town was going to keep me from hanging out with who I wanted to hang out with. I'm not sure if it was embarrassment or good judgment, but I never told Sandra about the conversation with my dad, or how people in town may be talking.

Spending so much time together each evening, Sandra and I were naturally getting closer. The topic of dating had to come up eventually, and it soon did. Sandra wanted to know what I thought of black and white people dating. She had told her father about me, apparently, and asked her dad the same question. Her dad told her it was no problem for him at all. She asked me how I felt about it.

I stammered. The swirl of emotions in my heart and confusing thoughts in my head had neglected to settle into a clear idea of where my intentions stood regarding Sandra. There were times I wanted to reach over and kiss her, I admitted to myself. But I didn't. Why not?

"I don't know," I said. "I guess, all things being equal, it's probably better if black people and white people don't marry, because their kids will face a lot of discrimination on both sides."

Sandra's expression at that point must have looked exactly like mine did when confronted with my father's accusatory questions at the dinner table.

Wow. Had those words just come out of my mouth? I wasn't even sure what I meant to say. I tried to rebound. "I mean, if two people love each other and definitely want to get together, they should. I'm just saying, it would be more difficult."

But the damage had been done. Not only had I clearly rejected her feelings; I was now hiding behind racist ideology and cowardice as justification—the same ideology and cowardice that, just days earlier, had driven me to fury when I heard it from my dad. My hypocrisy hit me immediately as I saw tears well up in Sandra's eyes.

✳ ✳ ✳

I really hate online dating. Like many older singles, I didn't have a lot of options for meeting folks after my divorce. I'm on the introverted side to begin with, and I also don't enjoy the bar scene or really any scene that screams "Hey, I'm lonely and would like to meet someone." Unfortunately, most churches are so oriented toward married couples that it's hard to even meet a single person of any type, much less find someone you would like to ask out. Eventually boredom reigned victorious over self-consciousness, and two years after my marriage officially ended, I swallowed my humiliation and created a personal profile on two online dating sites.

At first, I felt hopeful. There is a certain comfort in logging in and seeing people in your age group who also took the leap and put themselves out there. After answering several questions about background, interests, and "deal breakers," I put myself on the market.

And by *market*, I do mean market. If you haven't partaken of online dating services, let me tell you: it feels like selecting a new pair of shoes on Amazon. For all the talk of "forty-seven foundations of compatibility" or whatever the promised magic algorithm entails, you're still presented with a screen full of faces. Some thumbnail pictures scream "trying too hard" or "not trying at all." A few are natural and friendly. A surprising number are selfies taken in the bathroom mirror or in the car (do so few of us have even one friend who could take a nice pic of us to share?). It's a fascinating snapshot of humanity, these dating sites, even better than people-watching at the mall.

The most stringent criteria in my search included a strong orientation toward faith. Being one of those nice Christian boys, I'd like a nice Jesus girl, please. No smokers. Should I feel guilty about checking off a minimum educational attainment? I considered my own image in the mirror and admitted it would be hypocritical to not check off "a few extra pounds" on the acceptable body type list. That's about it. In keeping with my budding journey toward an existence where race did not dominate my filter, I left the "race and ethnicity" section completely open, with no restrictions.

Years went by. Every few months I would log into one of my dating site accounts, click through the humanity, get frustrated, and vow never to return. Several months later I'd log in again, always adjusting the radius tradeoff between increasing the pool of qualifiers versus narrowing it to a realistic distance to nurture a relationship. Let's face it; requiring a certain level of education reduced the pool a great deal, particularly in a rural region. When I narrowed the search to those within the Charleston, West Virginia, region, in which I lived at the time, I felt terror that someone I knew would see me on the site. Exposing to acquaintances that I was willing to shop myself on a dating site? That was a special realm of shame in my Appalachian-shy mind.

I reached out to mostly white women, who, based on West Virginia's demographics comprised the vast majority of profiles presented. When I expanded my geographic radius, I said hello to some women of color who appeared in the new batch of recommended profiles. Hardly anyone of any race responded. It turns out online dating is just like old-fashioned dating, only you get rejected at a much faster rate from many more people. What a great age of technology we live in!

Fast forward to Nashville. Finally, a larger metro area where the likelihood of an acquaintance stumbling upon my profile was next to none. The pool of qualifiers seemed to mushroom. It still felt like an online meat market, but the market had just expanded. Plus, if you can't find a Jesus girl in Nashville, you might as well hang up your favorite "I'm hip and classy but down-to-earth" dating shirt for good.

One day I gazed upon the friendly, smiling face of OpenHearted, at the time a forty-two-year-old woman from Murfreesboro, a town about forty-five minutes away from Nashville. The pictures in her profile showcased her big brown eyes, long black hair, and warm smile, and they stopped my mouse in its tracks.

Relationship status: Divorced. Have kids? Yes, and they live at home. Seeking men aged thirty-five to fifty (whew, I barely made the cut). Faith: Christian-Protestant. Education: Graduate degree. I scanned the rest of her profile and felt a tinge of excitement about our shared interests and values. In her own words section: "I do not seek value through performance, I believe that I am enough just the way I am; and I am looking for someone who has a similar belief. I know this is probably hard to find because we live in a world driven by performance. But I am sure there's someone out there who feels the same way :-)."

Then, my "in" presented itself: "I love to read Donald Miller's blog," OpenHearted had written. "If you like his writing, we might have something in common :-)." Smiley faces are good. I like a profile with appropriate levels of smiley faces. Plus, Donald Miller happened to be a successful author published by the company I now worked for in Nashville. I was actually scheduled to have lunch with him the next day. Naturally, I had to play the Donald Miller card.

The Lord had set this up too perfectly for me not to use all the weapons at my disposal.

I scanned the rest of her profile pictures one more time before crafting my ever-important introductory email. I noticed her light brown skin that went along with those big brown eyes. I glanced at her profile again.

Race/Ethnicity: "I'll tell you later" was her entry.

✶ ✶ ✶

The dating site OKCupid has been tracking trends in online dating for several years. Not surprisingly, their massive database of dating preferences and behaviors is painting a picture of how race influences relationship possibilities in a way that would never be known if we relied on individuals to tell the truth in personal surveys.

Perhaps not surprisingly, OKCupid found that the majority of people placed a premium on dating members of their own race.[1] Yet they also were able to track, based on the real behavior of thousands of users on the site, where cross-racial "premiums" or "penalties" existed, such as the higher ratings white men gave for Asian women (even slightly above white women), or the much lower rating Asian women gave to African American or Latino men compared to those they gave to Asian or white men.

The study is full of fascinating and often discouraging tidbits, including somewhat predictable findings like the fact that a higher number of politically conservative users than politically liberal ones are overt that they are not open to dating certain races. However, while politically liberal folks more often checked openness to dating multiple races, their actual click-and-response data demonstrate just as much bias toward their own race or toward lighter races. Also, since the site allows users to select more than one race, they found that any person of color who added "white" in combination with another race increased their average rating, even from members of their own racial categories.

Interestingly, OKCupid found that while the responses to profile questions such as "Do you strongly prefer to date someone of your own race?" trended to become less racially exclusive between 2009 and 2014, *actual* dating behavior on the site remained the same. Shakira may say hips don't lie, but in reality, mouse clicks tell a fuller version of the truth in the world of dating.

As a marketing research geek, I've learned how brutal data can be. They tell you things you just don't want to hear, much less believe. OKCupid's dating data betrayed just how difficult race has made the lives of people with darker skin in the most intimate areas of life. For example, African American women were rated as less attractive than Asian and Latina women even by African American men. The light-skinned cultural ideal of beauty has real, heartbreaking implications that affect millions of women of color.

Although the rate of interracial marriage has grown from about 5% in 1980 to 17% in 2015, the power of racial stereotypes, racial associations between class and status, and the lack of exposure to different ideals of beauty across races have planted seeds of relationship preferences that have proven difficult to shake.[2] If we humans did not let race-based biases into our dating selection, from a purely statistical perspective we would see about a 44% interracial marriage rate.[3]

By this point in my life, I truly didn't care what race a woman might be who was absurd enough to go on a date with me. Although early in my first year of college I had let fear lead me to shy away from dating an African American friend, later in college I had one serious relationship with a Korean American young woman. I even went home to meet her Korean mother, which she warned me would be a somewhat intimidating experience (she was right about that). I also dated a Filipina-American girl for a brief time. I don't recall any of the strange looks or awkward questions from friends or family members about dating the Asian women that I received from simply walking down the street with my African American friend Sandra in Glenville, or going to the movies with my African American friend Shelby in Morgantown, who would often get called "Oreo Cookie" by some of her friends when spotted with a white guy like me.

✳ ✳ ✳

I responded to OpenHearted's profile. "So, does having lunch with Donald Miller tomorrow count for something?" By now, you've probably guessed I'm referring to the "friend" I introduced earlier, Soni.

My shameless "I know your favorite author" bait was cast, and it quickly caught hook. Soni responded within an hour. After some fun back-and-forth email banter establishing that we appreciated each other's sense of humor, we agreed to meet for breakfast the next weekend.

At that time, I still had no idea what race or ethnicity she was. I noticed her unique accent and she offered, without my asking, that she had grown up in Spain but was born in India. She said she put "I'll tell you later" because she didn't feel like she fit pre-selected categories and didn't want to be labeled. She felt more Spanish in culture, in many ways, than Indian, but now she was an American citizen who had lived in the United States for twenty years.

What I noticed perhaps most of all on that first date was Soni's warmth and sincerity. I could tell this woman was something different, something special. I would soon learn from her friends that they thought she was pretty darn special also, and that I had better treat her well. I consider it a good sign when a woman's friends let you know they will cut you if you don't treat their friend properly.

Over the ensuing months, Soni and I discovered our prayers were similar with regard to finding someone with deep spiritual foundations, and that perhaps God had just answered our prayers. We talked on the phone every night. We saw each other as much as our work and parenting schedules would allow. When you're older and wiser, you learn to get to the heart of things, sharing the good and the ugly that you've experienced along with the pros and cons of what you bring to the table. I mean, if the person you're considering can't handle your baggage and you theirs, let's just not waste each other's time, right? In the words of blues man Keb Mo, "I got a suitcase baby, I take it everywhere I go." It turns out that we could easily carry each other's suitcases without any problem.

Soni shared with me what it was like to grow up in Indian culture, including within the small, tight-knit community of Indian families living in her Spanish city of Valencia. She shared her youthful desire to chart her own life, and her rebellion against the cultural practice of arranged marriages. She shared what it was like to be an immigrant to the United States and her experience living in the South. With her accounting degree, her baptism into Christianity, her prior marriage into a Southern family, and her two daughters' attendance at a private Christian school, Soni had, in many ways, successfully assimilated into mainstream American life, all with a minimum of perceived harassment or discrimination.

Then came the 2016 election season.

Our first date was in June, and as we swapped details about ourselves, we learned each other's political leanings. I had moved squarely into an independent, moderate-to-liberal point of view, depending on the issue. She was also independent politically, with perhaps a more conservative perspective. Along with the rest of the country, we were tracking the presidential campaign and the rise of Donald Trump as the Republican nominee.

As our relationship grew closer and I got to know her two daughters, Soni shared more personal details of her life with me. As the campaign season heated up, and especially as the presidential candidates' battle played out on our social media feeds among friends and acquaintances, Soni began to share observations and experiences that concerned her. First was the alarming trend of friends, often from her church or private Christian school relationship circles, sharing anti-immigrant sentiments that mirrored those of candidate Trump. After experiencing years of acceptance among white Christians, Soni felt the sting of underlying or sometimes overt intolerance and judgment from within her faith community. With the broad strokes of anger and judgment embedded in their posts, these friends seemed to be entirely oblivious to how they would be affecting Soni as an immigrant citizen. There was little nuance wrapped in the anger, just as people angry over radical Islamic terrorists after 9/11 often labeled the targets of their anger broadly as "Muslims."

Second, she and her daughters began experiencing outright hostility while out and about in the community in which she had lived for the last seven years. A door was slammed in her face by a man wearing a "Make America Great Again" hat as she tried to exit a donut shop. Hostile stares during trips to grocery shop at Wal-Mart. Odd looks while strolling through The Avenue shopping center in her town of Murfreesboro.

As my love and concern for Soni and her daughters grew with each passing month, each new negative experience she shared deepened my own level of anxiety and frustration. Her pain became my pain. I was already discouraged by the pass that my evangelical friends had given Trump for his many misogynistic, ethnocentric, and just plain racist comments. It was as if all the "values matter" claims of churchgoers during prior elections were thrown by the roadside during the GOP primary season, and now the white, Bible-believing world was lined up squarely behind a candidate who knew next to nothing about Christian theology and exhibited even less interest in living by biblical values. (To be clear, this is not to say that I was a Hillary Clinton supporter either. After all, the Clintons and other Democrats had been on the forefront of "tough on crime" legislation in the 1990s that had sent an inordinate number of African Americans to prison over petty crimes or relatively small drug offenses at a far higher rate than white people. The whiteness that I was in the process of shedding had permeated both parties, just in different ways and with different consequences.)

By the night of the election, watching the returns with my daughters, I had an even more personal and emotional concern over a Trump victory. Many of this man's most ardent supporters would highly prefer that the woman I now loved—a woman who had contributed greatly to her church, community, and employer—not even be in the country.

✦ ✦ ✦

Soni and I had been dating for five months when Thanksgiving rolled into view. We now faced one of those big relationship milestones: meeting one another's family. Seeing how Soni's family lived in Spain and mine lived six hours away, she got the honor of running that gauntlet first. We packed up the SUV with our four vivacious daughters—who were soon practically demanding that we get married—and headed to the small West Virginia town where my brother and his wife generously hosted Thanksgiving dinner each year. My sister-in-law and mother seemed ecstatic to meet Soni and her girls, which made my heart happy. My brother and I traded jokes at each other's expense via text messages planning the visit, as we are wont to do.

Maybe it was the turkey-induced semi-consciousness, but throughout our introductory Thanksgiving as a couple, I found myself getting a little emotional looking across the cramped living room full of children growing up too fast. My amazing daughters and nieces, my rambunctious and precocious nephew, Soni's two beaming daughters taking in a whole new set of potential relatives: all were surrounded by doting grandparents and parents. It all seemed to fit perfectly. Nothing about the range of physical attributes of the people in the room, from my brother's red hair and freckled skin to Soni's jet black hair and beautiful brown face seemed out of place at all.

It was hard to believe that at the beginning of my life in 1966, race was a barrier to marriage in sixteen states, including my home state of West Virginia. At that stage of American history, 3% of marriages were interracial (mostly in northern and western states). Twenty years later, I had spurned the feelings of an African American young woman and, if I'm honest, denied my own feelings for her under the cover of racial anxiety. Fifty years from my birth, and I was now in love with a woman of Indian ancestry, and almost one-fifth of marriages in the United States were considered interracial.[4] It felt like a lifetime, because it was. However, in the scheme of history, the changes in racial attitudes relating to interracial relationships happened overnight.

I thought of Sandra. It saddened me greatly, but in some ways my experience with her in Glenville and now my relationship with Soni bookended my journey from small-town self-consciousness with race to a completely different mindset. Where was Sandra now? Was she happily married? Did she have children? How much had race—including my excuses for not being willing to consider dating her—shaped her life and identity? And would race somehow inhibit the trajectory of my future with Soni?

I had long ago forgiven my dad for that dining room table incident over Sandra. Appalachian families, and certainly the James family, don't often talk through uncomfortable incidents from the past. But through unspoken ways, I knew he regretted his anxieties that led to that incident. He died far too young for me to explore this with him, as I now wish I'd done. I realized how frail and susceptible we are to how others view us. He was and always will be one of the most Jesus-like people I've ever been around, and I miss him greatly. I realized more recently that I wouldn't have had any of the experiences with people of color and a passion for justice if it weren't for his example and decisions. I needed to forgive his regrettable reaction to peer pressure, just as I needed to forgive my own failure with Sandra. Yet this fog of whiteness had led an otherwise amazing man to yield to its pressures. If he had succumbed, how could I hope to overcome it?

* * *

The Greenbrier Resort in White Sulphur Springs, West Virginia, is a source of great pride for most West Virginians. As early as 1778, wealthy visitors, including five of the country's earliest sitting presidents, visited the area nestled in the Allegheny Mountains to partake in the healing spring waters. By 1858, the huge "Old White" hotel was built but was soon consumed in the Civil War conflict, with both Union and Confederate armies commandeering it for use as a hospital or military headquarters. There isn't much about my home state that is considered "fancy"; the five-star Greenbrier Resort is the rare exception.

Soni and I decided to hold a small, family-only wedding at The Greenbrier, primarily so that my aging mother could be sprung from her assisted living facility and make it to the celebration. With its ultra-colorful Dorothy Draper interior designs and Christmastime decorations, it was a stunning backdrop for our vows and intimate, low-budget wedding party (as low-budget as one could be at The Greenbrier; we decided to save our pennies to take our new family to Spain to spend time with Soni's side of the family at a later date). Our four daughters were striking in their beautiful dresses as we shared vows with them as well as each other to blend our families. Soni took my breath away as I first saw her in her wedding dress, and she took it again when she worked references to the West Virginia Mountaineers into her vows. She knows the way to my heart, and truly, I am blessed to be married to this woman.

In such an exclusive venue as The Greenbrier, it was hard not to notice the privileges and contrasts associated with the history and current patterns of the place. Just a few short decades ago, our interracial marriage would have been disallowed in the region in which it sits. Now, our Greenbrier wedding concierge was cheerful and helpful, making us feel welcomed and special. However, we noticed that all the bellmen were African American, a tradition from segregation days that was continued as a kind of hand-me-down custom; it was similar to how the White House staff roles are filled through word-of-mouth and sometimes passed down through generations of primarily African American families. Other roles, however, including front desk staff and store clerks, were entirely staffed by people of European origin.

Grand paintings of former presidents and former guests such as Princess Grace of Monaco adorned the walls next to chandeliers that were featured in *Gone with the Wind*. Photos of famous golf pros, movie stars, and political giants were featured in the classic side rooms and writing parlors. The Greenbrier, with its "Old White" main grand hotel, most definitely lived up to its name; no photos or paintings celebrated famous guests of color from prior generations. Despite its welcoming of a marriage between two lovebirds of Indian and European heritage, it still held highly perceptible symbols of white privilege and practices, down to who was slotted to fill certain roles to serve guests.

Soni was thrilled with the wedding, and so was I. But as the African American bellman carted our luggage to the grand entrance to pack in the car, after the African American parking attendant had driven it up to meet us, I was reminded again that stripping my life of whiteness in a world still very much structured around made-up racial castes would be extremely difficult.

13

Deonta's Book Report

> White is a metaphor for power, and that is simply
> a way for describing Chase Manhattan Bank.
>   —James Baldwin, *I Am Not Your Negro*

When I turned forty, I left Microsoft and moved back to my home state of West Virginia to be closer to my family and to run my own boutique marketing consulting firm. One afternoon our small team, which included Crystal, was sitting in our favorite conference room, which included wall-to-wall whiteboards on which we were constantly sharing ideas through the magic of dry-erase markers. A young, tall, thin, and well-dressed African American man opened the door to our office and entered, smiling big. Through the door of our conference room we saw him enter the office and stand at the front desk, and we invited him in and asked what we could do for him.

As it turned out, Deonta' Landis was a recent graduate of West Virginia State University, a historically black college and university (HBCU) located just twenty minutes down I-64 in Institute, West Virginia. He explained that he was interested in an internship and wanted to drop off his resumé. I'm not sure if it was our desire for distraction at the moment or Deonta's natural exuberance, but we invited him to take a seat so we could ask him some questions. Deonta' probably wasn't expecting to be interviewed on the spot, but it was clear from the moment he walked in that there was very little that daunted him. He exuded a positivity and confidence that I knew, from years of interviewing and hiring dozens of young people, was rare.

At the time, I had a habit of assigning my team members a "book report" each month. They were to read through a business- or marketing-related book and bring back a brief overview of what they learned so we could all benefit from the knowledge. Often, we would take the Power-Point slides from these presentations and build them into our marketing workshops. Since it also became clear that Deonta' was a talker and we needed to get back to business, I decided to challenge Deonta' to present a book report for us. I gave him a week to pick a book and come back to present to our team as a way of evaluating the applicability of his skills for our organization. Usually little challenges like that are a good way to weed out who is truly committed and who isn't. Deonta' enthusiastically accepted the challenge and bounded out the door.

After three days, I received a call. "I'm ready!"

"Are you sure you don't need some extra time? We gave you a week to complete it," I replied.

"No, sir. It's up to you if you're all available, but I'm ready now," said Deonta'. Deonta' almost always said "sir" or "ma'am," which is a Southern cultural thing, I figured.

We welcomed Deonta' back to our little conference room on a Thursday. As our team gathered, we settled in for what we expected would be a nice, raw, and probably not very effective presentation typical of an inexperienced college student.

Deonta' stood up in his crisp shirt and tie, took a deep breath . . . and blew us away. He had chosen the book *Neuromarketing: Understanding the Buy Buttons in Your Customer's Brain*. It was a fairly advanced topic, one that our own team sometimes struggled with when working with our own clients. Deonta' presented his Power-Point slides with clarity, enthusiasm, and understanding. He looked us in the eye. He zeroed in on the important points and made sure they were highlighted. He used his own words instead of just reading off the slides, a mistake many presenters make. He was confident and amazing.

We may have thrown him off by our stunned faces, because at the end he smiled and said, "How'd I do?"

It may be relevant to point out that my book report assignments were often met with groans from my team members. They understood the value of them, but during our busy days and weeks serving clients, it could be a real chore to finish them each month. As a practitioner of the "mess with them a little" school of management, I would sometimes succumb to the temptation of needling my team with joking comments such as "You put those PowerPoint slides together about five minutes ago, didn't you?" All in good fun, of course. So naturally, I looked at my team after Deonta' was finished and said, "He just made your book reports look *pitiful*."

Deonta's presentation had utterly blown away the quality and depth of our normal book report presentations—yes, including my own. I didn't necessarily have the money in my budget to bring on a paid intern, but we really didn't have a choice after that. I offered Deonta' a part-time paid internship on the spot.

Later, I learned more about this engaging young man. He had grown up with his grandparents in the small North Carolina town of Creedmoor and became a star wide receiver on his high school football team. After a full scholarship offer to North Carolina State University didn't work out, Deonta' assumed his future college career was over before it started. However, through an alumnus connection, he ended up accepting a conditional offer to play football at West Virginia State University in Institute, just down the interstate from our office in Charleston. The Yellow Jackets have generally been regarded as a mediocre NCAA Division II program in the Mountain East Conference, which is a significant step down from the Division I Atlantic Coast Conference in which NC State plays.

Deonta's transition to college and West Virginia wasn't an easy one. Growing up without his parents, his primary guidance had come through his grandmother, who kept him in church where he played drums for the choir and in a gospel group. Perhaps most impressively to us, at the time Deonta' was raising a daughter as a single father; a single father who was a full-time college student and All-American student athlete. Through sheer determination and faith at levels most of us don't possess, Deonta' had mustered up the courage to enter our little office and boldly present his talents.

✱ ✱ ✱

What has it meant for me to be considered white in our culture's network of schools, workplaces, and banks that provide—or prohibit—access to the American Dream? It's easy to oversimplify why an individual may reach a certain level of economic success or why he or she may not. Despite years of seeking to promote equality and diversity in the workplaces in which I've enjoyed pursuing my own dreams,

I had failed to truly ponder this question. Where would I be, right now, with my own mix of career successes and failures, if I were not white?

When I considered my advantages, I had to be honest that they were extensive. I was born into a middle-class, educated, two-parent family, which research has shown to set me up for success in educational attainment.[1] My parents were both college graduates (thanks to those generous GI Bill benefits discussed earlier) and were in fact teachers themselves. I went to kindergarten three straight years from age two through four because my mom taught it and drug me along. (By the time I was five, I guess I had tested out of official kindergarten, so I took that year off.) Piles of research demonstrate the connection between early language, reading, and math skills and future academic success.[2]

Although brought up in a relatively poor rural county, I attended elementary, middle, and high schools that were fully funded by West Virginia's statewide taxation (unlike other states and localities that primarily fund schools through property taxes, perpetuating the gap in school funding between rich and poor districts) and stocked with committed, caring teachers. I lived in an extremely low-crime community—essentially almost no serious crime at the time, save for a fight or two in the high school hallways. Recent evidence shows that exposure to even one violent crime in a neighborhood can have a negative effect on a child's academic achievement and motivation.[3]

I had always assumed I would attend college, and I did, at West Virginia University through a mix of easily obtained student loans, part-time jobs, and contributions from my parents. I stayed at WVU to finish up my master's degree on a full scholarship with a stipend while also working part-time. I was living so large during that last year of college, and credit was easily available to me, that I purchased my first brand-new car at the beginning of the semester with no help from my parents.

Before I graduated, I sent out resumés to a few targeted potential employers through our university's career services center. Since my name was an Anglo-sounding "Jeff James," I had about a 30% higher chance of earning an interview than if I had a "nonwhite" sounding name, like say Deonta', Juan, or Miguel.[4] By literally walking in the door unannounced, Deonta'-style, and presenting a weak resumé—high points of my work experience at the time? Shoe salesman at a department store and door-to-door encyclopedia salesman—somehow, I landed a part-time job at IBM my senior year of college, which I kept throughout my master's program.

Near the end of my graduate program, I was offered a $45,000 starting salary from a large industrial company in Houston (that equates to $85,000 in 2019 dollars). Instead, I decided to join a relatively small software company for $20,000 less in salary. In other words, I apparently felt secure enough to make a risky, lower-salary choice, with confidence in my future.

Hailing from Appalachia, where it's a mortal sin to brag or call attention to oneself, it pains me to list out these "accomplishments," but bear with me as I paint a picture of the rest of my career experience. With an underlying feeling of "I'm getting away with something here" impostor syndrome, this small-town white boy rode the wave of success experienced during the 1990s and 2000s by that relatively small software company: Microsoft. During that time, I received multiple promotions from my white managers. After leaving Microsoft in 2007, I ran my own marketing consulting firm for eight years, with varying levels of successes and failures. Currently I'm a vice president in a mid-sized publishing company that is owned by a very large, publicly traded multinational corporation.

Some will review my above journey and judge me quite privileged, and they would be correct. Others will praise me for working hard, getting good grades and "going for it" when I took a risk and attended WVU over my hometown Glenville State, or turning down a slow-growth industrial company and choosing Microsoft; they also would be correct. Others will evaluate me as perhaps not working as hard as I could have (I can't get that comment from my ninth-grade English teacher out of my head) or, if they investigated my career closely, suggest that I have made some stupid mistakes. All the above would be true.

The point of this exercise, for me, was to consider what elements of my journey were enabled or advanced by my whiteness, and what would my life moving forward look like if I gave that up (*if* I could give it up) in the arena of economic opportunity in our country?

What likelihood would I have had to land a plum job at IBM by walking in right off the street in the 1980s, or getting job offers in tech companies like Microsoft that were well over 90% white at the time? Would I have been promoted as quickly and as often? During times of career setback or business failure, would I have had a family with resources to bail me out? Would banks and other creditors have given me as much flexibility in paying them back? As we've reviewed earlier, the answer: not likely.

And now that I am fifty, what advantages do my children have after growing up in the environment—built upon the benefits provided me at birth—that I have been able to provide them?

✳ ✳ ✳

The dynamics of race in the workplace can feel like walking on fire-crackers. I once proactively and privately engaged a human resource executive to set up a meeting to discuss diversity in our division of the company. Her instantly defensive, suspicion-laced reaction would have led you to believe I came in asking "Why does our company hate black people?" All I asked for was a conversation to generate ideas on how to proactively improve diversity within our ranks; and this was a white guy asking! I could only imagine the reaction to a person of color who brought up such a topic. This HR leader would even tell you that she shared my commitment to building a diverse workforce, but the instant defensiveness seemed telling in how we may have defined that goal or pursued it differently.

Racial assumptions and distrust are rarely discussed in corporate settings, but they are just below the surface and are always coloring how we interpret workplace dynamics. These tension-filled assumptions can lead to some discouraging experiences, such as when the same HR executive mentioned three or four times in a meeting, "As long as we're still talking about hiring the most qualified people"—as if diversifying our workforce came with the expectation that standards would be lowered, and as if our past hiring practices (really, any company's hiring practices) weren't steeped in subjectivity on what determined who "the most qualified people" were and how they ended up in our interview pipeline.

Being the champion of equality that I had always considered myself to be, I took some satisfaction in my hiring record when it came to diversity. If I compared myself to my peer managers, I had what I considered a fairly progressive understanding of and commitment to diversity in the workplace. I knew that effective initiatives were not about bringing in token "diversity hires," or filling quotas. I knew it was about identifying diverse talent pools and working harder to ensure qualified people of color were in the recruiting pipeline, *then* hiring the best candidate in that more diverse pool. I admit to feeling a tinge of accomplishment in the fact that among the fifty or so people I've hired in my career, between 20 and 25% of them have been people of color and a majority of them have been women. In the arenas that I've worked in—primarily technology and publishing—that is a much higher rate than the diversity levels in those industries overall.

Great; so, I'm a champion of diversity in the workplace. That doesn't necessarily mean that, as a white male manager, I had a clue about how to handle an incident that occurred during my last role at Microsoft. It was a scenario that unfortunately plays itself out too often in organizations all over the country, day after day.

MJ was a marketing manager on my team; in corporate vernacular, she was a "rock star." I had taken notice of her marketing skills and positive reputation while we worked in neighboring sales districts; she in New York, I in Philadelphia. We in the Philadelphia office were always comparing ourselves to our New York peers. MJ always seemed to be leading best-practice initiatives and catching the eye of executives. The daughter of two immigrant doctors who came to the United States after persecution in their native country of Haiti, MJ was sharp, focused, organized, witty, and not shy about selling and implementing her ideas.

I had learned early on at Microsoft that as the talent on your team goes, so goes your team. So, when I was hired into my last role there, as a director in Microsoft's Redmond, Washington–based headquarters, I sought out MJ to join my team. After a persistent effort on my part, she agreed to make the leap to a corporate role in which she would be working directly for me.

It's important to understand that the culture in the tech industry and specifically at Microsoft was more aggressive and freewheeling than in many industries. The halls were filled mostly with Ivy League MBA smarty-pants, and then a few people like me who came from more humble beginnings but had learned to work tenaciously to rise up the ranks. I'm not saying the environment was full of frat boys or that every meeting was a no-holds-barred cage fight, but let's just say you would have had a difficult time thriving at Microsoft in those days if you were a wallflower. Above all, the culture believed itself to be a pure meritocracy, and for the most part, I bought into that myth.

How else would a small-town kid from a non-Ivy school like me have made it this far?

As in many large corporations, at Microsoft you had to knit together cooperation from multiple teams to get anything done. Progress required a great deal of patience, focus, persistence, and informal influence beyond your direct reports. Common to many projects with many moving parts is that after an initial quick start, things begin to bog down. Actual deadlines have to be met, and it's at this point that teams either sink or swim. Will "virtual" team members, who formally report to other departments, go back to doing what they were comfortable doing each day or what their boss pulled them into? Or will they stay committed during the toughest stages of a cross-team project? Often, the question for a team leader comes down to: Do your colleagues like you enough to keep working on the project you're coordinating?

As was my habit, I challenged my new marketing team with some bold goals. I assigned MJ one of our most ambitious tasks: integrating data from across dozens of different customer databases. I attended a few meetings of the cross-division team that MJ had pulled together. The challenges were thorny but achievable. But it was clear that some frustration was sinking in. There was some tension in the room, and I began to hear from MJ about the obstacles she was facing. Certain team members who committed to clear deadlines and deliverables weren't getting them done on time, and this was happening consistently.

Without going into additional details that would only interest corporate techies, I can say that the project was taking longer than hoped. The project dragged on, and end-of-year personnel review time rolled around. The outcome of these reviews of work performance by managers can range from raises and promotions to a simple "Nice job, keep up the good work" to the far more uncomfortable

"Here's what you really need to improve if you want to keep your job." Considering that at Microsoft basically everyone was inherently ambitious and hard-working, a simple "Nice job" almost came across with the same effect as "You stink."

At the time, Microsoft and many tech companies had a "stack-ranked" review system, in which peers were compared against each other to see who earned a higher review rating. This system can successfully weed out poor performers but can also lead to unhealthy internal competition and squabbling among managers over whose employee deserved one of a limited number of high review ratings. Also, in a complex environment in which progress can be challenging to measure unless you're in sales or a similar metrics-oriented role, a manager's or peer's feedback can be wildly subjective.

In the case of MJ, feedback from some of the virtual team members she was leading had filtered up to their respective managers. Although I could sense some tension within the team during my occasional participation in their meetings, the details of the team members' complaints didn't fully make their way to me until review time. In essence, the team members characterized MJ as a "difficult" person to work with. From their point of view, the delay on the project was tied to her unrealistic expectations of them; they blamed their lack of motivation to make progress on the task on MJ's style of leadership.

A group of white men was resisting the leadership of an African American woman. Given all that we have covered so far, from the infrequency of people of color (and women) in leadership roles to how human brains provide gaping holes receptive to bias and misunderstanding, this shouldn't have been surprising, unfortunately.

In my observations during those meetings, I could tell that MJ was not shy about asking about the status of deliverables and questioning those with assigned action items why they were delayed. She was not holding meetings to discuss planning a happy hour gathering;

this was a significant project with far-reaching implications, and she was expecting results. There were times that I, too, winced at the sharpness of her words to the group; but frankly, the team members seemed to deserve an occasional tongue-lashing, what with their lack of focus and delivery. And relative to white male managers who also weren't shy about calling people out, her tone was completely in line with the company culture's norms. They had committed to the project but didn't seem to be treating it as a high priority within their daily activities, and MJ was letting them know that.

As was the process, I turned in my recommended review score to my boss, who then had to rationalize all the scores and negotiate with *his* peer executives about who ended up with the top scores and the corresponding rewards—salary increases, stock option grants, and promotions. I requested a top rating for MJ based on the quality of her work across all her performance objectives, including but not limited to the database project. Within a few days, he came back to me with the obstacles he faced in securing the score for her I had recommended. "Hey man, I don't think I'm going to be able to get this rating for MJ approved."

The feedback from the virtual team, shared through their own management and on up the chain, had torpedoed my plan to reward MJ. The question was, how valid was the negative feedback? If she truly ran the team inappropriately, that was certainly cause for giving her a lower score. Any manager of any race has to both challenge and win the hearts of a team, especially when that team is made up of members who report to different managers. It was a classic challenge at a huge company like Microsoft. In this case, did MJ fail? Or was she the victim of a group of white males who, whether consciously or subconsciously, chafed at being led by an African American woman— and a confident, authoritative one at that? Would a white man in the same situation have faced the same rebellion?

I was disappointed and pushed back to my boss. MJ deserved the top performance rating, in my opinion, and she deserved our support. Whether it was a lack of desire on my boss's part, or just the reality of the situation he was in with his peer executives who had to barter review ratings at this time of year, the answer was clear: nope. A lower score would have to stick, and my job was to report to her why she didn't get a higher rating.

When I delivered the news to MJ, she was understandably upset. She reiterated how she had laid out the goals, made clear and balanced assignments, received the team members' buy-in, and then had to tolerate people who didn't deliver on their commitments. And yes, she went there: clearly, in her assessment, this was about bias and the inability of these white men to follow direction from a black woman. In addition, the rest of her work, which consisted of several other projects, was excellent. But because of the complaints of these white men, she had not only received a lower score; she also had to face seeing the "reason" behind it in the "things to improve" section of her written review. Essentially, it's the systemic way in which women, and specifically women of color, often get formally labeled as "difficult to work with."

Within the framework of building a diverse workplace, it's also what many white male managers dread. I hated what had happened, and I knew that she was upset with me and saw me as part of the problem. After all, I was her manager. I had consistently given her positive overall feedback throughout the year, along with some in-the-moment coaching on how to work with these men. She expected and deserved my advocacy, yet I was caught between delivering the company line and the reality of her positive performance. As best I recall, I stammered my way through a half-defensive, half-empathetic explanation of the situation. Which is to say, I handled it poorly.

Would I or any other white male have experienced the back-door rebellion at review time that she faced? I honestly had no idea.

Microsoft had a reputation for backstabbing among teams, and certainly many a white male had been torpedoed by the environment. Then again, most managers were white men.

I had proactively recruited MJ. I had sung her praises repeatedly to my boss and made it known that she was a fast-rising talent that we as a broader organization should keep an eye on. I wanted her to thrive, and I knew she had the talent and drive to do so.

After this experience, I felt drained, frustrated, and powerless. And I can only imagine how much more drained, frustrated, and powerless MJ was feeling. At times I felt I should have fought much harder and put myself on the line to secure that higher score. At other times, I realized comments about her perceived abrasiveness from multiple members of the team were difficult to dismiss and I would have had to leap above my boss or even my boss's boss to fight the good fight. Even then, who knows how it would have turned out?

Difficult. I think that word was what really triggered MJ's feelings about the whole situation. Was she really "difficult"? Situations in the workplace are so subjective and difficult to define, much less prove, that it becomes a battle of perspective. Words delivered from mouths attached to certain genders and races could be interpreted as "decisive" or "accountable." The same words coming out of a mouth attached to a different gender or race could be construed as "abrasive" or "demanding."

My relationship with MJ wasn't the same after that review. She was bitter about the situation, which is totally understandable. I felt hurt at the time that she didn't give me the benefit of the doubt that I had fought for her. But had I, really? If I would not have been "white" at that time, and if I was to be not "white" now, how would I handle the situation if it happened again? How *should* I handle it?

✳ ✳ ✳

Years later I reconnected with MJ. It was gratifying to catch up after many years, and she graciously agreed to revisit this period in our lives. She recounted what happened in her life and career after I left the company. She and other African American employees began realizing that many of them had received similar derogatory performance reviews and had experienced difficulty securing promotions at the same pace as their white peers. Additionally, at a team-building event offsite that involved customizing go-carts and then racing them, one of the teams decorated their vehicle with a Confederate flag. After more than six months of formal complaints to HR, the executive in charge of the event was given a mild reprimand . . . and then promoted not long afterward.

MJ left the company after a couple more years. When we caught up, she was thriving as a successful vice president at a different software company. The executive team includes African Americans and other senior-level leaders with diverse backgrounds.

Job opportunities in America don't come from a government assignment. But clearly neither do they come from a completely unbiased, merit-based system. Any good career guidance counselor will emphasize that the least likely way to get a good job is by sending in your resumé to a corporate job posting; it's the proverbial needle-in-a-haystack approach that has a minuscule chance for success. Unless you work in a job that can be measured purely by numerical production or elite technical skills, most likely your advancement will have many subjective elements to it, including forming relationships with superiors who feel "comfortable" with you or who champion your success. To even get considered for an interview, most career coaches will encourage you to "work your network." In other words, you better know somebody on the inside.

If close relationships are mostly developed along racial, gender, and economic lines, and if relationships form the pathway to career success, is it any wonder that diversity in certain industries and among the upper ranks of management has been so frustratingly slow in improving? Without the external pressure of public opinion or threat of government audit, how much progress in access to opportunity for people of color and women would there be today?

The Equal Employment Opportunity Commission receives between 70,000 and 90,000 formal legal workplace discrimination complaints a year, with roughly one-third of them related to race and another 9% related to national origin.[5] The bar for winning a discrimination charge against an employer can be extremely high, requiring evidence of intent and a historic pattern of discrimination. These cases can take years to resolve, and for those that do go to trial (most are settled before that phase), the complainants win about 1% of the time.[6] It's been estimated that for every formal complaint they receive, there are many incidents that never get reported. How would the situation that MJ faced, which had no explicit hostile racial over-tones but plenty of implicit ones, be evaluated?

In reality, who has the time, the emotional energy, or the desire for backlash to fight these recurring micro-battles? Meanwhile, day after day, the biased lenses of race influence how team members and managers get hired, managed, and rewarded.

A benefit of thinking more deeply about race and my own career is that I am able to process these experiences through a broader lens. This journey has helped me connect the dots and open my eyes to deeper realities about those situations that I either didn't take the time to ponder or was unwilling to think about.

A realization struck me as I was reviewing the memories of MJ's story. I recalled that during the same period, under that same unit man-ager we reported up through, I was dealing with two other employees on my team who I evaluated as being poor performers. I did what most would consider good managerial behavior: I set clear goals and expectations for them, and I gave them feedback on how they were—or weren't—meeting them. In their case, they weren't meeting them, and I was clear in our one-on-one meetings about that.

These particular employees complained to my boss that I was holding them "too accountable," and during review time, they shared their point of view in my manager feedback form. How did my manager handle these complaints about *me*? In many ways, these employees' concerns were similar, in terms of being protests from poor performers about how they were led, to the reviews of MJ's leadership.

"I think, considering their quality of work, they aren't happy about being managed well, Jeff," my boss told me. "I'd be worried if they *didn't* complain. Don't worry about it; keep holding them accountable."

Things that make you go "hmmmmm."

✱ ✱ ✱

After my consulting firm had run its course and I had moved to Nashville, Deonta' moved his young family to Atlanta. In addition, he leveraged his experience at our little company to land a digital marketing role, then got promoted to e-commerce program manager for North America at a large software firm that provides tax and accounting tools. In his role, he leads cross-company initiatives that include a bunch of marketing and techie jargon stuff that comes with a great salary. In short, he's a big deal. He's doing his thing and kicking butt. This talented, driven, committed young man could have taken many different forks in the road. One of the forks in the road that was presented—more accurately, that Deonta' *created*—was walking into our office that day. He parlayed that ad hoc opportunity into a career that pays him well, provides for his family, and lays the groundwork for a bright future.

How many Deonta's are out there in America? How many, after facing difficulties early in life, didn't get a second chance but instead went off to a low-skilled, low-paying job or got hauled off to prison? How many young black men *didn't* happen to pop into an office full of people who weren't intimidated by an unannounced visit?

I really have no idea. But it seems now to be my responsibility—and America's responsibility—to provide more forks in the road of opportunity for people of all backgrounds. If we stick with the same pattern of closed-circle hiring practices within our own race-homogenous networks, we will continue to miss the Deonta's of the world. If we don't dismantle how whiteness throttles opportunities for millions of people, the talented MJs will still face an uphill battle in advancing to the executive suite and then miss out on opening doors to similar opportunities for others. America will continue to be weighed down by an economy not firing on all cylinders because significant pockets of talented humans aren't presented with their own forks in the road of opportunity, and we'll continue our constant political battles over what to do about the aftermath.

It seems to me my job—as a potentially former white person who happens to hire a few people now and then—is to add a lot more prongs on the forks. I know Deonta' and MJ will be doing that too, as they continue rising in the ranks of leadership.

PART III

Free at Last?

14

Knowing Too Much

> Race doesn't really exist for you because it has
> never been a barrier. Black folks don't have that
> choice. . . . This invisibility is political.
> —Chimamanda Ngozi Adichie, *Americanah*

I woke up on my birthday and looked in the mirror. My droopy, sleepy eyes had dark rings under them, and my skin displayed the tell-tale liver spots and odd markings that confirmed, yes, I was indeed fifty years old.

Life is so short. Where did the time go? How did my babies start getting driver licenses, taking ACT tests, and heading off for colleges? What *is* that on my forehead?

With life's Indianapolis 500 pace, it seemed sad that so much of it is spent on creating, noticing, and enforcing differences. *Our* neighborhood. *Our* country. *Our* borders. *Our* jobs. *Our* church. *Our* race is strangely wrapped up into our understanding of all these. Looking back on my fifty years, I thought it all seemed so limiting.

It had been over four years since I had received Crystal's challenge to give up being white. For most of this period, I had no idea how to go about it objectively, but I felt it was time to assess my progress. Was I still "white"?

At the beginning of my journey, I defined how I would evaluate whether I would continue to be considered a white person or not. I realized that we're friends with who we're friends with, married to who we're married to, work where we work, and live where we live because the forces of race and class have led us here. If I held a worldview unfettered by whiteness, racial assumptions and made-up norms would not be primary determinants of how I made choices or spent time across the spectrum of pursuits that make up life. "White" people would no longer be "my people." Belonging would have to be determined on other factors beyond race.

No. I'm not white anymore.

How could I be? I know too much.

✳ ✳ ✳

My deep dive into human history has shown me that race as a concept was invented by humans. In his bestselling book *Sapiens*, Yuval Noah Harari notes that many of the constructs we humans operate under on a daily basis—government, economics, culture—are only "real" because we agree to pretend they are real in our imaginations. To him, this is what enabled *homo sapiens* to break out as the dominant species we are today. This collective societal pretending led to profound advantages that led humans beyond our tribal clans and into larger collaborative societies. Of course, these shared mythologies can also lead to great destruction. Race, I had discovered, is a giant destructive shared falsehood. A societal pretending.

Not only that, the race designated to be at the top of the heap due to circumstances of time and technology—white—was invented by a process of collusion between European merchant classes, academics, and clergy with the intent to secure and protect their self-imposed notions of superiority over other children of God during an era of unprecedented economic power-grabbing. "Euro-origined" people in power, during the relatively thin slice of history in which they have been on top from a military and economic perspective, developed this pernicious cycle of race-based superiority theory.

When other cultures from other bands of history were on top, I imagine they may have had their own justifications for why they were inherently more valuable than those around them. But their eras did not coincide with the period in which humans found a way to explore and conquer far-reaching lands. If the progress of certain technologies in ammunition, shipbuilding, and navigation had emerged earlier, or later, perhaps the world would hold up different skin tones as the ideal. But that's not what happened, and that's not the point.

Not only did these scarcity-minded race-inventors set themselves up over others in their quest to hoard resources; they also set us up to limit ourselves from the abundance of collaborating with broader perspectives and insights. We've all heard the perhaps mythical stories of hospitable Native Americans who helped the Pilgrims learn how to grow corn. How many other cross-cultural insights and collaborations have been lost throughout the centuries—insights that could have led to more abundance and opportunity for everyone? Racism, empowered by its foundational theories of race, embraces scarcity mentality to the extreme, and unfortunately it can work in the short term to achieve certain goals at the expense of others. The scam has worked well for the inventors and perpetrators. Many who are considered white have had the nerve to claim it was all God's will for us to dominate the world and claim heavenly blessing on this racial currency of power and privilege.

No matter whether you're an atheist believer in naturalism and the creative powers of random chance or a believer in a Creator with a purpose, the point is that parsing out human beings based on 0.1% difference in DNA affecting skin tone and hair—and then assigning levels of worth to humanity through made-up evidence—is evil. Modern science doesn't justify it; ethics and philosophy don't justify it; good theology doesn't justify it. Our brains may seem wired for self-centered categorizations and value-slotting, but our spirits know better.

Unlike other animals, *homo sapiens* can override our System 1 scarcity brain reactions with a System 2 abundance outlook. For a naturalistic-minded person, brain science is giving us tips every day for how to retrain our mind. For a believer, the challenge comes with the promise of help and direction from God. The biblical narrative lets us know that God will provide, and there is more than enough provision in the world for people, especially if they cooperate with God and other humans.

Participation in a system that has caused such needless, unjustified suffering among God's children is immoral. We're so quick to identify and reject other sins, but this racism stuff is one of the devil's craftiest schemes. It's so tricky that we can even continue to participate in it even when we think we're against it. Once exposed, however, it's critical that we begin the undoing process. The health of our souls, not to mention our peaceful existence on this shared planet, depends on it.

The question I had finally answered for myself—and the one all who benefit from this system must ask ourselves—is whether we are going to continue to be perpetrators of this system or architects of a more just and prosperous future. I had hesitated to answer my own question definitively throughout these past four years—partially because, on the face of it, it still sounds a little ridiculous. Give up whiteness—really? After all, everyone else who's been so deeply trained in the ways of our race-based worldview will still see me as white, with all its privileges, whether I claim it or not. Honestly, I was also intimidated by that blip of "post-racial" idealism that spread after an African American president was elected. I knew how quickly that euphoria had dissipated the minute he attempted to govern in our still deeply race-conscious country, and how aggressively the pendulum had swung during the next election back toward the other end of the white identity continuum discussed earlier.

Finally, my hesitation was also due to the fact that, like many aspects of life, we never seem to be 100% of anything. As soon as we stake a claim on who we are, too many contradictions pop into view and make us look like hypocrites. I've been a Christ-follower for decades, but I still doubt, and I still don't act very Jesus-like all the time. I consider myself fairly intelligent, but I still make stupid decisions. I like to think I'm generally a nice person, but I can lose my temper and send a snarky text to my ex-wife or judge someone driving too slowly on the highway. We never seem to maintain 100% of any particular attribute. If I can't be sure I'm 100% of those other things, can I ever consider myself having given up 100% of my whiteness?

A key aspect of Christian theology, however, has helped me come to a conclusion about this journey to reject whiteness and racial classification. In the Christian faith, there is the idea that our position before God is secured by Jesus and his death and resurrection. Once we accept that gift, our stance is one of complete forgiveness and eternal life. Our position doesn't change based on our feeble human emotions, circumstances, or weaknesses. Once we accept this gift from

Jesus, it's ours. We can never go back to not being God's reclaimed child. Henri Nouwen, the celebrated priest, author, and professor, said it this way: "Spiritual identity means we are not what we do or what people say about us. And we are not what we have. We are the beloved daughters and sons of God." Once you accept that status, it's yours forever. It's your identity.

The "process" of living like God's reclaimed child is ongoing and full of stumbles, however. There are days I forget who I am and act like a guilty, angry outcast. But then, I remember—or rather, God reminds me—that I am God's. He is mine. That's not changing.

I think there's a parallel with race and whiteness. Although the world may entirely reject my decision to emotionally, intellectually, and spiritually reject whiteness (and the framework of race altogether), I can still stake my position as a raceless person. It will be a process, and I may never entirely shed all those culturally baked, hair-trigger responses programmed into my mind to be "white." But I've found throughout my life, and particularly through these last four years, that those responses, when consciously identified and purposefully rejected, can diminish surprisingly quickly.

"Be sure that whatever you are is you," said the poet Theodore Roethke. I am who God made me to be. Nowhere do the Scriptures suggest that I see my identity as white or Euro-American. All the rich spiritual identity teachings of the Bible tag me with many labels: as an adopted son (Ephesians 1:5), as his child (John 1:12), as a branch from his vine (John 15:1), as a friend (John 15:15), as not condemned (Romans 8:1), as an heir of God's kingdom (Romans 8:17), as a saint (1 Corinthians 1:2), as a temple and the home for God's Spirit to dwell (1 Corinthians 6:19), as a new creature (2 Corinthians 5:17), as free (Galatians 5:1), as God's workmanship (Ephesians 2:10), and as a citizen of heaven (Philippians 3:20). I could go on . . . but wow. That's a pretty great start to an identity.

Nowhere in the long list of identity descriptors does God elevate race or ethnicity as something to be grasped, sought after, or stamped upon us. Yet in so many ways, in our world race stands with gender and class as the primary devices for dividing, ranking, and relegating humans to levels of value. Many would throw religion into that list, and they'd probably be right. But my simple reading of Jesus's words and life obliterates these distinctions.

Jesus told the rich man to go and sell all his possessions and that he would find life. It wasn't that wealth itself was inherently evil; in fact, resources used to enable good are quite empowering. But the rich man, like most of us too weak to resist, had intertwined his identity to wealth so closely that it was easier for a camel to go through the eye of a needle than it was for him to trade wealth identity for heavenly identity. Whiteness has been the powerful currency of power and identity for Europeans and the American majority, even when we didn't realize it. It has been our treasure on earth, inhibiting our more abundant God-given treasure. I was eager to continue the process of trading treasures.

✦ ✦ ✦

Three elements of my claim to racelessness do continue to confound me. The first: it is only in a culture that assigns particular freedoms and privileges to those considered white that I even have the option of giving up whiteness. Quite a dichotomy, isn't it? In our culture, I'm free to give up whiteness only because I'm white.

However, is this true? Could someone of African or Chinese descent choose to give up her race and focus more on her ethnic and culture identity, if so desired? Theoretically, in the same way that I have chosen to reject broad racial categories, yes, she could. It's just that in response, our society would continue to impress negative stereotypes and consequences on the 0.1% of her DNA determining outward appearance. In my case, however, society will continue to overlay unmerited privileges despite my protests that I'm no longer eligible for them. My challenge is to leverage any privilege assigned to me to deconstruct barriers that keep everyone from enjoying the same privileges; a person of color choosing to give up racial classification has the challenge of ensuring the development her own self-worth and the worth of other people of color, despite our ongoing fog of racial classifications and assumptions. In other words, the race lie I need to shed is one of "more than"; another person's race lie to shed may be one of "less than." Both are lies not to be believed any longer.

A second major challenge is that it will be a continual struggle to operate without racial assumptions in daily ways, especially from the standpoint of how others react to me with their pre-set race-based lenses. One of the biggest expressions of those assumptions has to do with the language we use to describe other humans. "Black" and "white" have become so embedded in our culture that you can hardly sign up for a student loan, buy a house, or fill out a survey without being led down the path of choosing from a list of check boxes full of false choices. A woman at the Tennessee Department of Motor Vehicles reminded me of this when I registered for my first Tennessee driver's license. I decided not to check any of the race categories on the form, and she handed it back to me to complete. "I choose not to identify with any of the racial categories," I said, somewhat hesitantly, from lack of practice in this form of resistance. She looked at me over her glasses; not really in a condemning way, thankfully, but in a "Oh, you're one of those people intent on making my day interesting" way. I checked "Other" and handed it back to her.

When I want to point out someone in a crowd, and the person happens to be the only African American person among others, I still get self-conscious when I say, "That guy in the red shirt" instead of

"That black guy over there." Race and skin color can still be tempting to use as the laziest of identifiers. But I've chosen to resist that temptation, and it's becoming more natural.

From this point on, I've also committed to rid my vocabulary of the descriptor "white." Yes, the vast number of those with European ancestry and light-skinned features—the definition of "white" found in the dictionary—will refer to themselves as white for a long time to come. But, as of the writing of this chapter of my life and this book, I've decided not to refer to myself or other Euro-Americans with a false descriptor any longer.

Third, and most concerning, is the notion that shedding my race may be a subconscious attempt to shed my responsibility to undo what those designated as white have done—and are still doing—to others in different race-assigned categories. Over the past four years I added much depth to my understanding of the malevolent origins and applications of race theory and the prejudice-laced power to enforce it over others. Now, conveniently, I want to walk away from my white designation? Now that the full weight of implications of what European ancestors and current European-origined peers are still doing in this country, I want to distance myself from this race? How expedient of me.

Yet in revisiting my motivation to fully explore Crystal's challenge to prick a pin in the balloon of my whiteness, I feel strangely secure. It's true: I don't want to identify with whiteness for all the reasons outlined so far. But I do want to dedicate myself, side-by-side and in humility with others far more knowledgeable in their lifelong struggle against racism, to undoing what has been done. To reject the false label, with all its false privileges, is one rebellious step toward collapsing the whole structure. It's a rejection, yes. But it's a rejection that brings on a commitment to rebellion, not withdrawal.

After much prayer, I feel compelled to take on the danger identified by James Baldwin: "To act is to be committed, and to be committed is to be in danger. In this case, the danger, in the minds of most white Americans, is the loss of their identity." Upon the challenge of my friend Crystal and the support of many others, I have purposely chosen to confront my false identity and claim a revised version. With that new identity comes a responsibility to acknowledge and obliterate what those in my ancestral communities did to establish and benefit from the false god of whiteness and its assumed superiority.

✦ ✦ ✦

There is a fascinating spiritual truth that the Apostle Paul describes in his first letter to one of the earliest churches in Corinth. He compares our bodily existence here on earth to that of a seed and its shell.

> How foolish! What you sow does not come to life unless it dies. When you sow, you do not plant the body that will be, but just a seed, perhaps of wheat or of something else. But God gives it a body as he has determined, and to each kind of seed he gives its own body. Not all flesh is the same: People have one kind of flesh, animals have another, birds another and fish another. There are also heavenly bodies and there are earthly bodies; but the splendor of the heavenly bodies is one kind, and the splendor of the earthly bodies is another. (1 Corinthians 15:36–40 NIV)

We live in husks, Paul appears to be saying, shells that must at some point die in order to pave the way toward our eternal bodies. Elements of the seed determine the type of fruit that comes from it; but the fruit looks nothing like the seed. What "seed" was God trying to plant with gender and other physical differences? Paul claims in Galatians that there is "neither Jew nor Gentile, neither slave nor free, nor is there male and female" (Galatians 3:28 NIV).

Through this spiritual and social journey, I've come to realize that all physical differences are elements of our temporary seed shells that need to die. For there to be true unity among those made in God's image, false distinctions must be set aside. Whatever physical differences God has seen fit to create or to allow through natural processes, we are not to use them as barriers or categories of value. God may have invented different skin tones, sexual organs, facial features, or hair texture; God didn't invent the evils of division and unequal worth that humankind decided to assign to them.

When I claim to be giving up my whiteness, this is what I'm claiming. It's not a desire to darken my skin or change my appearance. I'm not seeking to adopt or appropriate another race-based or region-based culture. I am claiming to shed all the false value, power, and differentiation that has been attached—with disastrous effects—to the invented category of humanity called *white*.

What am I not giving up? Being Appalachian. Having ancestral roots—according to DNA, my dad's scrapbook, and Ancestry.com—in the British Isles and a smattering of southern Europe. Being John and Sharon's son and Doug's brother. Being an American—in a "we hold these truths to be self-evident" mold with Americans who have their ancestries from every corner of the world, rather than in the narrow Eurocentric, British colony, and white racial identity sense. Being a father, a husband, a friend. Being on Team Jesus—the version that feeds off of and shares his grace and truth, not the one that seeks to build up more of the very power structures he came to obliterate. In many ways, the shedding of whiteness—of race—frees me to explore and embrace all those things on a much deeper level.

Probably the most emotional aspect of this journey has been my conversations with friends who are slotted in that broad "people of color" category in today's nomenclature. These interviews were deeply emotional for me, but, I believe, also for them. The generosity of my friends in sharing their thoughts about what it's like to be some-one considered "other" by the majority of citizens—citizens who con-sciously or subconsciously consider America a "white" country—was humbling. They shared some hurtful, heartbreaking experiences, as you've experienced in this book. What struck me was how positive and hopeful they were, despite these experiences. What really floored me was how many of these friends thanked me for listening. For most of them, no friends with European ancestry had ever asked them how they felt on these issues, even during the recent flareups of racial hos-tility. To be clear, some of their "white" friends had brought the issues up, but often in confrontational "Whose side are you on: Black Lives Matter or the police who protect us?" tones.

During our conversations I asked my friends what they thought about my journey to give up whiteness. All of them expressed the opinion that it was a fairly bold and positive pursuit, one they thought could yield progress among those who considered themselves white. I also asked several of them what they thought of giving up their own assigned races, whether they be African American or Asian. Most hesitated but then answered no. To give up their racial identity at this point in history would mean devaluing the immense struggle that oth-ers before them, and others beside them today, have gone through to establish that their designated race has equal value.

Those reactions made sense to me. People of color had the overlay of race theory and prejudice forced upon them. Every signal sent by our society, even today, has roots in those cultures and pulses out the same message of "You're the other, and you're not equal." Now, just because one white guy has more fully discovered the roots of this evil, they're supposed to go along?

Again, James Baldwin's words ring powerfully: "What white peo-ple have to do is try to find out in their hearts why it was necessary for them to have a n***er in the first place. Because I am not a n***er.

I'm a man. If I'm not the n***er here, and if you invented him, you the white people invented him, then you have to find out why. And the future of the country depends on that. Whether or not it is able to ask that question."[1]

My responsibility now isn't to go and convince people of color that they aren't their perceived race just because I've decided I'm not white anymore. That very act would be an attempt to put myself back in a role of an oppressor. My job is to continue pricking as many more white balloons as I can—balloons that, when fully inflated, lead to seeing others not just as others but as [insert racial epithet here]. Then and only then—maybe, dear Lord, maybe—those who have been told for generations they weren't "us" will feel safe enough to trust that this whole destructive scheme is finally over. Maybe then, more will be ready to lay down their categories too. Centuries of "otherness" won't be undone anytime soon, least of all by me; to think otherwise would be ridiculous.

Yet, as others have noted, every avalanche begins with a dislodged snowflake. Maybe a rebellious snowflake that rejects its whiteness can help start the flow.

15

One Day at a Time

You must do the things you think you cannot do.
—Eleanor Roosevelt

A drone whirred above me. As my eyes were drawn upward, I spotted several law enforcement officers pacing the rooftops of the two- and three-story buildings that surrounded the Rutherford County Courthouse. Peering back to street level, I observed a second wave of officers dressed in combat gear with semi-automatic rifles joining those already in position, circling the courthouse.

Even as a newcomer, I knew this wasn't a normal scene in the small but fast-growing city of Murfreesboro, Tennessee, the city in which I would soon move after my marriage to Soni. Then again, it's not every day that the Ku Klux Klan and various white nationalist groups decide to hold a public rally in your community. There was the League of the South, a group calling for a second secession of Southern states and that recently held a celebration commemorating the assassination of Abraham Lincoln. There was the Traditionalist Worker Party, whose stated goal is to "establish an independent white ethno-state in North America" and only allow immigrants into the country if they were from European origins. And there was the National Socialist Movement, who openly praise Adolf Hitler and align their philosophy with Nazism. It was quite a change from my ultra-diverse Una neighborhood back in Nashville.

After the mayhem these and other groups generated in Charlottesville, Virginia, in 2017, the emboldened leaders of hate and separatist groups decided to target other small cities in the South to keep their cause in the news and attract more followers. They chose Shelbyville, Tennessee, on this cool fall morning, and that afternoon they planned to hold a second rally in Murfreesboro, where I now stood.

"We've been here marching for the white people's rights," one of the groups' spokespersons said to a reporter. "Making a stand and bringing awareness to what's going on. Like the shooting a black man walking into a white church shot up several people [sic] . . . you don't hear hardly nothing about that on the news. One white man walks into a black church and it's national news forever. We just bring awareness to the stuff that's going on and maybe we can wake up the general public and just open their eyes."[1] (Let's be clear: the first incident he mentioned was in fact well covered by the Nashville regional news and nationally as well.) In interviews leading up to their planned rally, leaders of these groups would mention perceived slights to Euro-American folks but never mention their stated long-term goals.

I've never been a hit-the-streets protestor type. I like to think it's because I'm an introvert. But sadly, maybe it's because I just hadn't been passionate enough about anything to protest it. As more of a people watcher than a slogan shouter, I remember being fascinated by the energy and hint of danger at huge rallies in Philadelphia, when Nelson Mandela or Bill Clinton came to town in the 1990s. But I just didn't feel the desire to join in the fray.

Lately, however, I was feeling a significant stir. Some seeds had been planted long ago through Circle of Hope and its penchant for tweaking my traditional small-town Appalachian Baptist church preference to lay low. The soil of my heart and mind was tilled further through friendships with Crystal and others who seemed tireless in their fight for justice. As I thought more about it, I realized that my passion for justice was also inflamed by being the father of two daughters who, as teenagers, had already been the target of misogyny in the hallways of their schools, and now the expansion of my family with an India-born wife and her two exceptional daughters. Love for my friends and family of color, the desire to fight for a safer and more affirming country for my daughters and wife, and the lingering shock of observing my churchgoing friends support a president who consistently, unabashedly denigrated women and minorities: the combination was developing a late-blooming activist's heart in me.

My first timid foray into street-level activism was to join the national women's march shortly after Trump's inauguration. It was a massive display of resistance against the misogyny of the candidate and campaign, and it was extremely energizing to join in as my daughters and I traded pictures through our phones—theirs from Charleston, mine from Nashville. At the very least, I wanted them to know I stood with them.

Joining the resistance rally against the hate groups in Murfreesboro was a little different. After the violence in Charlottesville, it took a little more consideration. What was the risk? Would there be more violence? Soni and our daughters expressed their concerns about me attending; the objections of five amazing women in your life should give anyone pause. In the end, though, how could I not go and stand up to this upsurge in open hate-group activity, especially in the very town in which my new family members—family members that these groups were advocating not be allowed to reside in their "white homeland"—lived and that I would soon be joining? Some father and husband I would be if I couldn't overcome a little trepidation.

✦ ✦ ✦

I had decided I wasn't white anymore. What now? What would my daily recovery from whiteness look like? Would my daily existence change in any significant way? And if others happened to join me in this journey to shed whiteness, what would that begin to look like in our society?

Having lived in the diverse Una neighborhood of Nashville, I knew that living in Murfreesboro would be a challenge in maintaining my brain's receptivity to diversity again. A burgeoning suburban city about forty-five minutes from Nashville, the city had rocketed from 44,922 citizens in 1990 to well over 150,000 in recent population estimates. It also had a precarious history with race and diversity. A statue commemorating Confederate war heroes stood proudly in Murfreesboro Square. In 2010, the Islamic Center of Murfreesboro sought to build a new mosque in the city and received both political resistance and vandalism. Arsonists torched construction equipment, and someone spray-painted "Not Welcome" on its future site sign.[2] Ultimately, however, a Rutherford County judge reaffirmed the Muslim community's right to build their mosque on the site in 2011, and some churches, including the one Soni and I were now attending, stood by the Islamic community in support.

The home to thousands of Nissan manufacturing plant employees and twenty thousand Middle Tennessee State University students,

Murfreesboro did have its bands of diversity. About 16% of its citizens were African American and 6% were Hispanic or Latino. Soni's experience living in the region had been mostly positive. But the sting of anti-immigrant comments during the last presidential campaign, and the occasional racist comments toward her daughters by other kids, seared her heart and made her far more wary.

The truth was that unless I was purposeful about resisting the reencroachment of dominant white culture around me—at work, in my new city, in social and entertainment media—I could easily slip back into whiteness. I decided to develop some strategies for nurturing an ongoing white-free approach to life.

Perhaps the most personal and challenging would be to purposely expand the social and faith networks in which I spent the majority of my time in order to develop relationships that weren't primarily Euro-American. As an introvert, I found it tough enough to make friends of any substance. Superficial acquaintances, sure. But the kind of friendship that leads to evenings out as couples, or helping each other out with a home maintenance project on the weekend? Those are tough, especially for someone at my age.

As for neighborhood and community, that decision was made for me, at least for the short-term. After the wedding my daughters and I moved into Soni's house, because the school the girls attended was just five minutes away. I noticed a few families of color, including African Americans and Indian Americans, living near to us in this middle-class neighborhood. To the extent I could motivate my introverted self to be social, at least my immediate surroundings were conducive to a diverse new friend pool.

From a political and patriotic perspective, I felt sound in my approach over the last few years. I was firmly independent, and I simply didn't trust either Democrat or Republican party machines, which were polluted by lobbyists and massive influence from a handful of wealthy donors. But how could I move beyond voting and simple social media posts to invest myself in real change that could foster the movement toward equitable, effective policies? I decided to make a list of policy positions and offer my marketing and communications skills to see if they could help move the needle. My list started with practical issues, such as education equity and community policing, and I began to pray and seek out opportunities to support them. I knew how to develop some buzz and communicate ideas; I began to feel excitement about investing those skills toward real change.

My revised definition of "us" would need to lead me to broader conclusions about how our criminal and social justice system works. With the many inequities in the system, I would now feel the same passion and act when those inequities impacted any portion of humanity, not just the narrow Euro-American, evangelical tribe from which I came. If Muslims were being discriminated against because of their faith or ethnicity, I would advocate for them as vociferously as if Christians were being discriminated against. If a drug law sent a higher portion of African Americans to jail compared to Euro-American citizens for the same crime, I would now work to call it out and challenge politicians to fix it. If certain types of government entitlements such as tax breaks or incentives favored the Euro-American or the already-wealthy to the exclusion of others, I would help resist such policies.

During my prayer time, I started feeling a call toward supporting what many Euro-Americans consider radical and unaffordable: reparations. Reparations for groups that have been profoundly impacted by generations of unjust policies from our government, namely African Americans and Native Americans, would not undo the generations of injustice enacted upon them. But it was far beyond time for our country to fill in the footprints that the Foot had stamped on communities of color, and I knew from the results of the GI Bill and massive government investments that exclusively benefited citizens considered white that the benefits could be huge and long-lasting. That didn't make me a socialist, as I knew some would accuse; I felt it made me an advocate for practical public investment and restorative justice. I had no idea where that would go, but it felt exciting to explore.

At work, I would renew my efforts to illuminate the opportunities that could be realized for our company with a more expansive and diverse business strategy, including author acquisition, target customers, and hiring practices. For my down time, I made a list of media options, from podcasts to Netflix series, that could keep my mind dialed into a broader media narrative.

Yes, it was obvious that my ongoing changes would have to be purposeful, even more purposeful than the last four years had been in exploring life without whiteness.

Perhaps the most illuminating and exciting realization was how this approach to life aligned with a more holistic and accurate understanding of following Jesus. I hungered for a deeper, richer faith beyond the often-rote evangelical experience of Sunday worship, small-group prayer and Bible discussion, perhaps reading a few Christian living books here and there . . . and then changing very little about how I lived or the world around me. Shedding the idolatry of whiteness in the real world and in my daily experience would require action, and action would require a plan. "What good is it, my brothers and sisters, if you say you have faith but do not have works? Can faith save you?" said the Apostle James, the brother of Jesus (James 2:14 NRSV). It was time to get to work.

Foundational to all these aspirations was a realization that I would not be able to grow in a state of isolation. Communities built on whiteness had shaped my addiction to it at church, work, and in neighborhoods; a different kind of community, one with diversity and equality at its core, would have to help me in my recovery. Despite my introverted personality, I had to build deeper relationships with people who would continually challenge and encourage me, and where I could do the same for others. As noted, it was discouraging that it wasn't easy to find that community already in existence in most churches. Whether I could find an existing pocket of other recoverers or needed to create one, this was perhaps the cornerstone for all the other goals.

✳✳✳

On the chilly morning of the white supremacist rallies, I prayed and thought about the decision to participate. I wanted to check my own motivations. Was I drawn to challenge the racists' protest to engage in a confrontation for confrontation's sake, or from a sort of morbid fascination to observe hate-filled loudmouths? No; I needed to show up. I needed to see for myself what these people were preaching, and I needed to be a face of resistance.

As the hour for the rally approached, anxiety crackled in the growing line of counter-protestors waiting to be let into the fenced-off protest area. It became abundantly clear that the local city, county, and state law enforcement teams had done their homework. Whereas the Charlottesville mayhem seemed to take that community by surprise, the Murfreesboro law enforcement community had a dizzying array of security processes and resources in place. The security perimeter surrounding the protest area was thicker than an airport, and what seemed like hundreds of well-armed police and sheriff's officers lined every street in Murfreesboro Square. Streets themselves were blocked by cement mixers and garbage trucks so that no rogue car could mow down protestors as had occurred in Charlottesville. Protestors from each side were herded into the town's square through different entrances and were separated first by rows of fencing and then by rows of rifle-toting officers. It felt like I was in the middle of an Israeli–Palestinian conflict area, and I found the impressive display both comforting and concerning.

The long, slow security check process had the effect of letting out the air of the protest balloon. Even when the young antifa ("anti-fascist") radicals made their presence widely known, with their coordinated chants and all-black matching outfits, their energy level was soon deflated as they waited in line like everyone else. Some of them looked a little bored and dejected by the time they made it through the security line and waited for their friends to join them.

After several hours of this, I noticed that no racist protestors had shown up yet. Their side of the security fence around the courthouse was empty. Three clever racists did make it through the anti-racist security entrance and whipped out a Confederate flag as they strutted through the crowd of largely hippies and hipsters. Immediately the antifa crew smelled some action and surrounded the insurgents, shouting them down. Mounted city police quickly surrounded the young racists with their horses and guided them out of the area.

Later, two or three older racists appeared in their staged area and engaged the hundreds of anti-racist protestors across the fenced buffer with taunts. Bored and ready for some sort of engagement, several of the younger anti-racists swarmed to that corner of the square and returned chants and insults. Standing on a bench to improve my view of the skirmish, I found it somewhat comical to behold: hundreds of anti-racists versus a small cluster of racists, with hundreds of thousands of dollars' worth of security staff, equipment, and drones to keep the peace.

That was the extent of the clash so far, and it was now midafternoon. I looked at my watch. When was this battle finally going to take place, anyway? Were white supremacists normally late? I took out my phone and checked Twitter, which I had been tracking through the day for updates on what happened at the earlier racist demonstration in nearby Shelbyville. A hundred or so racist group members had indeed marched that morning in the neighboring town twenty-five miles down Route 231, but apparently they were discouraged by the levels of security and their inability to bring in their characteristic shields, torches, rifles, and other typical white nationalist items into the march as they had been allowed to do in Charlottesville. Overwhelmed by the measures set up by police and the many hundreds of anti-racist counter-protestors, the groups' leaders decided to call it a day and cancel the Murfreesboro portion of their protest.

It was certainly anticlimactic. As I wearily walked back to my car, I felt a hint of satisfaction and maybe even joy that so many citizens in my new community had shown up strong and derailed the momentum of these white supremacists. Racist groups had been emboldened after the chaos of Charlottesville; this seemed like a major victory that doused those fires. The whole day had seemed surreal to me. These were the types of cultural battles that raged when I was born in the 1960s; now, here we were all over again. As a white person for the past fifty years, I had felt a pass to decide whether or not to enter these battles. Now, having shed that label, I knew I didn't have that luxury any longer. Those still clinging to whiteness, especially on the segregationist edge of the continuum, would be back again to fight another day. For me, *not* resisting was no longer an option.

❊ ❊ ❊

We humans love power. We're addicted to it because it is such an attractive short-term antidote to fear. As fear courses through our minds and bodies, little doses of power we experience throughout the day soothe our insecurities and give us the false impression that we're in control. Beyond a feeling of safety, scientists have found that dopamine is released in our minds during activities that stroke our ego. But just like illicit drugs, the effect of this addiction to short-term feelings of power are highly destructive.[3] The historian Henry Adams wrote, "The effect of power . . . on all men is the aggravation of self, a sort of tumor that ends by killing the victim's sympathies." This addiction to power fuels the abusive husband, parent, coach, teacher, police officer, and local politician. Power literally causes brain damage and limits a human's ability to empathize and see things from another's point of view.[4]

Perhaps the biggest eye-opener on my journey, particularly over the last four years, is that the invention of race was one of the most powerful developments in the history of power-seeking, and whiteness is one of the most pernicious weapons in the arsenal. So many satisfying dopamine hits of superiority and power get sent to those of us who are considered white when we walk down the street, watch television, or sit in a classroom or meeting. I and other white-categorized people have been raised as whiteness-addicts without even realizing it. And as any addict will tell you, getting sober is a long, tough road.

This realization was, frankly, chilling. My whole life I have failed to rid myself of an addiction to sugar; how in the world could I seriously attempt to get sober from my addiction to whiteness? Nobody wants to admit they are an addict of any sort, much less to racism. But as I thought about it, isn't that why so many Euro-American folks become extremely defensive when racist thoughts or actions are revealed in our own lives?

We don't consider ourselves addicts; the whole idea is offensive. Respectable people aren't addicts, right? But just watch how we—I—act when our addictions to power are called out in the homeowners' association meeting, or the decision to reorganize the company, or the PTA meeting to discuss the new school zoning plans. In fact, I felt that defensiveness recently, when one of my daughters pondered aloud whether I had truly given up whiteness because I still felt entitled to sit in a Starbucks to use their wi-fi even when I hadn't ordered anything, and because I sometimes dropped into a hotel or restaurant to use the restroom even when I wasn't a customer. My earlier awareness of how race plays tricks on the brain and leads to an addiction to whiteness came back to me with a punch in the gut.

How does an addict set themselves free? The answer, according to various recovery groups—alcoholics, narcotics, sex addicts, co-dependents, and others—is that you can't set yourself free. To paraphrase the first two steps of the Twelve Steps program: "We admitted we were powerless [over whiteness]—that our lives had become unmanageable," and "[We] came to believe that a Power greater than ourselves could restore us to sanity." Austin Channing Brown, in her exceptional book *I'm Not Here*, noted that after slavery "America could have put to death the idea of Black inferiority. But whiteness was not prepared to sober up from the drunkenness of power over another people group." Like every other addict, I had to seek God's power to change.

Only the hope of greater joy can motivate someone to embark on a lifestyle of such massive change. I have yet to buy into the joy of being healthy in order to give up my sweet tooth. But somehow, my willingness to shed whiteness—theoretically much more ridiculous and difficult to attempt than changing my diet—was implanted with a seed of joy from relationships with people of color throughout my life. Now it feels like that seed is finally blooming into a state of resistance to race as a primary identifier in my life and an embrace of justice as a way of life.

It's been a challenging experience full of missteps, misstatements, and mistakes. I'm sure it will continue to be. But now? It feels right. Like a jogger who has overcome the initial pain of pounding the pavement to train for a marathon can sometimes find a "runner's high," the training for unity and equality with all other humans brings me joy.

After gaining the confidence to come out as a formerly white person, I posted on Facebook a note about the scientific community's current assessment that all humanity's common ancestry is rooted in East Africa. The first response was from an African American friend. "Hello, my brother."

Hello, my sister. It's worth the journey to give up whiteness.

EPILOGUE
THAT'S WHAT STARTED
THIS WHOLE THING

I have to admit, I was nervous about sending my documentation of the last four years to Crystal. Her text message had launched this challenge, and I was a bit anxious about what she would think of what I learned and the conclusion I had come to. If there is one thing you can count on, it's that Crystal will share what's really on her mind.

Crystal had gone through many changes in her own life over the last four years. I didn't see her very often after moving to Nashville, and I missed her wild ideas and our far-fetched collaborations.

I emailed her a draft of my manuscript and reached out to prompt her response.

> What did you think of the book?

> Wait, dating sites work?!! Sign me up.

I hope you weren't joking with that text yrs ago cuz I spent four years on this thing, lol

I was comforted to read about my role in WV, to know that someone else saw my frustrations. My pain was/is not in vain. I feel validated and I hope others will too.

I'm glad. We had some challenging moments through the years. But I learned so much from you. Thanks for letting me share it.

I met with a WV senator the other day who insisted he wasn't a racist because his brother adopted a Haitian boy . . .

. . . he grew up poor, in a coal camp like his two best friends -- who were black.

A self proclaimed God fearing West Virginian who is not a racist "because" . . .

But every day he's at the Capitol defending inequality by compromising a black policy agenda . . . then saying - we have a black person on our board, in our office . . . at the table. Etc.

Well. I was probably him a lot of my life.

I'm always aware that you can only meet people where they are and that is me included.

I don't know. But I hope this book finds an audience in people like the Senator. He's trying . . . I believe . . . to understand and do what is right in God's eyes, his constituents. But, I think he would have a hard time seeing God as a Black man.

Do you still think I'm white?

I never DID think you were white. That's what started this whole thing LOL

Others will still think you are. You have to use that. I could say the same things you are and it would fall on deaf ears. And it's because of this - whites talking to whites - that this book offers weight.

That kind of sucks. But I understand. Thank you friend.

Wow. Be careful what you text your friends, they might write you into a book!

BTW am I getting royalties for this text?

RECOMMENDED RESOURCES

Ajourney of this sort requires trustworthy guides. This list barely scratches the surface of great resources that exist from amazing authors, academics, prophets, preachers, and reporters. I'm indebted to so many, but here are several sources that were especially meaningful and helpful by planting and answering questions in my mind.

History

The History of White People by Nell Irvin Painter (W. W. Norton & Company, 2010). This comprehensive, fascinating review of the formation of race and whiteness was very influential in helping me understand how, from the get-go, race was rooted in the biased, pseudo-scientific lens of European history.

Slavery by Another Name: The Re-Enslavement of Black Americans from the Civil War to World War II by Douglas A. Blackmon (Doubleday, 2008). This book is a gut-punch to any belief that slavery ended in the United States with the end of the Civil War and passing of the Thirteenth Amendment.

The New Jim Crow: Mass Incarceration in the Age of Colorblindness by Michelle Alexander (The New Press, 2012). Alexander shows how that Thirteenth Amendment loophole has left a devastating, ongoing trail of injustice, particularly for African Americans, and led to the rise of the prison-industrial complex.

The Half Has Never Been Told: Slavery and the Making of American Capitalism by Edward E. Baptist (Basic Books, 2014). Well-documented evidence that America's economic might rests largely on the backs of enslaved people. Warning: It becomes very difficult to argue against at least some form of significant reparations for descendants of enslaved people after reading this more complete history of our country and its corporations.

Stamped from the Beginning: The Definitive History of Racist Ideas in America by Ibram X. Kendi. Kendi is exhaustive in his documentation of how racist ideas shaped American history and power. His description of segregationist, assimilationist (which is a racist position), and antiracist categories was very educational.

Parting the Waters: America in the King Years 1954-63 by Taylor Branch (Simon & Schuster, 1988). After reading this book in college, it firmly established Martin Luther King Jr., John Lewis, Diane Nash, and other civil rights leaders as my personal heroes. Confronting the violence and indignity of Jim Crow was and always will be one of the most heroic acts in history.

Bury My Heart at Wounded Knee: An Indian History of the American West by Dee Alexander Brown (Vintage Books, 1987). Originally published in 1970, this classic was the start of filling my embarrassing void of historic knowledge about Native American experience. I have committed to educating myself far more about American experiences beyond Euro-American and African American.

Christian Theology and Life

I'm Still Here: Black Dignity in a World Made for Whiteness by Austin Channing Brown (Convergent Books, 2018). Brown's exhaustion with white people and her "creative anger" over a white church and society that seek assimilation far more than they seek equality and justice was significant confirmation to me that whiteness itself needs dismantling.

The Color of Compromise: The Truth about the American Church's Complicity in Racism by Jemar Tisby (Zondervan, 2019). If you are a Christian believer with humility and a desire to understand the history of American Christianity and its sinful resistance to equality, this book will break your heart and hopefully motivate you to be the change that is hundreds of years overdue in the church.

Divided by Faith: Evangelical Religion and the Problem of Race in America by Michael O. Emerson and Christian Smith (Oxford University Press, 2000). I read this soon after my Damascus Road antiracism awakening, and Emerson and Smith show how evangelical Christian good intentions and even hard work can make matters worse unless whiteness itself is set aside.

Be the Bridge: Pursuing God's Heart for Racial Reconciliation by LaTasha Morrison (WaterBrook, 2019). There is a time for looking back and repenting, and a time to roll up the sleeves and move forward. Morrison provides a beautiful, practical roadmap. This just might work. Sign me up.

Racism, Whiteness, and White Privilege

Between the World and Me by Ta-Nehisi Coates (Spiegel & Grau, 2015). Few articulate the personal pain of racism and our country's stark use of power over black bodies more than Coates. His writing can communicate a hopelessness that any person of faith can't help but resist, but there's no doubt reading this book will slap you out of any denial of how historic and present-day realities affect individuals living under them.

White Fragility: Why It's So Hard for White People to Talk About Racism by Robin DiAngelo. DiAngelo describes how an addict reacts when challenged with their addiction, and why it's so hard for white people to admit they have a problem.

Waking Up White and Finding Myself in the Story of Race by Debbie Irving (Elephant Room Press, 2014). This was one of the first personal narratives that revealed an awareness of white privilege by a white author that I remember reading. Irving's courage in revealing her mistakes and misunderstandings gave me some additional courage to do that same.

White Like Me: Reflections on Race from a Privileged Son by Tim Wise (Soft Skull Press, 2008). Wise makes no bones about being a polemical writer and speaker, and he shares razor-sharp personal and cultural critique about whiteness and its privileges.

Dying of Whiteness: How the Politics of Racial Resentment Is Killing America's Heartland by Jonathan M. Metzl. While the story I've shared in this book documents the impact whiteness has had on me personally and what I have learned about its effects on people of color through the generations, Metzl documents how the policies of protecting whiteness have measurably harmed the very people they were designed to support—those who consider themselves white.

Roots of Justice: https://rootsofjusticetraining.org. Roots of Justice, Inc., is a nonprofit organization established to carry forward and broaden the work founded by the Damascus Road Antiracism Training Process, which I mention in the book. Change comes with deep, roll-up-your-sleeves work, and Roots of Justice is doing just that.

ACKNOWLEDGMENTS

As a book publisher, I often read the acknowledgments from our authors. Honestly, they can get a little sappy. But after more than four years of diving into uncomfortable truths, holding dozens of emotional conversations, reading stacks of books, clicking on hundreds of articles, and sitting through countless evening and weekend hours trying to capture it all on the page, I get it. Authors deserve a few sappy pages to share their gratitude.

First, I would like to thank someone who I don't know personally but who planted seeds of disorientation, dismay, and determination that came to fruition through this book. Ewuare X. Osayande—poet, political activist, and intersectional antiracist educator—rocked our eager, naïve white minds one evening in a little church on Locust Street in Philadelphia in the mid-1990s. I'm sure he's rocked many others' minds before and after. Never underestimate the power prophetic words can have, even if you may never know the extent of their impact. Mr. Osayande, thank you for your challenge to go back to my white world and do what I could do to advance anti-racism. Thank you, Pastor Rod and the Circle of Hope community, for having enough faith and passion to pursue a more authentic way of following Jesus and inviting Mr. Osayande to challenge us.

Thanks to my agent—and now boss!—Don Jacobson, who shared the vision and passion of this book in a way that gave me the hope all authors need. We needed that hope when it took more than a year to find a home for it! I look forward to collaborating on other world-changing projects, as the Lord wills.

Speaking of a home, thank you Lil Copan, for the courage to take on an odd, perhaps head-scratching project about challenging race and undermining whiteness. Thank you to all the Broadleaf Books administrative, editorial, marketing, publicity, and sales team members for your support, but especially Valerie Weaver-Zercher, my stellar editor. A great editor brings that special mix of qualities that shepherd a book in the right direction while keeping an insecure first-time author believing that maybe, just maybe, he's a decent writer. Valerie, you have been an encouraging, wise partner. Thank you.

My amazing wife and partner, Soni, whom I love greatly, is responsible for ensuring this book actually got finished, with her prayer, encouragement, feedback, and sacrifice. She sent me off to Starbucks on many evenings and weekends to keep writing. You are a true rock in my life and I'm so grateful God brought us together.

Sonora and Shelby, I've always cherished our long philosophical and spiritual discussions. You are world-class daughters, and you amaze me with the depth of your hearts and minds. I've always believed I was getting away with something too good to be true by being your dad. Bella and Gabby, how lucky could one guy be to be blessed with such wonderful bonus daughters? Your warm acceptance, enthusiasm for life, and exuberant love are a thing to behold. When the four sisters get together to laugh, sing, hug Pasha, or play Minecraft, it makes Soni and me so happy. We love you so much.

Thank you, Mom, Dad, Doug, and Lori, for putting up with my antics and strange adventures. You're a really great family to be a part of; I'm so grateful for you and love you dearly.

Often there are so many people who played a huge role in your life or in a book's existence that it's easy to opt out of naming them, for fear of leaving someone out. I'm going to take a risk and attempt it, because all my friends who educated and trusted me with their stories of hope and struggle in a world designed around the myth of whiteness deserve my personal thanks. Morgantown clay pit friends, Speedy, Susie, Sandra, Chanja, Shelby, Sunil, Jenny, Steve, Audrey, Martine, MJ, Eneida, Dave, Ruth, Kenyatta, James, LaRue, Calenthia, Gigi, Erica, Jonathan, Maurice, Sandra, Alix, Amanda, Tiffany, Deonta', Chantel, Sujani, Erika, Alex, Mark, Belle, Kevin, Bhana, Sandra, Ron, D.P., Michelle, Eva, Miguel, Jessica, and Karen: Thank you so much. If this book lessens the need to explain things to just one more person, I'll have considered it all worthwhile.

And . . . Crystal. You are always up to something. As the most creative person I've ever met, I shouldn't have been surprised by your many ideas and challenges, least of all this one. I hope I did it justice. You are an inspiration to all of us. Much love and gratitude.

Most of all, thank you, Jesus. You'll soon heal us all; I'm sure of that.

NOTES

CHAPTER 1: CRYSTAL'S TEXT MESSAGE

1. Sharmila Choudhury, "Racial and Ethnic Differences in Wealth Holdings and Portfolio Choices," Social Security Office of Policy website, April 2002, https://tinyurl.com/yx533nvs.
2. An additional odd twist is that Williams later recanted her story of sexual abuse and torture, even though the perpetrators were convicted based on physical and verbal evidence from the accused's own testimony. See Michael Martin, "Megan Williams Recants Claims of Sexual Abuse," National Public Radio, October 22, 2009, https://tinyurl.com/urcmkc3.

CHAPTER 3: THE MEASURE OF WHITENESS

1. "On Views of Race and Inequality, Blacks and Whites Are Worlds Apart," Pew Research Center, June 27, 2016, https://tinyurl.com/jxtk762.
2. "What Is the Science of Happiness?" Berkeley Wellness, November 9, 2015, https://tinyurl.com/rvkpx9e.
3. "Fact Sheet: Health Disparities and Stress," American Psychological Association, accessed January 7, 2019, https://tinyurl.com/t7az83j.
4. Rakesh Kochhar and Anthony Cilluffo, "How Wealth Inequality Has Changed in the United States Since the Great Recession, by Race, Ethnicity and Income," Pew Research Center, November 1, 2017, https://tinyurl.com/tjkdxtg.

5. Nicholas Carnes and Noam Lupu, "It's Time to Bust the Myth: Most Trump Voters Were Not Working Class," *The Washington Post*, June 5, 2017, https://tinyurl.com/ybmv7lel.

6. "Why I Voted for Trump," *The Washington Post*, updated November 23, 2016, https://tinyurl.com/ju9bp6j.

7. Samuel H. Williamson and Louis P. Cain, "Measuring Slavery in 2016 Dollars," Measuring Worth, 2019, https://tinyurl.com/6wn22af. It's important to note that this study is not attempting to place a dollar value on human life or on any enslaved individual's suffering as a result of forced servitude; that would be offensive and, of course, impossible. It merely attempts to calculate the economic value of enslaved people's labor.

8. Stephen Yafa, *Big Cotton: How a Humble Fiber Created Fortunes, Wrecked Civilizations, and Put America on the Map* (New York: Viking, 2005).

9. Rachel L. Swarns, "Insurance Policies on Slaves: New York Life's Complicated Past," *The New York Times*, December 18, 2016, https://tinyurl.com/wg65c7x.

10. Tracy Jan, "White Families Have Nearly 10 Times the Net Worth of Black Families. And the Gap is Growing," *The Washington Post*, September 28, 2017, https://tinyurl.com/y9luwejz.

11. Lincoln Quillian, Devah Pager, Ole Hexel, and Arnfinn H. Midtbøen, "Meta-Analysis of Field Experiments Shows No Change in Racial Discrimination in Hiring Over Time," *PNAS* 114, no. 41 (September 2017): 10870–875, doi:10.1073/pnas.1706255114.

12. Samantha Artiga, Julia Foutz, Elizabeth Cornachione, and Rachel Garfield, "Key Facts on Health and Health Care by Race and Ethnicity," Kaiser Family Foundation, 2016, https://tinyurl.com/y3u3gcv6.

13. Findings: The Results of Our Nationwide Analysis of Traffic Stops and Searches, The Stanford Open Policing Project, Stanford, CA, 2016, https://tinyurl.com/ruqzpo8 (accessed February 2, 2018).

14. Christopher Ingraham, "Black Men Sentenced to More Time for Committing the Exact Same Crime as a White Person, Study Finds," *The Washington Post*, November 16, 2017, https://tinyurl.com/quyg9a2 (accessed January 13, 2018).

15. Brian Thompson, "The Racial Wealth Gap: Addressing America's Most Pressing Epidemic," *Forbes*, February 18, 2018, https://tinyurl.com/ubx7kqx (accessed February 19, 2019).

16. Reuters/Ipsos/UVA Center for Politics Race Poll, University of Virginia Center for Politics, Charlottesville, 2017, https://tinyurl.com/v2netsv (accessed March 29, 2018).

17. Geoffrey T. Wodtke, "The Impact of Education on Inter-group Attitudes: o Multiracial Analysis," *Social Psychology Quarterly* 75, no. 1 (2012).

18. Art Markman, "What Does Guilt Do? The Role of Guilt in Repairing Relationships," *Psychology Today* (May 2012), https://tinyurl.com/y556r356 (accessed August 15, 2018).

CHAPTER 4: PLATO AND PECKING ORDERS

1. Robert W. Sussman, "There Is No Such Thing as Race," *Newsweek*, 2014, https://tinyurl.com/oku3gzz (accessed August 13, 2018).

2. The Human Genome Project, National Human Genome Research Institute, Washington, DC, 2019, https://tinyurl.com/y2kfn252 (accessed May 2, 2017).

3. Vivian Chou, "How Science and Genetics Are Reshaping the Race Debate of the 21st Century," *SITN Boston*, April 17, 2017, https://tinyurl.com/y75n5rbl (accessed October 28, 2018).

4. John Hawks, "Three New Discoveries in a Month Rock Our African Origins," *Medium*, June 7, 2017, https://tinyurl.com/yxt7xcsd (accessed December 9, 2018).

5. Jennifer Raff, "What Does DNA Tell Us About Race?" *Forbes*, April 25, 2019, https://tinyurl.com/r5gdbac (accessed May 25, 2019).

6. Chou, "How Science And Genetics Are Reshaping the Race Debate of the 21st Century."

7. A corollary question may be: Have scientists identified genes that are correlated with intelligence? Yes, they have. But the genetic diversity of humans and the impact of environment on these genes, compared to say, adaptations that would lead to skin color or height differences, lead scientists to predict that we'll not see a certain "race" (again, a category that genetically doesn't even exist) with more genetically derived intelligence than another. See Nina G. Jablonksi and George Chaplin, "Skin Deep," *Scientific American*, October 2002, https://tinyurl.com/s5pkf2v (accessed June 14, 2017).

8. Kevin Mitchell, "Why Genetic IQ Differences between 'Races' are Unlikely," *The Guardian US*, May 2, 2018, https://tinyurl.com/y9vq88zv (accessed April 30, 2019).

9. Keith Bradley and Paul Cartledge, *The Cambridge World History of Slavery: Volume 1, The Ancient Mediterranean World* (Cambridge: Cambridge University Press, 2011).

10. Thomas F. Gossett, *Race: The History of an Idea in America*, new edition (New York: Oxford University Press, 1997).

11. Nell Irvin Painter, *The History of White People* (New York: W. W. Norton, 2010).

12. Plato, *Plato: Republic, volume I: Books 1-5*, trans. Christopher Emlyn-Jones and William Preddy.

13. Aristotle on inequality, *Works and Days*, https://tinyurl.com/qkqd58s (accessed March 2, 2018).

14. C. N. Trueman, "The Lifestyle of Medieval Peasants," The History Learning Site, December 18, 2019, https://tinyurl.com/y8327k4l (accessed August 27, 2018).

15. Adam Nagourney, "A Defiant Rancher Savors the Audience That Rallied to His Side," *The New York Times*, April 24, 2014, https://tinyurl.com/tn8xf3g (accessed February 11, 2018).

16. "The Capture and Sale of Enslaved Africans," International Slavery Museum, Liverpool, UK, http://www.liverpoolmuseums.org.uk/ism/slavery/africa/capture_sale.aspx (accessed May 27, 2018).

17. David Smith, "African Chiefs Urged to Apologise for Slave Trade," *The Guardian*, November 18, 2009, https://tinyurl.com/ybllg23l (accessed July 18, 2018).

18. "The Middle Passage," Digital History, https://tinyurl.com/lq9hlyt (accessed March 2, 2017).

19. Patrick Manning, "African Population, 1650–1950: Methods for New Estimates by Region." Paper presented at African Economic History Conference, Vancouver, BC, 2013. (Note: Before we moderns feel too superior in our ethics on slavery, do we in modern times take any more heed to where our low-cost clothing or plastic trinkets come from? The modern-day slave trade is alive and well. See http://slaveryfootprint.org/ to see how many slaves may be working on your behalf, based on your consumption habits. I found out that approximately 82 slaves, based on the current practices of human trafficking and forced labor in the world, contributed to making the products in my home.)

20. "The Gate of Teka-hra," Evinity Publishing, https://tinyurl.com/wdks7ec (accessed May 2, 2017).

21. "Oh, For a Heart Whiter Than Snow," Words: Eliza E. Hewitt, in *Junior Songs*, ed. John R. Sweney and William J. Kirkpatrick (Philadelphia: John J. Hood, 1892), no. 19. Music: William J. Kirkpatrick.

22. Bruce Baum, *The Rise and Fall of the Caucasian Race: A Political History of Racial Identity* (New York: New York University Press, 2006).

CHAPTER 5: WE HOLD THESE TRUTHS TO BE SELF-EVIDENT—FOR SOME OF US

1. Michael Guasco, "The Misguided Focus on 1619 as the Beginning of Slavery in the US Damages Our Understanding of American History," Smithsonian. Washington, DC, 2017, https://tinyurl.com/uulzhaw (accessed November 14, 2018).

2. E. R. Shipp, "1619: 400 Years Ago, a Ship Arrived in Virginia, Bearing Human Cargo," *USA Today*, February 8, 2019, https://tinyurl.com/y4g8ql5h (accessed February 27, 2018).

3. "A Timeline of Slave Law in Colonial Virginia," Sam Houston State University, Huntsville, TX, 2009, https://tinyurl.com/stnser9 (accessed February 19, 2018).

4. "The Declaration of Causes of Seceding States," American Battlefield Trust, Washington, DC, https://tinyurl.com/yxkhmm8x (accessed March 7, 2018).

5. Keri L. Merritt, "Land and the Roots of African-American Poverty," Aeon Media Group, New York, https://tinyurl.com/vwfzzgs (accessed September 7, 2018).

6. Survey of Consumer Finances (SCF), Board of Governors of the Federal Reserve System, Washington, DC, 2018, https://tinyurl.com/ydgm6kmu (accessed July 29, 2018); Tracy Jan, "1 in 7 White Families Are Now Millionaires. For Black Families, It's 1 in 50," *The Washington Post*, October 3, 2017, https://tinyurl.com/y78d2u8b (accessed December 2, 2018).

7. Recent Accomplishments of the Housing and Civil Enforcement Section, United States Department of Justice, Washington, DC, 2019, https://tinyurl.com/gmm9h5z (accessed June 22, 2018).

8. Brandon Weber, "How African American WWII Veterans Were Scorned by the G.I. Bill," *The Progressive*, 2017, https://tinyurl.com/r56d8ob (accessed May 27, 2018).

9. Chuck Leddy, "A Critical Look at the GI Bill's Impact," Boston Globe Media Partners, LLC, September 10, 2009, https://tinyurl.com/ujyjoyw (accessed November 28, 2018).

10. Edward Humes, "How the GI bill Shunted Blacks into Vocational Training," *The Journal of Blacks in Higher Education* 53 (August 2002): 92–104.

11. "How the GI Bill Changed the Economy," *MarketPlace*, 2009, https://tinyurl.com/yxkhmm8x (accessed March 7, 2018).

12. Paul A. Offit, "The Loathsome American Book That Inspired Hitler," *The Daily Beast*, August 26, 2017, https://tinyurl.com/v9avzha (accessed December 17, 2018).

13. Alex Ross, "How American Racism Influenced Hitler," *The New Yorker*, April 30, 2018, https://tinyurl.com/y62pebwv (accessed January 4, 2019).

CHAPTER 6: THIS IS MY BRAIN ON RACE

1. Project Implicit, https://tinyurl.com/jah6cj8 (accessed November 1, 2017).

2. David J. Kelly, Shaoying Liu, Kang Lee, Paul C. Quinn, Olivier Pascalis, Alan M. Slater, and Leizhong Ge, "Development of the Other-Race Effect during Infancy: Evidence toward Universality?" *Journal of Experimental Child Psychology* 104, no. 1 (2009): 105–14.

3. Kristina R. Olson, "Are Kids Racist?" *Psychology Today*, April 2, 2013, https://tinyurl.com/jxx9ado (accessed December 1, 2018).

4. Jeffrey Zacks, *Flicker: Your Brain on Movies* (Oxford: Oxford University Press, 2014).

5. Olson, "Are Kids Racist?"

6. S. Sangrigoli, C. Pallier, A. M. Argenti, V. A. Ventureyra, and S. de Schonen, "Reversibility of the Other-Race Effect in Face Recognition during Childhood," *Psychological Science* 16, no. 6 (2005): 440–44.

7. Karen Ravn, "Some Amazing Facts about Your Unbelievable Brain," *Los Angeles Times*, May 18, 2017, https://tinyurl.com/uyn2ses (accessed January 24, 2019).

8. Kristina Birdsong, "A Fun Way to Learn about Your Incredible Brain," *Scientific Learning*, 2016, https://www.scilearn.com/blog/10-facts-about -your-wacky-brain (accessed February 2, 2019).

9. John Gramlich, "5 Facts about Crime in the U.S.," Pew Research Center, Washington, DC, October 17, 2019, https://tinyurl.com/y4ubf6ro (accessed October 5, 2018).

10. Skye Gould and Dave Mosher, "How Likely Are Foreign Terrorists to Kill Americans? The Odds May Surprise You," *Business Insider*, January 31, 2017, https://tinyurl.com/y7gf8cc5 (accessed September 27, 2018).

11. Alex Nowrasteh, "Illegal Immigrants and Crime—Assessing the Evidence," Cato Institute, Washington, DC, March 4, 2019, https://tinyurl .com/y4y2uc2u (accessed June 12, 2018).

12. "Black Women Really Do Have High College Enrollment Rates (at Age 25+)," *Family Inequality*, June 10, 2016, https://tinyurl.com/qlkhzl3 (accessed November 15, 2018).

13. "Labor Force Characteristics by Race and Ethnicity, 2017," Bureau of Labor Statistics, Washington, DC, August 2018, https://tinyurl.com/tmx sjbh (accessed November 5, 2018).

14. College Student Employment, National Center of Education Statistics, Washington, DC, https://tinyurl.com/yxxe2ayz (accessed December 8, 2018).

15. Joe Davidson, "Implicit Bias Training Seeks to Counter Hidden Prejudice in Law Enforcement," *The Washington Post*, August 16, 2016, https://tinyurl.com/hh9dare (accessed March 2, 2019).

16. Daniel Kahneman, *Thinking, Fast and Slow* (New York: Farrar, Straus & Giroux, 2011).

17. Margaret J. Shih, Rebecca Stotzer, and Angélica S. Gutiérrez, "Perspective-Taking and Empathy: Generalizing the Reduction of Group Bias towards Asian Americans to General Outgroups," *Asian American Journal of Psychology* 4, no. 2 (2013).

CHAPTER 7: BRITISH ISLES AND COUNTRY ROADS

1. IMDB, https://tinyurl.com/y9y3cbfe (accessed May 29, 2019).

2. Ibram X. Kendi, *Stamped from the Beginning: The Definitive History of Racist Ideas in America* (New York: Bold Type Books, 2016).

CHAPTER 8: SHARP KNIFE AND UNA STARBUCKS

1. New American Economy, https://tinyurl.com/tkcndvu (accessed June 2, 2019).

2. Edward Glaeser and Jacob Vigdor, "The End of the Segregated Century: Racial Separation in America's Neighborhoods, 1890–2010," *Manhattan Institute*, no. 66 (January 2012).

3. A. von Hoffman, E. S. Beklsky, and K. Lee, "The Impact of Housing on Community: A Review of Scholarly Theories and Empirical Research," Joint Center for Housing Studies, Harvard University, 2006, https://tinyurl.com/rn44owc.

4. Jeff Nesbit, "If You Are Black, Chances Are Your Neighbors Are Too," *US News and World Report*, June 29, 2015, https://tinyurl.com/twh84fl (accessed June 17, 2019).

5. "Facts, Information and Articles about Andrew Jackson, the 7th U.S. President," HistoryNet, https://tinyurl.com/txj9osh (accessed June 1, 2017).

6. Brandon Rottinghaus and Justin Vaughn, "New Ranking of U.S. Presidents Puts Lincoln at No. 1, Obama No. 18; Kennedy Judged Most

Overrated," *The Washington Post*, February 16, 2015, https://tinyurl .com/zree6mm (accessed July 7, 2018).

7. Gale C. Toensing, "Indian-Killer Andrew Jackson Deserves Top Spot on List of Worst US Presidents," *Indian Country Today*, September 10, 2017, https://tinyurl.com/ydytm34b (accessed February 18, 2018).

8. Neighborhood Scout, https://tinyurl.com/ux6q5tu (accessed January 27, 2019).

CHAPTER 9: HAM'S CURSE AND HIPSTER CHURCH

1. Bob Smietana, "Sunday Morning in America Still Segregated—and That's OK with Worshipers," LifeWay Research, Nashville, TN, January 15, 2015, https://tinyurl.com/vj9f5ey (accessed November 20, 2017).

2. Bob Smietana, "Americans Agree U.S. Has Come Far in Race Relations, but Has Long Way to Go," LifeWay Research, Nashville, TN, December 16, 2014, https://tinyurl.com/s595xfx(accessed August 3, 2017).

3. Gene Rice, "The Alleged Curse on Ham," American Bible Society, Philadelphia, https://tinyurl.com/yx4zwzqr (accessed March 30, 2017).

4. Lizzie Wade, "Ancient DNA Reveals Fate of the Mysterious Canaanites," *Science Magazine*, July 27, 2017, https://tinyurl.com/twmwq6b (accessed February 13, 2018).

5. Justin Taylor, "A Conversation with Four Historians on the Response of White Evangelicals to the Civil Rights Movement," The Gospel Coalition, 2016, https://tinyurl.com/s3729nm (accessed February 8, 2018).

6. Michael Pasquier, "White Catholics Have 'to Talk about Race and to Admit Their Racism,'" *America Magazine*, July 27, 2016, https://tinyurl .com/tz5p7cu (accessed May 1, 2018).

7. Malcolm X, "Black Man's History," MalcomX.org, https://tinyurl.com /rpb2vzc (accessed June 19, 2018).

8. Global Christianity—A Report on the Size and Distribution of the World's Christian Population, Pew Research Center, Washington, DC, December 19, 2011, https://tinyurl.com/y6696ns3 (accessed July 27, 2018).

CHAPTER 10: BAD JUSTICE FOR GOOD JOBS

1. Christopher Graham, "Black Men Sentenced to More Time for Committing the Exact Same Crime as a White Person, Study Finds," *The Washington Post*, November 16, 2017, https://tinyurl.com/y7zpsh44 (accessed January 13, 2018).

2. Danielle Paquette, "One in Nine Black Children Has Had a Parent in Prison," *The Washington Post*, October 27, 2015, https://tinyurl.com/t5hjjne (accessed March 1, 2018).

3. QuickFacts: Gilmer County, West Virginia, US Census Bureau, Washington, DC, 2018, https://tinyurl.com/sqyzzpa (accessed June 1, 2019).

4. Peter Wagner, "Why Is West Virginia the Federal Prison Capital of the Country?" Prison Policy Initiative, Northampton, MA, June 10, 2014, https://tinyurl.com/uc4duu7 (accessed December 15, 2018).

5. Rich Morin and Renee Stepler, "The Racial Confidence Gap in Police Performance," Pew Research Center, Washington, DC, September 29, 2016, https://tinyurl.com/jxf28ql (accessed November 1, 2018).

6. Melissa Healy, "Blacks Are More Likely to Be Killed by Police, but That's Because They're More Likely to Be Stopped, Study Says," *Los Angeles Times*, July 25, 2016, https://tinyurl.com/taj442q (accessed October 17, 2018).

CHAPTER 11: FACEBOOK AND AFFIRMATIVE ACTION FRIENDSHIP

1. Christopher Graham, "Three Quarters of Whites Don't Have Any Nonwhite Friends," *The Washington Post*, August 25, 2014, https://tinyurl.com/r8mjkux (accessed December 29, 2018).

CHAPTER 12: OPEN HEARTS AND OREO COOKIES

1. "Race and Attraction, 2009–2014," OKCupid Blog, 2014, https://tinyurl.com/yxunlvyf (accessed February 21, 2018).

2. Gretchen Livingston and Anna Brown, "Trends and Patterns in Intermarriage," Pew Research Center, Washington, DC, May 18, 2017, https://tinyurl.com/y2tltptz (accessed March 1, 2018).

3. Aaron Sankin, "The Weird Racial Politics of Online Dating," The Daily Dot, January 18, 2015, https://tinyurl.com/qmpuwnw (accessed March 1, 2018).

4. Monda Chalabi, "What's Behind the Rise of Interracial Marriage in The US?" *The Guardian*, February 21, 2018, https://tinyurl.com/ybh2uq3u (accessed October 19, 2018).

CHAPTER 13: DEONTA'S BOOK REPORT

1. Emma Garcia and Elaine Weiss, "Education Inequalities at the School Starting Gate," Economic Policy Institute, Washington, DC, September 27, 2017, https://tinyurl.com/ydyn83ud (accessed August 1, 2018).

2. "Early Skills and Predictors of Academic Success," Hanover Research, Arlington, VA, November 2016, https://tinyurl.com/rwyvs6y (accessed May 25, 2018).

3. "How Day-to-Day Violence Affects Children's Educational Attainment," Institute of Labor Economics, Bonn, Germany, April 24, 2019, https://tinyurl.com/ve6jso4 (accessed June 1, 2019).

4. Dina Gerdeman, "Minorities Who 'Whiten' Job Resumes Get More Interviews," Harvard Business School, Cambridge, MA, May 17, 2017, https://tinyurl.com/y45ckypm (accessed December 1, 2018). See also Lincoln Quillian, Devah Pager, Ole Hexel, and Arnfinn H. Midtbøen, "Meta-Analysis of Field Experiments Shows No Change in Racial Discrimination in Hiring over Time," *National Academy of Sciences* 114, no. 41 (September 2017).

5. Charge Statistics (Charges filed with EEOC) FY 1997 through FY 2017, US Equal Employment Opportunity Commission, Washington, DC, July 31, 2018, https://tinyurl.com/ycr38gtg (accessed April 23, 2019).

6. Sean Captain, "Workers Win Only 1% of Federal Civil Rights Lawsuits at Trial," *Fast Company*, 2017, https://tinyurl.com/to5pa8p (accessed July 30, 2018).

CHAPTER 14: KNOWING TOO MUCH

1. "'Because I'm Alive': James Baldwin on Film," Walker Art Center, Minneapolis, 2017, https://tinyurl.com/uh76gb7 (accessed May 3, 2018).

CHAPTER 15: ONE DAY AT A TIME

1. Natalie Allison, "White Lives Matter rally: Who Are the Groups Involved, and What Do They Believe?," *The Tennessean*, October 23, 2017, https://tinyurl.com/svzqube (accessed February 2, 2019).

2. Elisabeth Kauffman, "In Murfreesboro, Tenn.: Church 'Yes,' Mosque 'No,'" *Time*, August 19, 2010, https://tinyurl.com/u53stq5 (accessed August 12, 2018).

3. Ian H. Robertson, "How Power Affects the Brain," *The Psychologist* 26, no. 3 (March 2013), https://tinyurl.com/ya6cjh9o (accessed June 17, 2018).

4. Jerry Usseem, "Power Causes Brain Damage," *The Atlantic*, July/August 2017, https://tinyurl.com/ybcq7zyk (accessed June 2, 2018).